John le Carré

Twayne's English Authors Series

Kinley E. Roby, Editor
Northeastern University

TEAS 496

John le Carré

LynnDianne Beene

University of New Mexico

Twayne Publishers ▪ New York

Maxwell Macmillan Canada ▪ Toronto

Maxwell Macmillan International ▪ New York Oxford Singapore Sydney

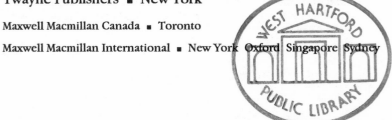

John le Carré
LynnDianne Beene

Copyright 1992 by Twayne Publishers

Twayne Publishers   Maxwell Macmillan Canada, Inc.
Macmillan Publishing Company   1200 Eglinton Avenue East
866 Third Avenue   Suite 200
New York, New York 10022   Don Mills, Ontario M3C 3N1

Macmillan Publishing Company is part of the Maxwell
Communications Group of Companies.

Library of Congress Cataloging-in-Publication Data

Beene, Lynn.
  John le Carré / LynnDianne Beene.
    p. cm. – (Twayne's English authors series; TEAS 496)
    Includes bibliographical references and index.
    ISBN 0-8057-7013-5 (alk. paper)
    1. Le Carré, John, 1931- – Criticism and interpretation. 2. Spy
stories, English – History and criticism. I. Title. II. Series.
PR6062.E33Z64 1992
823'.914 – dc20   92-18671
                                             CIP

10 9 8 7 6 5 4 3 2 1

Printed in the United States of America.

For Donna, Penny, and

the spy who loved us

Contents

Preface

With his typical irony Graham Greene has his self-congratulatory novelist, Quin Savory, comment that "a novelist depends on other men; he's an average man with the power of expression. 'E's a spy." Such is the case with the object of this brief study, David John Moore Cornwell, known more popularly as John le Carré. Le Carré is the master of his own brand of contemporary espionage fiction. British reviewers acknowledge le Carré's position as a skilled novelist writing within a clearly defined tradition. American critics, on the other hand, argue that his place is properly with novelists of recognized status and reputation.

There are resemblances between le Carré's fiction and that of John Buchan, Erskine Childers, Herman Cyril McNeile, and, to the surprise of some reviewers and critics, William Le Queux and Ian Fleming. Like these genre novelists, le Carré writes artful thrillers filled with resourceful agents, animated narratives, the technical details of espionage, and entangled political affairs. He also has strong ties to the mainstream fiction writers. His densely plotted fiction favors Charles Dickens's eccentric characters, Joseph Conrad's tortured ambiguities, T. E. Lawrence's graphic descriptiveness, and Greene's moral irony. Yet no matter how complicated his labyrinthines are, his narratives always hold one agent out above all others, one man whose underlying idealism cogently argues what actions befit an honorable man.

Reviewers and critics miss the truism aptly captured in Savory's observation. David Cornwell is an average man whose power of expression, even when unruly, makes him the unique novelist John le Carré. His social and political didacticism – the substance of his worried mind and the topic of all his writing – is born of a deep sense of commitment to human beings and the individualism they must embrace. It is here that le Carré's fiction defines him as a "spy," because readers see a worried, conscientious man peering into the deformed hearts of those who would betray his people and warning us of their games and snares. His lessons seldom vary, perhaps because his concerns are seldom alleviated.

Underlying this study is the view that le Carré is a didactic novelist whose work spans genre and mainstream fiction. While my analyses draw heavily from the texts of British reviewers and American critics, I try to let le Carré's fiction and judgments speak for themselves, without extended critical commentary. Although themes, characters, and even some situations repeat in le Carré's fiction, I've organized the study chronologically so that readers will get a sense of how and why le Carré chooses to elaborate rather than vary his fundamental approaches. Chapter 1, a brief recapitulation of le Carré's childhood and publishing career, sketches the biographical information necessary for an interpretation of his fiction. Chapters 2 through 6 consider le Carré's literary works, and chapter 7 suggests how these works separate the le Carré novel from typical espionage fictions and urges a full reappraisal of le Carré's position in contemporary literature.

■

Words on a page can only inadequately thank the many people who encouraged and helped me with this project. Special thanks go to Ivan Melada and Lewis De Simone for their reassurances, to Fred Warner for knowing how best to wield Moscow Rules, to Krystan V. Douglas and Juliette Cunico for coffee and criticisms, to Gary Scharhorst for knowing his style, to Kinley Roby for his careful editorial guidance, to Michelle Marsee Loeblich for her sharp eye and good humor, and to Alfred the butler for interpreting my clandestine messages. Finally, a special thank-you to David W. Frizzell, without whom this book would undoubtedly awkward read.

Chronology

1931	David John Moore Cornwell (John le Carré) born in Poole, Somerset, England, on 19 October to Ronald ("Ronnie") and Olive (Glassy) Cornwell.
1936	Olive deserts family after Ronnie serves first jail sentence for fraud.
1945	Ends education at St. Andrew's Prepatory School, Pangbourne.
1947-1948	Leaves Sherborne for University of Berne, Switzerland.
1949-1950	Joins Army Intelligence Corps as part of National Service. His brother, Anthony, graduates from Cambridge University with a law degree and leaves for America. Ronnie runs for a seat in Parliament to avoid active duty.
1950	Charlotte Cornwell, David's half-sister, born.
1952	Enters Lincoln College, Oxford University, to study modern languages.
1954	Marries Alison Ann Veronica Sharp ("Ann").
1955	Nearly broke, leaves Oxford to teach at Millfield Junior School, Glastonbury, Somerset.
1956	Graduates from Oxford with first honors in modern languages, particularly German.
1956-1958	Tutors at prestigious Eton College. Son Simon born. Reunited with his mother for the first time in 21 years.
1959-1964	Joins Foreign Office as second secretary at the British embassy in Bonn. Sons Stephen and Timothy born.
1960	*Call for the Dead.*
1962	*A Murder of Quality.*

1963	*The Spy Who Came in from the Cold.*
1964	*The Spy Who Came in from the Cold* published in the United States, receives British Crime Writers' Association Golden Dagger and Somerset Maugham awards. *Call for the Dead* and *A Murder of Quality* published as *The Incongruous Spy*. "You Can't Sack a College Boy" published in the 27 November *Spectator*.
1964-1966	Is consul in Hamburg for Foreign Office.
1965	*The Looking-glass War*. Film version of *The Spy Who Came in from the Cold* released. Receives Edgar Allan Poe Award from the Mystery Writers of America for *Spy*.
1966	Profits from *Spy* allow him to quit Foreign Office and become a full-time writer. "To Russia, with Greetings," an open response to Russian criticism of *Spy* and *Looking-glass War*. "The Spy to End Spies."
1967	Film version of *Call for the Dead*, *The Deadly Affair*, released. "Dare I Weep, Dare I Mourn?" appears in the 28 January *Saturday Evening Post* and is later produced by ABC television for its "Stage 67."
1968	*A Small Town in Germany*. "What Ritual Is Being Observed Tonight?" appears in the 2 November *Saturday Evening Post*. Settles in Cornwall despite tax disadvantages.
1970	Film version of *The Looking-glass War* released. His play *The End of the Line* produced at London's Armchair Theatre on 29 June.
1971	*The Naive and Sentimental Lover*, his lone venture into nongenre fiction. Divorces Ann Sharp.
1972	Marries Valerie Jane Eustace, editor at Hodder & Stoughton. Son Nicholas born.
1974	*Tinker, Tailor, Soldier, Spy*.

1975   Ronnie Cornwell dies without reconciling with his sons. Bantam Books reprints *Tinker, Tailor, Soldier, Spy* and acquires rights to all le Carré's books except *A Small Town in Germany*.

1977   *The Honourable Schoolboy.* "George Smiley Goes Home" (novel excerpt) produced by BBC television (published in *The Bell House Book* in 1979). Receives James Tait Black Memorial award for *The Honourable Schoolboy*.

1978   Receives Crime Writers' Association Gold Dagger for *The Honourable Schoolboy*.

1980   "Siege." *Smiley's People. Tinker, Tailor, Soldier, Spy* produced as miniseries by BBC television.

1981   Writes introduction to *The Philby Conspiracy*.

1982   "Memories of a Vanished Land." With John Hopkins writes screenplay of *Smiley's People* for BBC.

1983   "Betrayal." "Exiles in the White House." *The Little Drummer Girl*.

1986   *A Perfect Spy.* "The Clandestine Muse," speech at Johns Hopkins University on spies and espionage fiction.

1989   *The Russia House.* Writes screenplay for *A Murder of Quality*.

1991   *The Secret Pilgrim*.

Chapter One

Creating Secret Sharers

I honestly do wonder, without wishing to be morbid, how I reached this present pass. So far as I can ever remember of my youth, I chose the secret road because it seemed to lead straightest and furthest toward my country's goal. The enemy in those days was someone we could point at and read about in the papers. Today, all I know is that I have learned to interpret the whole of life in terms of conspiracy. That is the sword I have lived by, and as I look round me now I see it is the sword I shall die by as well.

— *The Honourable Schoolboy* (1977)

Readers accustomed to espionage fiction as pure entertainment are disturbed by John le Carré's work, which eschews Richard Hannay's unequivocal nationalism and James Bond's blatant disregard for moral standards. In le Carré's world, "our" side is undistinguished from "their" side. "We" can be incompetent, fumbling, and mindlessly destructive; "they" can be decent, conscientious, and dedicated. Le Carré's operatives, although often efficient, are pawns in an espionage chess game where betrayal is the basic tactic. Once caught in the game, their only escapes are betrayal (John Avery, Charlie, Barley Blair), death (Alec Leamas, Jerry Westerby) or, worse, self-realization and angst (George Smiley, Charlie).

Le Carré's messages atypically match the espionage fiction genre. Betrayal of and by security institutions, bureaucracies, ideologies, or country is expected but seldom excusable; betrayal of individuals or of self is unforgivable. Yet both are understandable and predictable, and both guarantee wrenching loneliness. These messages are reminiscent of Joseph Conrad and Graham Greene – not John Buchan or Ian Fleming – and were fostered by the erratic interplay of le Carré's family and his espionage vocation.

Enter David John Moore Cornwell

In 1931 John le Carré was born David John Moore Cornwell in the genteel coastal town of Poole, Somerset, "in a mouldering, airless house with a 'for sale' notice in the garden."[1] His childhood was a series of stern lessons on morality, frustration, abandonment, and broken promises that nurtured in him a distrust of institutions and a bend toward secrecy.

His grandfather, a builder, nonconformist lay preacher, and mayor of Poole, rigorously imposed his standards for respectability on David and his older brother, Tony. From his grandparents young Cornwell gained a religious temperament that defined for him ethics, responsibility, and moral behavior.

The premier influence on the future novelist was, however, his father, Ronald Thomas Archibald Cornwell (1906-75). Ronnie was an epic con man of little education, immense charm, extravagant tastes, but no social values – a man who could have made an excellent double or triple agent had he been at all trustworthy. In his quest for social prominence and wealth, Ronnie "pulled some wonderful cons in" le Carré's name.[2] He raced horses, sold fraudulent products and nonexistent companies and property, and skimmed thousands from unsuspecting marks. He sought Parliamentary office as a Liberal candidate to avoid his military service and, until his death, had a Micawber-like ability for creating both "a temporary problem of liquidity" and personal betrayals.[3]

Early in David's life his father's shady business ventures caused the family to fluctuate between wealth and financial disaster and brought Ronnie a prison sentence for fraud. Shortly after this imprisonment, when David was five, Ronnie's wife, Olive (Glassy) Cornwell, abandoned her husband and young sons to live with one of Ronnie's business associates. David saw her again 21 years later. His father's unorthodox financial ventures and criminal convictions brought stern judgments but few explanations from his grandparents; David therefore created his own reasons for his father's absences. Cornwell imagined that his father was "some great spy who went off and did nationally vital things."[4] His father's impositions and his grandparents' efforts to conceal them created "a condition of subterfuge," and Cornwell learned that dishonesty rather than loyalty begins at home.[5]

When he was not philandering or moving the family around, Ronnie was determined, by whatever means, that his sons would achieve the strong independence and social status he never found. To these ends, he sent Tony and David to public schools 30 miles apart, schools that he could not pay for.[6] Like Aldo Cassidy in le Carré's nonespionage novel *The Naive and Sentimental Lover* (1971), Ronnie shamelessly deprived his sons of a stable childhood. To compensate, David and Tony became crucially dependent on each other, frequently leaving their schools to meet, share what food Tony had scrounged, and invent their own sense of family.

As a wary and increasingly secretive schoolboy, Cornwell saw his father as an incidental, unreliable visitor at school – a father whose promises to take him away for Sunday holidays were seldom kept. David remembers how he "would come down to the end of the drive [at school] and wait, and my father wouldn't appear, and rather than go back and lose face I would just walk around and miss lunch and come back and pretend at 5 o'clock that I'd had a great day. Duplicity was inescapably bred into me" (Kanfer, 67).

In the mid-1940s Ronnie enrolled his younger son in the exclusive Sherborne School, the scene for James Hilton's *Good-Bye, Mr. Chips* and the caliber of school preferred by Sir Anthony Blunt, Guy Burgess, Donald Maclean, and Harold ("Kim") Philby. For two years David was a model student, conforming to Sherborne standards and absorbing the sense of ethics English public schools seek to inculcate. Sherborne became, however, one of the many institutions that disillusioned him. For David the wartime British "public" schools – more private institutions for the privileged class – offered gross repression, not education: "The preponderance of socialist parents who today patronize the private system suggests to me that the flight of confidence from the public sector is somewhat more rapid than the reverse trend" ("In England," 34).[7]

Young Cornwell's life at Sherborne was marked by traumas and propaganda, details he threads repeatedly in his fiction. He endured occasional "official" floggings – those done by the headmaster – for such punishable offenses as untidiness or failure to carry his Bible properly. Violence existed throughout the system. Le Carré attributes his partial deafness in one ear to a blow he suffered from one Sherborne teacher, Mr. Farnsworth.[8] He sketches himself in his description of Bill Roach, the spy in training central to *Tinker, Tailor,*

Soldier, Spy (1974), as a boy who turns his anxieties into covert means of protecting individualism against institutionalized repression. The privileged schoolboy, "a natural watcher," laments his inadequacy at all tasks, "even the daily routine of the school." He blames himself for imagined shortcomings, most of all "for the break-up of his parents' marriage, which he should have seen coming and taken steps to prevent."[9] Always uncomfortable, Roach condemns himself as "abnormally wicked or divisive or slothful," traits that must have induced his parents' rift. Nevertheless, Roach's ability to love others promises a faint hope for his adulthood, and Cornwell's retreat into fiction salvaged him.

Obligatory boxing matches and frequent war films emphasizing the courage and virtue of the privileged classes indoctrinated David with the rewards of violence and of defending his honor and Britain's. He laughed openly at the lower-class accents that he secretly knew identified his family, and he accepted that his future, his proper place in British society, was a part of Britain's imperial past. As members of the privileged public school class, he and his fellow students would carry on England's glorious tradition by taking their places in the government, the church, or the military service. In brief, David and his classmates trained to rule an empire that no longer existed. Slowly repulsed by such blind nationalism, Cornwell escaped into literature, history, and his imagination.

School life was punctuated with infrequent holidays with his father and brother, holidays that were less vacations than opportunities for Ronnie Cornwell to try out his latest con. Young Cornwell bitterly remembers how he and Tony spent one vacation sweating "in a cellar in Aberdeen, squidging figs and prunes" into a sludge that they later rolled in glucose "to be sold by my father as laxative pills. We really believed in those pills, I remember. We believed in them as we believed in God, school, victory over the Germans, and in my father. Those pills were faith and duty all at once, and we rolled them for England."[10] This experience, together with countless others of Ronnie's stratagems, confirmed for Cornwell a world of secrecy, conspiracy, fraud, and betrayal, where survival depended on "an infinite capacity for suspicion" (*Tinker, Tailor*, 315).

Weary from his inconsistent family life and repressive schooling, young Cornwell was "already very concerned with institutions which were outside my family" and how those institutions betrayed those they touched.[11] The novelist le Carré frequently dissects betrayal and the passing of honorable action in postimperial Britain by blending his criticism of institutions with his painful yet secret war with his father. Institutions – educational, bureaucratic, or artistic – are sourceless, bigoted collectives whose operations emulate Cornwell's childhood bedlam. Le Carré's successful fictional operatives learn the betrayal inherent in collectives, but they pay dearly for their realizations. Alec Leamas, the protagonist of *The Spy Who Came in from the Cold* (1964), dies on the Berlin Wall, refusing further betrayals; Jerry Westerby of *The Honourable Schoolboy* (1977) is murdered at Smiley's implicit order for choosing love over operational success; George Smiley's spirit metaphorically succumbs as his dopplegänger literally crosses from East to West; and the surnameless Ned of *The Russia House* (1989) and *The Secret Pilgrim* (1991) finds that local heroes tarnish definable ethics. Novel after novel underscores the danger of crossing hostile frontiers, both in fact and in vision, for the journey leads darkly to a full and deadly appreciation of betrayal's twisted depths. Double agents as well as colleagues and family betray friends, class, country, and, most important, love for institutions as petty as the ones they publicly represent.

Le Carré's artistry was as painfully bought as his education. Although he won a poetry contest when he was 13, David Cornwell's early attempts at fiction were quickly discouraged. His first story, prompted by his fondness for animals, was a tragedy of "an old, heroic racehorse who was ridden to victory by an unscrupulous jockey who had loaded his whip with buckshot." But the story was ridiculed by Sherborne's headmaster who, on discovering that David had convinced the school secretary to type the manuscript, angrily returned it, telling the boy that he should find his own resources to type such "trash" (Dean, 306). For Cornwell, this repression, like so many others, encouraged deception.

By 1947 David Cornwell could no longer tolerate Sherborne. He retreated briefly to an Anglican monastery and refused Ronnie's orders to return to Sherborne. His father, furious at the dishonored schoolboy's decision, eventually allowed his son to live in Switzerland with relatives. Cornwell traveled through Europe before enrolling in the University of Berne. These travels and his subsequent study of languages at Berne introduced him to European culture – and British espionage. The experiences provide the basic narrative for his autobiographical novel, *A Perfect Spy* (1986), in which Magnus Pym, writing to his son on the event of Magnus's father's death, tries to justify his life of betrayals. As a student Cornwell was attracted, like his anguished protagonist George Smiley, to the style and moral questioning of German writers, such as Hesse, Schiller, and Goethe. Setting out to understand German culture and letters, Cornwell ended by possessing them as a second soul and using them as a touchstone to question the values of his own culture.[12]

Unlike his father, Cornwell entered the National Service, where his language facility and knowledge of Europe ensured his posting as an intelligence officer in Vienna.[13] In addition to "low-grade intelligence work," Cornwell interviewed refugees who poured into Austria and debriefed defectors the Service coaxed across the Czechoslovakian border. Ironically, Cornwell, from a consistently unstable home, questioned people who had never had homes, who knew too clearly the tragedies of war because they "had been in prison or prison camps almost since infancy" (Abley 1983a, 34). In Austria he faced irony as well as grief: he met British pilots who had bombed Berlin in 1945 only to airlift supplies to that city in 1948. He spent "a great deal of time with extraordinary victims of half a dozen wars. Estonians, for example, who had been imprisoned by the Germans, fought for the Germans, been imprisoned by the Russians, imprisoned again by the Americans" (Kanfer, 67).

Cornwell took these memories with him when, his National Service duty completed, he returned to England and entered Lincoln College, at Oxford University, to read modern languages and linguistics. His studies took him deep into the psyche of other cultures, particularly German, and his novels' protagonists George Smiley, Jim Prideaux, John Avery, and Magnus Pym share his professions as both agent and linguist. Believing he would someday take up the life Ronnie envisioned for him – the Oxford don associated with exclusive clubs and august institutions – David spent four years studying German at Oxford, taking first honors in modern languages. While at Oxford he married his first wife, Alison Ann Veronica Sharp ("Ann"), the daughter of a much-decorated RAF air marshal and one of the few people not beguiled by Ronnie's charm.

Forced by his father's bankruptcy and his own debt to leave school, Cornwell accepted a teaching position offered him by an "insider" at Millfield Junior School, another institution satirized in his fiction. Ronnie, in the meanwhile, somehow maneuvered enough shady deals to secure his son's return to Oxford and his studies there. Despite his youthful disenchantment with the public school system and his Millfield experiences, Cornwell put aside his writing and, on graduation, accepted a poorly paid teaching position at the prestigious Eton College. Poverty dictated that, in his spare time, Cornwell freelance illustrating books, such as *Talking Birds* (1961) – an experience that enriches his descriptive passages of Berne, Hong Kong, and Palestinian training camps. Two years at Eton, however, confirmed Cornwell's educational cynicism: at its worst Eton was "unbelievably frightful . . . intolerant, chauvinistic, bigoted, ignorant. At its best, it [was] enlightened, adaptable, fluent and curiously democratic" (Dean, 306).

Cornwell knew he was talented, ambitious, and frustrated. Writing attracted him more than teaching; however, with a family, he needed a steady income. Abandoning both teaching and painting, Cornwell returned to his and all writers' "natural" profession: spying.

Enter John le Carré

From 1959 to 1964 Cornwell worked in various capacities for the Foreign Service in London, Bonn, and Hamburg. In 1960, as détente began to diffuse the cold war, Cornwell joined MI-6 – Britain's military intelligence version of the CIA – using as his cover the job of second secretary at the British embassy in Bonn. Bonn and MI-6 showed him, firsthand, double agents. Restless with his official duties and chronically in need of money, David Cornwell returned to fiction, writing on the train traveling to and from various assignments and, in the case of *The Spy Who Came in from the Cold*, in sight of the Berlin Wall. The Foreign Service forbade any employee to publish under a real name. Thus, for his first novel – the hybrid detective/spy thriller *Call for the Dead* (1960) – David Cornwell became John le Carré.[14]

Before le Carré few novelists considered espionage fiction more than entertainment. Nevertheless, such writers as Joseph Conrad in *The Secret Agent* (1907) and *Under Western Eyes* (1911), Somerset Maugham in *Ashenden* (1928), and le Carré contemporary Graham Greene in *The Confidential Agent* (1939), *The Power and the Glory* (1940), *The Third Man* (1950), and *The Quiet American* (1955) experimented with espionage as a means of presenting realistic characters who, as spies, define moral issues of honor, alienation, betrayal, guilt, and expiation. Critics generally censured these experiments: adventure thrillers could *not* be serious literature, and successful literary novels could not be "popular," because they unnecessarily complicated the genre conventions with character analyses.

When *Call for the Dead* appeared serious espionage fiction like Conrad's, Maugham's, or Greene's were exceptions. The popular spy novel was a mixture of fantasy, farce, and fanatic nationalism; its most successful practitioner was Ian Fleming; and the preeminent spy was James Bond, whom le Carré depreciates as an absurd "hyena . . . sustained by capital and kept in good heart by the charms of a materialist society."[15] His disgust stems from the myth Bond perpetrates and the obscenely passionate way alleged democratic patriots revere that myth. Unlike Fleming's dashing picture, Bond and his contemporaries embody "the ideal defector" and "ultimate prostitute" who replaces "love with technique" and questions only when – not whether – seducing people is ethically justified.[16]

In *Call for the Dead* le Carré seemingly answers the Bond myth with his first surrogate father, George Smiley, and his first bureaucratic corruption, the Cambridge Circus, "a very beautiful microcosm of English behavior and English society altogether."[17] Smiley is no James Bond. A short, fat, toadish scholar of German poetry, he is lured rather than recruited from Oxford for intelligence work. Bond's flashiness corrupts narrative realism; Smiley's anonymous appearance and insipid habits make him an unlikely but believable hero. Bond's sexual conquests are an anathema to George Smiley's cuckoldry: his wife's infidelities ironically complement his profession's faithlessness. Importantly, Smiley is a liberal humanist who endures only as long as he can question this humanism; Bond at best mouths superficial professional doubts.

Whether Smiley is a conscious revolt from Fleming's 007 hero is less consequential than his place in literature as a contemporary hero. With Smiley le Carré invigorates and enriches the mystery and espionage fiction born of Conan Doyle and Rudyard Kipling, refines the tradition of realism initiated in part by Conrad and Greene, and paves the way for later espionage antiheroes. Despite this contribution, clearly established with his first two novels, neither *Call for the Dead*, judged first runner-up in the British Crime Writers' Association awards, nor his second effort, *A Murder of Quality* (1962), received critical acclaim or more than modest sales.

All this changed in 1963 with le Carré's third and immensely influential *The Spy Who Came in from the Cold*. Le Carré, by now the financially strapped father of three sons, stayed reluctantly with his intelligence career and its regular salary. Still, he wanted to write and, he hoped, produce something of literary or artistic strength. Almost whimsically he had instructed his London accountant to wire him if his bank account ever reached £20,000, the amount he determined would release him from spying to writing. *Spy* earned this amount and far more. Detested by former CIA director Richard Helms for "undermining the very bedrock of intelligence" and praised by Graham Greene as "the best spy novel I have ever read," *Spy* sold more than a quarter-million copies, topped the New York and London best-seller lists for months, was translated into 12 languages, and by 1965 was made into a profitable if artistically indifferent Paramount movie with Richard Burton playing Alec Leamas. Now financially secure, le Carré was free to condemn the Foreign Service and privileged schools like Eton as institutions "so fortified against the outside world that they had no hope of personal contact with the people they were meant to govern."[18]

Spy additionally earned le Carré an international reputation as a serious novelist but lost him his family, a painful admission he acknowledged 20 years after his divorce from Ann Sharp. International acclaim for this novel overwhelmed him. He reveled in the attention, publicity tours, offers for everything from television shows to mistresses, and huge sums of money. His struggle to support a family disappeared while his effort to establish himself as a novelist took priority, an act Ann saw as antifamily. Public acclaim, le Carré's confessed self-doubt about his success, and domestic instability conspired to end the marriage and tempt him to more instability. Life after Ann included casual involvements, high-profile recognition, a tempestuous relationship with James and Susan Kennaway that lead to *The Naive and Sentimental Lover* (1971), and, in 1972, his second marriage, to Valerie Jane Eustace, an editor at Hodder & Stoughton Publishers.

Spy, however, was not a universal success. Polish authorities refused to acknowledge inquiries from le Carré's agent about its possible publication, and a Balkan editor censored long passages in the book and returned the tattered remains. In May 1966 le Carré responded to Soviet criticism of the book in an open letter (with the Flemingesque title "To Russia, with Greetings") to Moscow *Literaturnaya Gazete* critic V. Voinov. Voinov had branded le Carré a former spy who fanned the flames of the cold war by equating agents with contemporary heroes. In his response le Carré philosophically depreciates Voinov's conclusions by arguing that betrayal destroys institutions, human beings, and any possibility for heroism. Le Carré contends that since *Spy* is built around obvious paradoxes and mirror-image characters, the novel equates the morals and conduct of both sides: "They use the same weapons – deceit – and even the same spies (a point Mr. Khrushchev made long before I did)." Thinking liberals must question how long their democracies can "defend ourselves – you and me – by methods of this kind, and still remain the kind of society that is worth defending?" ("To Russia," 5). The contention dominates all le Carré's novels.

The international success of *The Spy Who Came in from the Cold* also raised questions about the nature of le Carré's Foreign Service work. In 1964 he claimed that his expertise with intelligence operations was drawn not from personal involvement but from his study of fictional and nonfictional spies, from his disenchantment with the inner sanctums of educational and governmental bureaucracies, and from his preference for realism and naturalism. Le Carré argues that writers create realism: "You only have to see a cat crossing the road and you should be able to write about what it's like to be hunted by tigers."[19] But his seemingly precise style incited critics to press the question further.

When asked 10 years later, le Carré again tried to shake off his spy-as-insider image. He finds that a novel's narrative derives not from the writer's vocational background but from the characters and their tensions writers invent: "The story of 'The Spy' was really a story of loneliness; it was a cold-war context which gave it the edge" (Cameron, 64). By 1983, however, le Carré admitted that his experience with British intelligence was influential. Although he declined to elaborate, he advised interviewers that, while overseas activities invariably entail secrets, "not all of them are half as enchanting as we fiction writers would wish them to be" (Bragg, 22).

Le Carré's espionage activities are secondary to the writing skills he gained working for the Foreign Service. He acknowledges how he benefited from the very bureaucracy and institutionalization that he deplores in his books. Even position papers written by "the smallest worm in the outfit" were copiously revised as each "wretched" clerk "adds his comments, eliminates loose words, questions style, questions the line of thought, until finally when it reaches the Ambassador he makes his own alterations and then it comes all the way down again" (Abley 1983a, 34). Le Carré claims that the practice disillusioned anyone with "any thoughts about the glory of" his prose style (Abley 1983a, 34). The wary, economical style he learned in the Foreign Office disappears, however, as he moves more into writing and further from his espionage vocation. His later novels sacrifice spare characterization to excessive description and innumerable eccentric characters.

The Looking-glass War (1965) recasts the cold war ideological impasse of *Spy* as the emotional deadlock born of old, impotent warriors' "hot-war" experiences. *Looking-glass* was followed in 1968 by *A Small Town in Germany*, a novel that waited almost 15 years before receiving critical recognition. Set in the Bonn offices of the British embassy, where David Cornwell served as second secretary, *Small Town* depicts the classic le Carré betrayal of an antihero/detective caught up in betrayal by his own side.

Also in 1968 le Carré's introduction to *The Philby Conspiracy* exposed his psychological fascination with Britain's most infamous mole and spymaster, Kim Philby. Philby, poised to be British intelligence's next leader, repeatedly justified his treachery as loyalty to cause; nonetheless, le Carré staunchly refuses to accept history or ideology as excuses for the heinous deceit. He condemns Philby as a "spiteful, vain, and murderous" man with no country, no credo, and no love who spied less for profit than to condemn his own class; however, he equally chastises the Secret Service and "the capacity of the British ruling class for reluctant betrayal and polite self-preservation."[20] Philby's motivations for betrayal haunt le Carré's fiction, suggesting the spymaster as one of Cornwell's secret sharers. Versions of Philby can be seen in Dieter Frey, the British-trained, German secret agent in *Call for the Dead*; in Jens Fiedler, Abteilung's dedicated deputy in *Spy*; and in Axel Axel, Magnus Pym's sympathetic partner in *A Perfect Spy*. Philby's motivations for betrayal enrich Bill Haydon's characterization in *Tinker, Tailor, Soldier, Spy* and Karla's throughout *The Quest for Karla*. And in *The Russia House* Philby's treasonous style makes up part of Barley Blair's moral exemplar, Ned.

Tinker, Tailor, Soldier, Spy, le Carré's most obvious retelling of Kim Philby's betrayal, continues the bildungsroman begun in *Call for the Dead* by reinstating George Smiley to find the Philby mole, "a deep penetration agent so called because he burrows deep into the fabric of Western imperialism" (*Tinker, Tailor*, 57). To bring sense to his and the discredited, demoralized Circus's political disorientation, Smiley increasingly adopts Karla's (his Soviet counterpart's) rigid absolutism. The change spiritually kills this man who continually evaluates his own relativism. Smiley confronts Karla in *The Honourable Schoolboy* and defeats his doppelgänger in *Smiley's People* (1980), but the price he pays is high. Although his victory over Karla is motivated by his sense of commitment, Smiley forces himself to win with his enemy's tactics. Succumbing to the absolutism of the-ends-justify-any-means, Smiley loses the moral superiority that set him apart from Karla.

In the midst of le Carré's success with the Karla trilogy, Ronnie Cornwell died "of a colossal heart attack . . . after a lifetime of perfect health and riotous self-indulgence, in an English country cottage, one summer's afternoon in 1975."[21] More than 10 years later in *A Perfect Spy* le Carré exorcises Ronnie's ghost. He admitted in an interview in the French monthly *Lire* that he "probably took refuge in the world of espionage to escape my father," and in his fiction he repeatedly strains to come to terms with his father and his childhood, for to "understand, explain and justify my father's betrayal of his milieu, class and society, one has to blame the institutions and the men behind them as well as the respectability in which I found temporary refuge when I fled."[22] As a result, Ronnie as he was and as the character David Cornwell remembers appears variously in le Carré's fiction as George Smiley, as Leclerc in *Looking-glass War*, as

"Sambo" Westerby in *Honourable Schoolboy*, as Charlie's absent father in *The Little Drummer Girl*, as Hugo Cassidy in *The Naive and Sentimental Lover*, and as countless duplicitious fathers scattered among his secondary characters. His fullest, most devastating realization, filled with a humor few le Carré critics acknowledge, is as *A Perfect Spy*'s father, Rickie Pym.

The success of the Karla trilogy, both in print and on television, halted le Carré's use of George Smiley as a character. Losing Smiley, however, freed le Carré for other projects. He turned his attention to the political situation in the Middle East. Writing *The Little Drummer Girl* (1983) and a series of newspaper critiques for the *Observer* on the Palestine Liberation Organization (PLO) and the hopelessly complex Middle East crises, le Carré used more than the headlines he reported. To gain a sense of atmosphere for the novel, he traveled to Israel, Lebanon, and the Palestinian camps, meeting with various players, including Yassir Arafat, in this complex and deadly theater. Le Carré used these radicalizing experiences to put a human face on the Palestinian imbroglio. The novel's protagonist, Charlie, loosely based on le Carré's half-sister, Charlotte Cornwell, demonstrates an astonishing change of character, behavior, and allegiances. These changes challenged le Carré to balance the Israeli and Palestinian perspectives in a novel where the motives of characters, rather than political or moral rhetoric, determine the action.

When le Carré completed *The Quest for Karla*, he complained that he had gone too far into a private world. *The Little Drummer Girl* was intended to dismiss one father figure, George Smiley, from his fiction even as the novelist struggled to dismiss the omnipresent Ronald Cornwell from his life. The very public *The Little Drummer Girl* left le Carré with his childhood demons, and so he took aim at those demons – himself and his father – in *A Perfect Spy*. The novel bears all the marks of a mature John le Carré work. It moves in contrapuntal style from the narrator's childhood through his recruitment, betrayals, and inevitable suicide; its characters, particularly Rick Pym, are Dickenesian in their vigor, humor, and eccentricities. But the novel's sense of betrayal cuts deeper than le Carré's earlier novels, if only because Magnus Pym betrays family, associates, and country for no ascertainable reason.

For *A Perfect Spy* le Carré probed the many links between love and betrayal by exploiting the doubling imagery he perfected in *The*

Quest for Karla. The exercise freed him at long last from his parental nemesis. That freedom brought joy. Le Carré "cried and cried when it was over," believing that "writing *A Perfect Spy* is probably what a very wise shrink would have advised."[23] For his twelfth and thirteenth novels, *The Russia House* and *The Secret Pilgrim*, le Carré turned again to the public world – and in *Pilgrim* to George Smiley – for character studies that humorously set espionage operations in former Soviet president Mikhail Gorbachev's liberalized, post-cold war world of *glasnost* (openness).[24] *Russia House* retraces familiar motifs and themes through vintage le Carré eccentrics who naturally gravitate toward dissembling. The story line, manipulated protagonist, taut structure, and controlled detail echo *The Spy Who Came in from the Cold*. Yet rather than a blatant political indictment, *The Russia House* is a black comedy of the manners of spies, indebted for its humor to *A Perfect Spy*'s caricatures. Barley Blair, a near-bankrupt British-publisher-qua-reluctant-agent, is seduced by his controller on a mission destined for failure – this time less by the agent's cynicism than by his determined escape from his British heritage of nation and destiny. An amateur caught in a professional's sordid game, he worries, learns dissembling expertly, and finds that by merely being a decent man, he acts heroically. His controller, Circus professional Ned, claims in *Secret Pilgrim* that he too has tried to act decently within the confines of Smiley's milieu. In this loosely connected series of reminiscences sparked by Smiley's address to impending Sarratt graduates, Ned traces the successes and failures that embittered but fundamentally honorable human beings like himself face working in a dishonoring profession that inevitably sires only compromise.

Russia House and *Secret Pilgrim* bring le Carré as a literary figure full circle. With them he embraces again a streamlined, realistic espionage fiction that is his forte. His writing "apprenticeship . . . finally over," le Carré places himself squarely within the genre, although "anybody writing now [has] to work a little harder and think a little harder" (Schiff, 189).[25] His fascination with spies goes beyond their adventures to their unique promise as representatives of the basic problems facing humanity. In seeking to reconcile the naive, natural state of action with the sentimental, contemplative world, operatives like Smiley, Westerby, and Ned entangle themselves in hopeless ironies. If they seek refuge in institutions and serve them with solitary reflection or unquestioning action, they forfeit their humanity. If they balance thought and action, as Smiley does in *The Quest for Karla*, they destroy their spirits as surely as they ravage others' lives. The only victors are those who continue the struggle.

The Spy Who Came in from the Cold, The Little Drummer Girl, Tinker, Tailor, Soldier, Spy, and *Smiley's People* illustrate le Carré at his best as obviously as *A Small Town in Germany, The Naive and Sentimental Lover,* and *A Perfect Spy* display his more pretentious side. Using his constant theme of the meretricious relationship between love and betrayal, he exploits the conventions of espionage fiction to show that no absolute standards of public or personal conduct exist. For le Carré, the consequent relativism results in cruelty or indifference; humanism, no matter how ponderously reexamined, cannot avoid inhumanity. Like Conrad, Maugham, Greene, and John Fowler, le Carré creates largely convincing characters whose often-unshakable faith in conspiracy leads uncontrollably to treachery. Readers may be lulled by the novelist's sometimes intentional, sometimes unintentional humor. But to enter le Carré's world, they are forced to recognize the inadequacy of abstract creeds, partly realized allegiances, and favored institutions. If readers leave his books with contradictory questions rather than impassioned solutions, the novelist has succeeded. For John le Carré, we have met the enemy, and we are they.

Chapter Two

A Brief History
of a Sentimental Man

A Spy is above all a man of politics. . . . [H]e must have the breadth of thought of a strategist, and meticulous powers of observation. Espionage is a continuous and demanding labor which never ceases.

"To Russia, with Greetings" (1966)

A World of Agents

Professional spies are mysterious, unpredictable, omnipotent, admirable yet criminal. Are they honorable patriots who compromise themselves for a just cause? Or are they liars, thieves, "a procession of vain fools, traitors" who play on the weaknesses of others to gain information?[1] Espionage fascinates because it promises secret, insider's information, and information in the twentieth century means power. Real-life spies, such as Gary Powers, Kim Philby, and John Walker bear witness to our capacity for deceit, but should they spy for us, we keep quiet. We want results; we don't acknowledge the methods. Fictional spies, such as Harvey Birch, Captain Hugh "Bulldog" Drummond, and Harry Palmer, mesmerize us, but our interest in every detail of their operations is academic. We're safe in the knowledge that the outcome stays between the book covers.

Critics claim that the relationship between spying and espionage fiction stems variously from biblical apocrypha, classical tragedy, Elizabethan intrigues, and the Industrial Revolution.[2] Whatever its origins, the seeds of the twentieth-century British espionage novel were germinated in the Edwardian age, a time when Britain, following its success in the Boer War (1899-1902) and prior to World Wars I and II, erroneously believed its empire invincible. To maintain political dominance, Britain became ever vigilant, especially for the ubiquitous German menace. By 1903 Britain and Germany were locked in a mutual suspicion that lasted for decades: Britain dreaded the newly developed German navy's challenge to British naval supremacy; Germany feared an unprovoked British invasion. Neither country seriously examined the consequences of its fears or trusted the other's diplomats. As a result, both countries' unrealized misgivings increased their shared misperceptions.[3] The door was further opened for a best-seller literature that capitalized on political turbulence.

Prior to this time a professional British intelligence bureaucracy did not exist. Influential leaders soon deplored this lacuna, arguing that intelligence organizations could protect Britain because only they could substantiate Germany's militaristic intentions. In the intelligence hysteria that resulted, a subcommittee of the Committee of Imperial Defence, under the chairmanship of Reginald McKenna Haldane, in 1909 recommended instituting the Secret Service Bureau to gather secrets from other countries, specifically Germany, and protect Britain's secrets from compromise. The Bureau's Home Office, forerunner of the military Security Service (S.S.), or MI-5, launched various espionage activities in Britain, and the Secret Intelligence Service (SIS), or MI-6, initiated counterespionage operations while gathering intelligence abroad.[4]

Fiction, as much as or more than actual political events, encouraged the creation of the modern intelligence bureaucracy. This bureaucracy in turn helped the modern espionage novel flourish in the second half of the century. A central contributor to this symbiosis was journalist, sometime spy, and hack novelist William Tufnell Le Queux (1864-1927). Half-French and half-British, Le Queux neither attended the proper schools nor attained membership in the correct clubs – the acknowledged trappings of nationalism. Nevertheless, British patriotism obsessed him. Convinced that envious Europeans had filled England with thousands of highly trained spies posing as waiters, bank tellers, barbers, and servants, Le Queux excited public opinion by inundating British agencies and newspapers with propagandistic reports, telegrams, pictures, and drawings. All that stood between Britain and its betrayal, the prolific Le Queux argued, was a small group of right-hearted but woefully ill-prepared amateur intelligence agents – himself, of course, one of them – who could no longer stand in readiness to defend their nation but must be called to arms immediately. For years authorities ignored him.

Le Queux's fervent nationalism and moral outrage did not stop at ominous newspaper editorials. Between 1890 and 1927 he encouraged the espionage profession through a variety of popular novels that combined his knowledge of military and political affairs, overly romanticized views of love and England, and shrewd sense of public opinion. With Field Marshal Lord Roberts, Le Queux published *The Invasion of 1910* (1906), warning of German plans for a naval invasion of England – plans he claimed he discovered through his voluntary intelligence network. *Spies for the Kaiser: Plotting the Downfall of England* (1909), Le Queux's next prophecy, grew, he maintained, from his interrogation of more than 5,000 German spies in Britain.[5] Other novels followed, each one delivering Le Queux's sensationalism.

Despite his influence on public opinion and policy, Le Queux was far from the best novelist to propose, in fiction, institutionalized intelligence operations. That honor goes to Erskine Childers (1879-1922) and John Buchan (1875-1940), who, along with more recognized figures like Rudyard Kipling (1865-1936), are credited with both encouraging the espionage frenzy and with establishing the literary criteria for the genre. Childers, an Irish-born clerk in the British House of Commons and a superb yachtsman, published *The Riddle of the Sands* (1903) when British attention was riveted on a possible German naval invasion. A sailing adventure, *Riddle* follows Carruthers, a bored Foreign Office clerk, and Davies, his somewhat mysterious friend, as they stumble into political intrigues initiated by European agent provocateurs. True Edwardian patriots, they reluctantly spy to preserve British institutions and to stimulate their intellectual curiosity, safely oblivious of bothersome ethical questions.

Political tensions and Childers's writing skills made his overly sentimental fiction instantly successful. Buchan's career thrived for the same reasons. *The Thirty-nine Steps* (1915), hastily written after the outbreak of World War I, and, later, *Mr. Standfast* (1919), purportedly based on contemporary diplomatic realities, aided Britain's war effort and continued the intelligence community's evolution. Predictably, the villains are German; the hero, Richard Hannay, an unassuming patriot; the politics, conservative; and the outcome, true to genre conventions and audience expectations.

Childers's and Buchan's better-written adventures outpaced Le Queux's potboilers. More important, their novels, and many similar ones, settled the criteria for spy fiction that were to remain until the cold war.[6] The genre laced careful plotting with two-dimensional characterization and repetitious description; it favored action adventure, facile romances, recurring settings and characters, clear moral guidelines, diverting games, and predictable outcomes. Staunchly British values were assailed by nefarious enemies – the French until the 1890s, the Germans until the 1950s, and finally the Russians. The psychology of loyalty and betrayal, the heart of contemporary espionage fiction, was peripheral. Loyal readers were seldom troubled by the conflicting demands of the individual and the collective. Instead, they relished the Great Game that excited Kipling's Kim, or they heroically battled for the integrity and values of the homeland and against vicious international villains capable of disguising themselves, sending coded messages, seducing honest women, and, when operationally warranted, treacherously murdering. Whereas criminals confirm the classic mystery detective's superior ability to solve ingenious puzzles, traitors reaffirm the legitimacy of the spy's values, culture, and difficult quests to prevent catastrophe.[7]

The uneasy peace between Britain and Europe was shattered by World War I, after which both Britain and spy fiction changed. Financially staggering from inflation and huge government debts, England feared a rearmed and belligerent Germany. World War II erupted a year after Prime Minister Neville Chamberlain declared, "Peace in our time!" Britain confronted its expected adversary – a stronger, wealthier Germany – and, unexpectedly, expanding unrest among British colonies.

To preserve the empire and secure the Soviet Union's entry into World War II, Britain and her allies formed an uneasy coalition with the Soviet Union in 1941, despite a deep-seated mistrust of post-Bolshevik Russia. Allied officials reasoned that Marxist Russia was the only block to German advances in Europe. They depreciated the security threat a possible Russian domination of Eastern Europe posed. After World War II the Allies, to pay their Soviet war debts, betrayed the peoples of Eastern Europe by dividing their homelands with the Soviet Union and consequently ensured decades of unrest and expanded espionage activity. Faced with depressed economic outlooks, a cynical citizenry, and a compromised national reputation,

British espionage agencies scrambled for scarce resources to maintain themselves and to best their richly funded cousins, the growing American intelligence complex.

Professionals in the intelligence services increased their importance – and their budgets – by reminding the tax-paying public of their agencies' wartime contributions and expertise while exploiting the public's deep-seated fears and patriotism. Between the world wars British intelligence service recruited Edwardian models from both Oxford's acclaimed colleges and Cambridge's less prestigious ones by promising these bright, presumably patriotic recruits honorable careers with an increasingly lucrative intelligence complex. Secretly, the Soviet Union also recruited from the same upper-class stock. Despite a trebled national debt, 800,000 wartime casualties, and, by 1963, the independence of 6 million of the country's tax-paying colonists, intelligence officials argued that their necessarily secret wartime successes evinced their infallibility at intelligence gathering, their patriotic superiority, and the continued greatness of the British empire – an effective cover for any spy or bureaucrat. To survive the peril of former-ally-now-enemy Russia, they argued, imperial pretenses must be maintained and clandestine operations increased. Facing the potential of new invasions or, worse yet, nuclear annihilation, financially strapped Britons paid.

Positive public sentiment began to fade when it was discovered that British intelligence, believed impregnable because its patriotism imitated unassailable democratic tenets, had been successfully penetrated by its own disillusioned nationals. Several young British intellectuals, members of the so-called Auden generation and sympathetic to Marxism, manipulated their places as proper British bureaucrats to thwart Britain's intelligence policies. By 1963, when *The Spy Who Came in from the Cold* was published, double agents Guy Burgess, Donald Maclean, and Kim Philby had defected to the Soviet Union, leaving England's confidence in its intelligence empire betrayed and the country's international reputation further diminished (see discussion in Chapter 5). Faced with a world of international tensions, sabotage, assassination, terrorism, and ultimate betrayal, intelligence operatives seemed impotent guardians of a declining society based not on reason, democracy, and a tacit class system but on duplicity. Western political systems looked as philosophically insolvent as

British coffers, for now not only the participants but the credo had gone mad.

With this heritage spy fiction developed two separate but unequal branches. On the one hand, such writers as Ian Fleming pursued fantastic, almost-farcical adventures. Fleming, a maverick stockbroker-turned-intelligence-planner, intended his James Bond series as an escape from the realities of cold war Britain. Bond is a contemporary throwback, an Edwardian-gentleman-agent-turned-midcentury-professional with his own office, secretary, and disgruntled boss. He is an urbane St. George, rescuing England from its protean enemies with modern technology and unbelievable tradecraft (i.e., espionage techniques) rather than battle-axes and swords.

In an economically and morally depressed Britain, even the escapist Bond literature comments ironically on England's decline. Bond chauvinistically squanders unlimited resources in defense of British values against Smersh, his and his service's fictional adversary. In a world seemingly poised for a third world war that Britain could not lead, Smersh, a totalitarian surrogate, is defeated as the British would wish for their richer and more influential enemies and competitors to be defeated; however, Smersh resurfaces each time stronger, more sadistic, and with more treasonous conspiracies for Bond to defeat.

On the other hand, some writers inquired from various perspectives into spying's inherent moral ambiguities. Alienated intellectuals replaced Edwardian staunchness with ideologies ranging from scientific probability, communism, and Marxism to Catholicism and skepticism. Many, notably Graham Greene, stayed with their conversions. In espionage fiction morality no longer had the Le Queux-Childers-Buchan certainty, and the gentleman agent image, appropriate for Edwardian England, gave way to the cold war operative as a suitable metaphor for postimperial alienation.[8] A few postwar writers recast agents as expendables of a manipulative system that, by separating individuals, subverts the value of individuality. Disaffected from the comfortable security of the greater good, these spies personify expediency and self-defined morality rather than society's pronounced virtues. They survive by betrayal, because as professionals they feign a detached interest in others while fervidly searching for their hidden knowledge. Presumably working within democracy's perimeters,

these operatives deride society's norms by violating both the letter
and the spirit of its tainted laws. They inevitably become outsiders,
either contemptuous of all or defeated by their own alienation.

One version of the alienated hero is W. Somerset Maugham's
Ashenden (1928), a gentleman agent who rejects the heretofore-
unquestioned motivations of Edwardian secret agents.[9] A middle-
aged man of letters, Ashenden lives as Maugham did in comparative
luxury and, like his World War I spy creator, challenges but does not
eliminate the romantic myth of the spy. Literary buff and social
opportunist, Ashenden enjoys the sense that as a British clubman his
presence can terrorize foreign agents. But far from Davies or Hannay, Ashenden is a pragmatist who suffers his Secret Service's
bureaucracy and his chief's ruthlessness. He can defeat most rivals
but relies explicitly on help from his agency and fears implicitly public exposure. He accepts – and pities – double agents as ordinary
types bribed to betray their countries. Because his field experiences
cost him his British naïveté and repay him with skepticism, Ashenden, more than Hannay or Bond, opens the way to George Smiley.[10]

Genre writers after Maugham abandon the gentleman spy and
his superficial morality altogether to present disenchanted characters
with often-questionable motives.[11] Eric Ambler's protagonists are
ordinary people – university professors like Charles Latimer in *A Coffin for Dimitrios* (1930) or engineers like Fraser in *State of Siege*
(1956) – who are swept up in espionage plots. Rather than auto-
matically defending the empire and its secrets, however, these amateurs slowly come to understand the conspiracies, reject involvement
in them, and flee back to their comfortable fictions. Len Deighton's
protagonists, such as his nameless, working-class antihero from *The
Ipcress File* (1963), are aging professionals complaining about late
paychecks, malfunctioning weaponry, slow bureaucracies, upper-
class supervisors, and incompetent co-workers. They defend private
moralities because all ideologies are bankrupt.

Contemporary writers manipulate the apparatus of espionage
fiction to concentrate on human weaknesses and to call into question not only the protagonists' motivations but the shifting morality
of a culture that condones espionage. Graham Greene, le Carré's
immediate literary influence, separates his "entertainments" from his
serious fiction, although his espionage "heroes," like all his protagonists, react to events primarily from self-centered interest. Betrayers

Wormold (*Our Man in Havana*, 1958) and Fowler (*The Quiet American*, 1955) undergo Dostoyevskian angst to appease their consciences much as nongenre protagonist Major Scobie (*The Heart of the Matter*, 1948) damns his soul for a faint hope of love. Greene's imposition of universal themes on a popular genre clouds heretofore-assumed distinctions between literary and genre fiction. Furthermore, his cynicism, more than Ambler's and Deighton's disenchantment, insists that readers evaluate moral issues, long ignored in spy fiction but pervasive in postwar democratic societies. As Joseph Conrad suggests in his character studies *The Secret Agent* (1907) and *Under Western Eyes* (1911), Greene surveys, through espionage, complex characterizations and symbolism.

Conrad's, Maugham's, and Greene's novels confirm how Le Queux's genre, even with its story-line restrictions, supplies contemporary writers with ready-made ethical impasses. Contemporary espionage fiction works within its popular predecessor's conventions and didacticism to enrich those conventions, obscure its propagandistic tone, and promote sophisticated novels of character. Unmistakable spy fiction, such as *The Invasion of 1910*, *Bulldog Drummond* (1920), or *You Only Live Twice* (1964), suggests political and historical events; however, espionage fiction, such as *Nostromo* (1904), *The Honorary Consel* (1983), or Adam Hall's Quiller series, interprets these events and their players.

John le Carré's novels react to Le Queux's propaganda and Fleming's escapism by refashioning, within the genre's basic conventions, the character motifs and themes of alienation that profit Conrad, Maugham, and Greene. His admirable protagonists confront the reality that, for all its seductiveness, the dynamics of espionage are incompatible with the human relationships that postwar democratic societies publicly sanction but privately undermine. Reluctantly, they concede their dilemmas but, finding no solace in acknowledged values and doctrines, are left adrift. Their approbation arises solely from their search for an internally consistent yet necessarily private ethical code that accommodates perpetual instability. Appropriate behavior, humiliation, loyalty, and betrayal become relative as events rapidly change attitudes and promote deceit.

In each of his novels le Carré warns that, as countries and their agents cautiously gauge their alliances, people must warily confront relationships. Like spies, all people fear insincerity, conspiracy, and

betrayal yet must embrace love if they are to survive. Individuals may
espouse moral attitudes to which they "subscribe perhaps
intellectually, but not emotionally."[12] These attitudes, however, concurrently alienate by minimizing the chance of emotional commitments and, ironically, protect by suggesting rationales for inexplica-
ble betrayals. This theme resounds throughout le Carré's fiction as
he guts espionage conventions to capture the estrangement that
eventually leaves people hollow and modern society marooned.

Précis to a Spy: George Smiley's Circus

Le Carré's earliest attempts at applying these metaphors are *Call for
the Dead*, a hybrid detective-spy novel that suggests its reluctant
hero as an isolated everyman snared in a difficult web of multiple
identities, and *A Murder of Quality*, a classic detective novel that critiques British society through the figure of a prostituted institution.[13]
Call for the Dead introduces le Carré's series hero, the diffident
intellectual-qua-aging-spymaster George Smiley, who epitomizes
British decency and the ineffectual efforts of an existential humanist
beset by the psychological and moral dilemmas his profession symbolizes.[14] Instead of spy fiction's required action, the novel begins
with a chapter-long history of Smiley, told mainly through other's
impressions. This strategy sets what becomes le Carré's standard narrative technique: he centers the story on a character, sets polar
opposites around him or her, and then exposes the inevitable colli-
sions that unmask characters' motivations.

The object of the moment is a perfect spy because, as his ex-wife
Lady Ann Sercombe indicates, he is "breathtakingly ordinary" yet
enigmatically attractive.[15] Lady Ann's intimate yet essentially solipsis-
tic view of "Toad" (her nickname for Smiley) paints him in relief
against the social milieu that sustains his profession and hints at why
this improbable couple should but can never prosper. Her aristo-
cratic connections secured her a position as Steed-Asprey's secretary, where, to her genteel family's dismay, she met and married
loner Smiley. The mismatch serves her morally diminished social
"Set" with a marriage they callously degrade and a divorce they emotionally trivialize. Typical of the Set's insensitivity and emotional
bankruptcy, her cousin Lord Sawley sexually degrades both Ann and

Smiley when he declares at their wedding that "Sercomb was mated to a bullfrog in a sou'wester" (*Call*, 1). Sawley's affront classes him with the first of le Carré's gray men, Maston, the sycophantic "Head Eunuch" of Smiley's aptly named service, the Circus.[16] Known to insiders as Marlene Dietrich, Maston is an "obscene cissy with his greying hair and his reasonable smile" (*Call*, 33), the epitome of the worst of the professional milieu that Smiley contrasts.

While *Call*'s narrator claims that Ann's love of and reasons for leaving Smiley are ambiguous ("if she hadn't left him then, she never could have done" [*Call*, 1]), Ann's attractiveness to Smiley is not. Extraordinarily beautiful, she is his fairy-tale princess come in a dream to turn, with a magic kiss, the shrunken toad into a desirable prince. She animates their marriage with a spontaneous joy for living and an authentic love for her husband. Life with Smiley's fantasized Ann promises balance, an existence where his bothersome paradoxes find improbable resolution, where her Set's prostituted ethic and his ambiguous profession reform themselves, where insensitivity to human motivations unravels, and where love is more than what can be betrayed.

Image and reality, however, often conflict in le Carré's fiction. Smiley disdains sterile traditions and ideologies, preferring life with Ann to any scholarly dedications. Yet over the eight-novel series he consumes her vitality, and she turns his dream into recurring nightmare. Imbalance between dream – embodied in the fairy-tale life Smiley envisions with Ann – and fact – embodied in Ann's infidelities – weaken Smiley and illustrate the futility possible in a common human experience, aspiration. When she quests for her own emotional replenishment (in *Call* she elopes with the first of her sundry lovers, Cuban motor-racing-driver Juan Alvida), Ann leaves a despairing Smiley psychologically hollow. He rightly sees himself as "lost luggage, destined . . . to remain unclaimed on the dusty shelf of yesterday's news" (*Call*, 3-4). Still, he returns to her even when she makes him "an offer which no gentleman could accept" (*Call*, 101), because he can sustain the love of a sentimental man only by drawing heavily from her emotional well-being. Smiley with Ann lives, albeit in emotional collapse, but without her he wanders a no-man's land.[17]

Why the Smileys attract each other is also unmistakable: both are rebels from the same hypocrisy that permeates her class and his craft. Smiley, the intellectual without lineage, seeks integrity in his life. Ann, the capricious, unfaithful chimera, seeks emotional distance from her caste. They would prevail if, separately or together, they could integrate contemplation (the naive) with feeling (the sentimental), an improbable reconciliation that forces weaker characters (even, periodically, Smiley) to escape to institutions or absolutes. Yet their traits as surely as their emotionally volatile interaction prevent the union. Smiley torments his personal relationships with endless ruminations, while Ann's flights into loveless affairs preclude sagacious inquiry. He endlessly laments that neither pure logic nor obscure mysticism can reveal people's motivations, particularly when they act violently, but he perseveres at unraveling that obscurity. Sometimes hostile, sometimes loving, she cuckolds him repeatedly, mirroring his weaknesses back to him and further tormenting him by exposing herself, her society, and his profession as distortions of him. It is only Smiley's increasing struggles and ultimate disenchantment that define him as a success. Ann, sketchily drawn, is never allowed voice to her conflicts and therefore never attains equanimity.

Deprived of Ann, Smiley immerses himself in obscure research on German love poetry. But his sense of service to country and the intellectual challenges espionage offer lure him back to the Circus. He rationalizes that the battle sustains meaning. Nonparticipation – for Smiley, a passive means of taking a stand – is discordant with Western thought and democratic systems. To maintain his sense of self in a world without love (Ann) or beauty (literature), Smiley must belong to an institution dedicated even superficially to preserving those ideologies. He needs his Circus almost more than it needs him.

Smiley through Ann's or the Set's eyes is not his only anomaly. The professional dream is Smiley as spymaster/supersleuth; reality is Smiley the toadish, middle-aged spy with "heavy spectacles and thinning hair," the one who spends too much money on ill-fitting clothes and deciphers secrets intuitively. To those outside his professional world, Smiley seems "a little, fat man, rather gloomy, suddenly smiling, and ordering a drink," rather than a powerful operative (*Call*, 128). Even insiders like Ailsa Brimley echo this image: Smiley is "the most forgettable man [Brimley] has ever met . . . the very prototype of an unsuccessful middle-aged bachelor in a sedentary occupation" (*Murder*, 21).

Smiley is intellectually superior to an Edwardian gentleman spy or a James Bond but physically unqualified as a worthy adversary for charismatic antagonists like *Call*'s Dieter Frey and emotionally uncomfortable in his profession. Furthermore, he misses as a super-sleuth and resolute detective. Again, le Carré presents the character comparatively. Using noteworthy powers of observation, Smiley in both *Call* and *Murder* collects information, recounts the facts under the heading "What do we know?," returns to the murder scenes to investigate, and analyzes clues and hidden motives. Yet he is unable to maintain a Holmesian emotional distance from his quarry. Nor does he make distinctions between right and wrong that are self-evident to his adopted assistant, retired Inspector Mendel. Though Mendel lacks Smiley's deductive prowess, he has resolved many of the paradoxes plaguing his friend with Holmesian simplicity: he contently raises bees in the countryside and distinguishes between honorable individuals and crooks from his hard-earned emotional wariness and common sense. Smiley is a scrupulous man and therefore deserves unflagging affection; Adam Scarr, Dieter Frey, and Bill Haydon are common criminals and therefore deserves a police officer's notice.

Mendel denies Smiley's supersleuth image in other ways. Whereas Smiley seems a "tired executive out for a bit of fun" (*Call*, 128), Mendel is indistinguishable from the criminals he pursues. He's a "thin, weasel-faced" loner who earned his stature through years of patient surveillance (*Call*, 22). Practice lets Mendel read people precisely and know, long before others do, when Smiley is in over his head. He readily proves his talents for subterfuge when he dupes the telephone exchange girl into revealing who placed the victim's, Samuel Fennan's, 8:30 call. He finds Adam Scarr, Hans-Dieter Mundt's British courier, and threatens him to get information. A straightforward man, Mendel has no time for Smiley's subtle interrogation methods. With a policeman's instinct he perceives Frey as a felon, not an ideologue; thus it is Mendel who anticipates Frey's escape from Sheridan Theatre, Hammersmith, and tracks him to Battersea Bridge. Whereas Smiley tolerates everyone, Mendel belittles those who exaggerate their misfortunes over unwarranted persecution but empathizes with those who sincerely suffered tyranny, such

as the Jews in World War II. After hearing and rejecting Else Fennan's confused but impassioned charges against Nazi terrorism, he
gruffly comments, more to himself than to Smiley, that his "dad was
Yid. He never made such a bloody fuss about it" (*Call*, 79).

Mendel also enjoys living in a way neither Holmes nor Smiley
can. Rather than Holmes's careless clutter or Smiley's lifeless
Bywater Street flat, Mendel's home has an "almost feminine neat-
ness" about it. He talks in effortless clipped sentences to everyone,
whereas Smiley, in balanced syntax, stays "bothered and awkward
. . . trying not to be clever" (*Call*, 41). Mendel's reverence for living
opens him to placidity. For all his disclaimers, Smiley acutely feels
others' impressions of him. Mendel is indifferent to others' opinions
of him because he is secure in what he thinks of himself.

The less obvious contrast to the spymaster/supersleuth image is
Smiley's own personality: he trusts HUMINT rather than TECHINT,
instinct over technology and tradecraft. Smiley senses something is
wrong when he receives Fennan's prearranged call to himself, literally a call for the dead. His instinct tells him Fennan, a Jewish-
banker's-son-turned-espionage-bureaucrat, was a good man despite
the Foreign Office's vague evidence, but his sentimentality hinders
him from identifying Else, Fennan's frail and fiercely private wife, as a
murderer. Smiley intuits that Else's "instinct was to defend" (*Call*,
30), but he never questions what Else is defending or what she
defines as normality. Whereas Holmes revels at his accomplishments,
particularly when he defeats Moriarty, Smiley agonizes, fathoming
how his investigation forces Mundt to murder Else. In Smiley's distorted circus, resolutions are not triumphs but examples of human
deceit and warnings of further trouble. Each time he defeats a Moriarty, Smiley keenly discerns the loss.

Call for the Dead

The action of *Call for the Dead* emanates from doubling contrasts
that induce crisis: past political facts (specifically, the Holocaust and
the Nazi's military aggressiveness) compete with present ones
(interagency rivalries and the illusive East-West war of words called
the cold war), duty and loyalty ambivalently become crime and perfidy, ultimate betrayal masquerades as unselfish love, and, most of

all, grim realities replace imperfect dreams. Currying favor with the minister and home secretary, Maston – "a barmaid's dream of a real gentleman" – insists that Smiley interrogate Samuel Fennan, a 20-year Foreign Office veteran anonymously accused of treason. By an improbable circumstance Dieter Frey, former British and now East German agent, sees them together. Smiley clears Fennan, but the clerk mysteriously dies, and Maston ineptly manipulates Smiley to cover up the alleged suicide. Always the glib paper pusher, Maston betrays Smiley's investigation for fear Smiley will find embarrassing security breaches that competing intelligence agencies would use to discredit the Circus's burgeoning professional status. Outraged, Smiley officially resigns but cannot concede Fennan's suicide.

Relying on his considerable interrogation skills and retired Inspector Mendel's legwork, Smiley reasons that Else Fennan murdered her husband because he unearthed her betrayals of him and of her adopted country. Before Smiley can act, however, Dieter, on orders from Hans-Dieter Mundt, murders Else and flees with Mendel in pursuit. In their violent confrontation at Battersea Bridge, London, Dieter – in his death – achieves the clear moral triumph over Smiley, tarnishing his mentor's position as a standard-bearer of free-world values.

With the possible exceptions of the brutal but shadowy Hans-Dieter Mundt (covernamed "Freitag" [Man Friday] from *Robinson Crusoe*), Inspector Mendel, and, in this novel, "polished and thoughtful" Peter Guillam, all the novel's characters unsuccessfully aspire to replace the past's painful realities with illusionary distortions. For Britain's receding empire and morality, Maston greedily supplants a professional intelligence service. The cultured, "inspired amateurism" of Steed-Asprey's and Jebedee's generation yields to his dream of the "bureaucracy and intrigue of a large Government department" (*Call*, 7). Fennan's youthful flirtation with Marxism gives way to his reluctant acceptance of democracy's tainted values. His wife and spiritual doppelgänger, Else, shrouds her memories of wartime atrocities and fear of a Nazi revival with not marital love but an equivocating allegiance to the apparitions called espionage and ideology. "[T]oo volatile, too swift to react, too brightly painted, too vain" (*Call*, 75), Dieter Frey (covernamed "Mr. Robinson") replaces the transfigured loyalties and the incomplete social answers that Smiley represents with an extreme faith in socialism. He trades one ideology (anti-Nazism) for another (communism) in his evolution from valued but untrustworthy British agent to a burgeoning East German spymaster.

As a reluctant hero Smiley finds himself caught between his desperate need to believe in loyalty, country, friendship, and love and his alienation born of history's lessons, contemporary affairs, and his habits of mind. The conflict traps him "Between Two Worlds," the title of *Call*'s last chapter, and leaves all dreams stillborn. Here as in later novels, Smiley is presented as stoically frustrated. If he could reconcile improbable paradoxes in a way that would adequately preserve their disparate elements, he thinks he would be content. Yet he acknowledges that even this belief is illusionary. The scrupulous spy who doesn't want to spy responds empathetically to friend and foe alike in an unmistakably amoral world. Although he nostalgically misses his contemporaries and uncomfortably assists their impotent successors, Smiley is unwilling to permanently abandon these bureaucrats or his profession.

Smiley's espionage career gives eloquent voice to these ambiguities and encapsulates the disparities between past and present, dream and reality. During the 1930s gentlemen scholars coyly recruited him away from his studies. All regarded him as a conscientious but undistinguished student who read obscure poets as "academic excursions into the mystery of human behavior, disciplined by the practical application of his own deductions" (*Call*, 4). While Smiley dreamed of "Fellowships and a life devoted to the literary obscurities of seventeenth-century Germany," his tutor Jebeedee "wisely guided [him] away from the honours that would undoubtedly have been his" and into espionage with its Edwardian perception of honor (*Call*, 4).

Smiley's first assignment was as a talent spotter (i.e., an agent who picks out potential recruits) at a "provincial German University," where, as an *"englischer Dozent"* (lecturer in English), he "lectures on Keats and vacations in Bavarian hunting lodges with groups of earnest and solemnly promiscuous German students" (*Call*, 5) and recruits new agents, including Dieter Frey, a student he always calls by his given name, suggesting an almost-paternal attachment between the men.

The world of beauty and truth (represented by Keats's poetry) and the lure of impassioned love (represented by the sexually active students) are incompatible with the requirements of Smiley's secret profession; the dry academic world is not. Spying requires the scholarly research skills of careful observation and analysis while concurrently requiring politically justified betrayals, the counterpart of education's critical inquiry. The contrast among the ethereal worlds of art and love, the demands of close scholarship, and the seedy realities of political necessity divides Smiley and informs him. He questions his morally ambiguous position as teacher/recruiter but also finds that this deepening understanding of beauty, gained through a study of literature, matches his growing aversion to unbending ideologies like Nazism, gained through his observation of Hitler's Germany. His ambivalence sharpens as he silently watches students sacrifice their heritage and the literature he loves (burning the works of "Thomas Mann, Heine, Lessing and a host of others" [*Call*, 6]) for unexamined dogma.

Smiley's university experiences promote in him a detached evaluation that threatens to transform part of him into a "bloodless and inhuman" operative (*Call*, 6). To avoid the pain such disloyalty to others brings, Smiley the sentimentalist recoils "from the temptations of friendship and human loyalty; he guards himself warily from spontaneous reaction," hates "the falseness of his life," masters such impulses as "the sudden unreasoning desire for a woman," and yearns constantly for "any drug to take away the tension of his life" (*Call*, 7). Fear promotes maturation, and Smiley's natural inclination to know, cultivated by his liberal humanism, turns him to his ignominious profession. His sentimentalism and essentially sympathetic acceptance of hotheaded students, would-be architects of impossible utopias, and burned-out idealists tempers him but keeps his spirit perpetually tortured.

The pain and insanity of a world war aggravate his troubled conscience and further make distasteful service permissible. After the war, his successful cover blown, Smiley is retired to England and academe. Soon "the revelations of a young Russian cypher-clerk in Ottawa" (*Call*, 7) show that the Circus blocks out the lessons of the past, and Smiley's court recalls him to their duty.[18] Edwardian wartime amateurs – Jebeedee, Steed-Asprey, and Adrian Fielding – are either dead or committed to other dreams, leaving contemporary bureaucrats to icily misunderstand their new enemies' commitment. The cold war has fabricated an operational never-never land that invigorates the Circus's new bureaucracy. Smiley rejoins to stay off its inevitable moral disintegration.

Smiley's interview with Fennan attracts Smiley to the clerk because, although le Carré doesn't draw a fully rounded character with Fennan, he sets the character up, in many ways, as Smiley's natural double. Roughly of Smiley's age and intellectual proclivities, Fennan is politically and emotionally betrayed. As a 1930s Oxford undergraduate, he was attracted to the "comfort and peace in the intellectual purity" Marxism promised; its "intellectual ruthlessness," "fearlessness," and "academic reversal of traditional strengths" (*Call*, 56) seemed to offer accessible solutions to politically Gordian knots. But ideology-turned-to-action polarized his disenchantment. Party members find Fennan, a Jew and a questioner, embarrassing; he estranges himself from them and their ideology because they are "not men, but children, who dreamed of freedom-fires, gipsy music and one world tomorrow" and who, without scrutinizing history, have "no power to resist the Eastern sun, and obediently turned their tousled heads towards it" (*Call*, 56). Their gullibility leads to violence, distrust, and disloyalty; his skepticism leads to measured recommitment.

Mirroring Smiley, Fennan allows "the disproportion between the dream and reality" to drive his close examination of both. His investigations lead him to ask a Smileyesque question: "What do you do when a dream has come true?" (*Call*, 56). His answers, congruous with political realities, disillusion him as they eventually will spiritually defeat Smiley. Marxism revealed no solutions, just bloody realities like Stalin's purges. Lacking Smiley's altruistic commitment, Fennan's only option is to abandon one precept for another. By "the sheer weight of his ability," he pushes aside his chosen masters' prejudice and enters the Foreign Office, eventually gaining minimal "success, prosperity, and integration" (*Call*, 56). He puts aside the "-isms" as schoolboys put aside their fantasies to accept sometimes unpalatable adult compromises prosaic to most espionage professionals.

Political dreams conflicting with official reality replay Smiley's emotional losses, and empathy with Fennan leads him to the clerk's assassin. Pondering Dieter's brilliance, Fennan's unrewarded dedication, Mundt's brutality, and Else's disillusion, Smiley sees how empty his life is without Ann. Could Fennan's life be empty too? Smiley studies his only wedding gifts, a Watteau sketch from reliable Peter Guillam and the best of Steed-Asprey's set of Dresden porcelain figures, a prophetic keepsake sympathetically depicting infidelity. In the "tiny rococo courtesan in shepherd's costume" Smiley envisions a duplicitous Ann with "her hands outstretched to one adoring lover, her little face bestowing glances on another" (*Call*, 97). The figurine's fragile perfection ironically comforts him as it underscores, in his mind, his psychic inadequacies and the pain of faithlessness – both Ann's and that of "this tiny shepherdess in her glass case."

The dual image of Ann as exquisite dream and disloyal reality crystallizes for Smiley the contradiction of Else Fennan as victimized Jewess and traitorous wife. Despite her obvious lies, Smiley intuitively resists seeing Else as the murderer because "there was no aggression in her, no will but the will to preserve" (*Call*, 30), but his distrust of his own intuitions prevails. Gazing at the figurine, he wills his dispassionate, academic nature to momentarily supplant his illusions. Hesse's words "Each is alone" resound to him as he twists suspects, isolated pieces in a speculative puzzle, "this way and that to fit the complex framework of established facts." The pattern will later be "re-formed with such assurance that it was a game no more" (*Call*, 98). In a passage reminiscent of Conrad, Smiley again laments the essential isolation that shrouds human motives: "We know nothing of one another, nothing. . . . However closely we live together, at whatever time of day or night we sound the deepest thoughts in one another, we know nothing" (*Call*, 30). Here, with confirming evidence surrounding him and Ann's image haunting him, he fights admitting indisputably bitter facts.

Smiley realizes how acutely hypocritical his unwilling investigation into Else Fennan's life is. He reveres his right to privacy and evades all questions about his parentage, marital life, or profession. Yet his vocation (spying) and avocation (research) demand encroachments on others' privacy through interrogation techniques at which he excels but which he would quickly brand insidious. This earnest defender of individual rights pries shamefully into Else's past and manipulates her in her grief to reveal her concentration-camp experiences and resultant failing health. Jealousy presses in on him, and he actively opens her raw wounds. Although Else professes indifference to her persecution from the Nazis and to her present widow's grief, their home suggests a closeness between the Fennans that Smiley can never achieve with Ann. Smiley uses this ambiguity to probe the depth of Else's past bitterness and present resignation, searching for the marital schism he suspects. She only partly conceals her intense hatred with half-truths and a litany of painful oppression.

Smiley's initial interview with Else informs on many levels. Else attempts to deflect his questions by dismissing him as "a mind without a body" and his destitute institution as populated by players of "a silly balancing trick of ideas" that degrades duty to bureaucratic tidiness (*Call*, 19). Stripped of her homeland, husband, and humanity, Else is impassive. Despite her age and frailty, she endures, hates, and refuses to let his absurd ironies slip by unnoticed. He, the oppressor, interviewed her husband "about loyalty"; now Samuel is dead, and she, long accustomed to oppression, accepts her lot. Smiley, rightly uncomfortable, falls back on Maston's lame duplicity. "I was given a job," he proffers, appealing to vague loyalty; "I was only doing my duty," he thinks, suffering his guilt (*Call*, 18). Cognizant of the duplicity, he demands from himself "Duty to *whom*, for God's sake?" and "Loyalty to whom, to what?" (*Call*, 18). The same questions and troubled resolutions raised in this interrogation tie the novel's political context to the incongruous conflict that climaxes it.

Smiley's respect for the emotionally tortured Else casts this villainess as a sympathetic character. Le Carré similarly allows Dieter Frey, the novel's other active villain, compassion by setting Smiley's affection for his former student in paradoxical contrast to the uncompromising ideologies the character espouses. Dark and mercurial, Dieter is a German Jew who betrayed his homeland for morally admirable reasons. He learned his tradecraft from Smiley as the spymaster's first Circus recruit, but in the arbitrary postwar political realignments he becomes his country's loyal agent, advancing a socialist order that grew from opposition to Hitler, and Smiley's enemy – a sad commentary the humanistic spymaster accepts.

Duty and loyalty, so obviously relative qualities in the political arena, mirror relative personal alliances, forcing these former colleagues to ultimate confrontation. But in their inevitable clash, Dieter seemingly values Smiley over his totalitarian commitment by remembering the friendship Smiley ignores. Facing each other in a nightmarish fog, a setting worthy of Dickens, Smiley, the vanguard of

British values, battles Dieter, a Byronic symbol of cold war ideology. Dieter would have murdered the helpless Mendel as remorselessly as he assassinated Else Fennan. Yet he stands back at Smiley's charge, refusing to wound his mentor mortally. Smiley, driven by rage, kills him.

On Dieter's murder, Smiley cries out, "Oh God, . . . who was then the gentleman?" (*Call*, 118). For the genre's conventionally simplistic answers, however, le Carré substitutes doubling incongruities. Dieter surfaced from Smiley's past and "fought to build a civilisation" by deceiving his teachers to serve his former oppressors. Smiley served his institutional masters and "fought to prevent him" (*Call*, 118). Though charismatic, Dieter scorns individuals for unthinking absolutism. But his death is enigmatic: he may have sacrificed himself out of love for Smiley or, just as abstrusely, committed suicide to serve his ideology, dying maliciously to feed this Western standard-bearer's destructive guilt. This scenerio repeats in Smiley's last case (*Smiley's People*), where his adversary Karla less ambiguously sacrifices himself and, through this open expression of love, consequently completes Smiley's spiritual ruin.

Smiley's anguish at murdering his beloved apprentice implies that not all absolutes are untenable or all morals only conventions. Under that political veneer Smiley's pain is all too human. Le Carré plays these political and personal levels off each other as mutual fantasies. Former enemies now reformed should be allies. But what if they are not? Friendship should be respected. But should it overcome caution if the friend is one you have trained to be pitiless agent and killer? Smiley's inability to decide who or what deserves veneration captures the humanist's dilemma in its ultimate ambiguity and cynicism.

As in all his actions, Smiley perseveres in his effort to solve Fennan's murder, hoping that the resolution will quell his conflicting feelings and acquit the Circus and, by extension, his country, a goal unquestionably absolutist and noble. Torturously, he reveals the conflict between his outward self – the dispassionate philosopher – and his inward self – the profoundly remorseful sentimentalist. Craving a fusion of disparities, Smiley only supplants compromise with imperiled vulnerability. Exposure translates to disaster; the resolution he so desperately seeks would be as much a dream-turned-nightmare as his Lady Ann. Smiley's concessions defeat him.

Smiley returned to espionage owing his professional allegiance to no one and to everyone; thus, he necessarily compromises values.[19] He openly favors individuals over the collective but is incomplete without the institutions of marriage, profession, and avocation. Even though he is "without school, parents, regiment or trade, without wealth or poverty," Smiley as much perpetuates the ruling class's prejudices, inculcated by his "unimpressive Oxford College," as he advocates empathetic appraisals of individualism. Rather than independence and idealism, he finds himself the raw material of the Circus's gray men of espionage. Rather than reestablishing stability, he fails to scotch any one particular incidence of evil. Smiley has unwittingly instigated the chaos that results in death and uncounted misery, and he agonizingly finds himself caught in an indeterminate, uncommitted reality.

Call for the Dead ends without order reestablished and without Western democratic principles affirmed or Eastern totalitarianism seriously questioned. Four people die for a mistaken impression. Mundt, East Germany's prized but brutal operative, vanishes. Maston successfully covers up the damage, extends his empire, and offers Smiley a choice position. But Smiley declines to accept Ann's proposed reconciliation, an offer he knows replaces his integrity with her passion and leaves him the trapped object of her tragicomedy.

A Murder of Quality

Cast as a traditional detective novel, the action in *A Murder of Quality* exceeds that genre's fundamental conventions, becoming social satire in its scrutiny of the many faces of hypocrisy. The genre choice is more than fortuitous. The novel, the darkest of le Carré's works, adroitly draws as symbols of duplicity the images of death that are so fundamental to mystery fiction. Additionally, le Carré orchestrates irony from the genre's basics by having expected circumstances result in acrimonious consequences. Smiley, clearly here the cerebral supersleuth, enters the quaint village of Carne to solve a seemingly irrational murder, exact righteous judgment, reestablish the society's status quo, and leave as unaffected and aloof as he entered. Through interrogations, lists of clues, intellectually subtle deduction, and luck, he unravels the case and delivers the perpetrator to the town's justice. But instead of intellectual satisfaction, Smiley's private, emotional reactions increase his vulnerability, and he finds himself again laboring to solve a murder surrounded by his conflicting awareness of human isolation and futile hopes for salvation. He leaves Carne, the scene of this symbolic nightmare, in moral defeat, suffering from a philosophical anguish this society fails to share.

Le Carré's inversions do not end with his series hero's role. The social milieu Smiley enters, a microcosm not just for the British public school system but for all closed societies, lacks redemptive characteristics. Carne, both "Town and Gown," symbolizes a closed society rich with bigotry masquerading as justification for aberrant behavior. It houses dishonorable individuals whose myopic choice to merge the past with the present perverts quality into snobbishness. The unassuming victim, Stella Rode, is a malevolent hypocrite and extortionist, perfectly at home in this community. No one laments her death. Her murderer, the honorable Adrian Fielding's homosexual brother Terence, is an oppressed, tenureless victim of his debased sexuality and Stella's blackmail schemes. To Smiley's sorrow, he is not a deviation but a pathetic expression of his society's decaying social structure. Fielding's continually dishonorable behavior bars an honorable end. He murders his favorite boy, the presumably innocent student Tim Perkins, to cover Stella's murder. Tim, however, is a social climbing cynic, and his death leads Smiley directly, and painfully, to Fielding. The murder is solved, but its irrationality is actually poetic justice. Carne's reestablished status quo merely perpetuates institutional hypocrisy.

Ailsa ("Brim") Brimley, Adrian Fielding's former secretary, calls on Smiley to journey to Carne, Ann's ancestral home in Dorset near Dorchester, because she's concerned for the safety of a woman she's never met. During the war Brim volunteered for espionage duty, for, like Smiley, she felt that her patriotism demanded service. After the war she took over the nonconformist (Baptist) newspaper the *Christian Voice*, founded by her former Circus supervisor. Brim's scruples derive from her resolution that individuals matter. She unselfishly cares for the *Voice*'s readers, humbly offering them good news to balance daily atrocities and, in her "Barbara Fellowship" column, answers to unsolvable problems. Ultimately, she perceives the

Voice's readers with a nostalgia that marks her memories of the Circus's glory days. But she is outside these communities, locked in her self-imposed editorial duties. Her compassion sets her in clear contrast to Carne's faithlessness, and her choice to live vicariously through her work aptly replays Smiley's attraction to institutions.

When loyal reader Stella (neé Glaston) Rode, daughter of magistrate judge Samuel Glaston, writes in fear of her husband's brutality, Brim calls Smiley away from his incessant ruminations to action. Her concern for Stella and her esteem for her former colleague Smiley blind her to the magnitude of her request. Smiley is again nursing psychic wounds from Ann's latest infidelity (she's run off with a 20-year-old ballet dancer whom Guillam calls the Welsh Apollo), and going to Carne only promises confrontations similar to Lord Sawley's ill-bred abuse. Despite his public objections and his private qualms at facing Ann's family, Smiley's loyalty to Brim compels him to go. But he arrives just after Stella is found brutally murdered. For a friendship rooted in the past, Smiley enters a world at present rife with ungoverned violence and duplicity to begin another of his somewhat dubious quests.

The horror Smiley finds in Carne is not of his own or of his gray professional world's, but it might as well have been. The village and its exclusive school for the sons of England's elite feed their mutual fraud.[20] The town is a backwater hamlet boasting not of its sense of community but of its police station, town hall, "serene and beautiful square of mediaeval houses," red-brick Tabernacle, shabby hotel (The Sawley Arms), and decaying preparatory school (*Murder*, 35). Carne's selectively remembered history betrays the society's decay. Residents claim an Anglo-Saxon-Roman heritage and speak proudly of King Arthur's stay as if such moribund traditions alone preserve the town's superiority. The claim is prophetic in that Carne is frozen in a darker time, one that encourages residents to speak of the Black Death as if it were "a fairly recent disaster in those parts, if not actually within living memory" (*Murder*, 84). Merging past with present fails to provide any fond reminiscence or perpetuate commendable ethics; instead, past and present conspire to give Carne a nightmarish quality and cast its residents as terrorizing vampires. Moreover, this unwillingness to delineate between past and present obscures Carne's waning class system.[21] The town's "quality" has been sapped by the school's pretentiousness, and its residents – whether they sustain or envy the snobbery – willingly trap themselves in time. By nourishing a defamed past that created a rigid caste system, they compel themselves to present destructive acts.

The deathlike images circumscribing the school complete Carne as a metaphor and underscore the psychological losses characters suffer when they welcome prepackaged identities, advanced by their surroundings, over difficult, sentient introspection. Amid the "black angels come for the burying" and the "undertakers mutes," the students, carrying their "tuck boxes like little coffins," and their tutors trudge toward Carne School returning for Lent Half, the second half of the school year, so-called because "terms are not elegant things" (*Murder*, 7). These young "black-coated boys" will someday take their mentors' places "always in mourning." Even the weather, a descriptive force le Carré exploits in every novel, accentuates the enervation found in Carne's people and their apathy. During Lent Half Carne is cold, with blustery winds, icy roads, snow, and overcast skies, giving the impression that a "cloud of gloom was as firmly settled as ever over [its] grey towers" (*Murder*, 8). The residents no longer know of themselves but only of their surroundings, for they – like so many of le Carré's bureaucrats and toadies – embrace an institution with the power to ennoble or debase and allow it to devalue their lives.

For spies, the only valuable intelligence is that with clear ancestry. This axiom immediately calls into question Carne's illusionary parentage. Outsiders to the school cynically attribute its academic influence to its undocumented royal heritage. Only common consent ascribes Carne's lineage to Edward VI (1537-53), the nine-year-old who succeeded his father, Henry VIII, to the British throne, only to die six years later. Had he lived, Edward probably would have been remembered not for his educational achievements but for his rigidity, religious zeal, and obstinacy, an apt legacy for Carne's rigid class system. With equal hypocrisy insiders attribute Carne's status to the now-contemporary "conviction that Great Schools, like Tutor kings, were ordained in Heaven" (*Murder*, 7). Like Carne, these institutions produce future Mastons and Lord Sawleys; thus the school appropriately includes "the young Prince" and Lord Sawley's son as well as lesser intellects, such as slow-witted Tim Perkins. Despite pressures to rejuvenate itself, Carne stubbornly upholds its discredited heritage by incestuously educating only its own with only its own.

Furthermore Carne actively sanctions its misleading academic claims. A rustic, country bumpkin's school until late in the nineteenth century, Carne entered the new century obstinately transmitting outdated patrician values to a ruling class so inbred that it is "distinguished by neither talent, culture nor wit; kept alive for one more generation the distinctions of a dead age" (*Murder*, 13). To this ignominious end, Carne's master reinstates meaningless protocols, such as the seven Canonical Day Hours "Prime, Terce, Sext and so on. A surfeit during the Half, abstinence during the holidays, that's the system, like games" (*Murder*, 60). These educational affectations are condoned by the school's staff and cynically appropriate for its clientele. In place of knowledge Carne offers tokens, "parchments in Latin, seals in wax and Lammas Land behind the Abbey . . . property, cloisters and wormwood, a whipping block and a line in the Doomsday Book" (*Murder*, 7). And in place of meaningful direction it offers tawdry equivocation. The words of its Latin motto, *Regem defendere diem videre* (To Defend the King Is to See the Day [*Murder*, 21]) imply royalty, honor, and loyalty, but its sense replicates the school's and the empire's hollowness.

Carne replicates its educational purpose in its self-professed charge of inducing personal scruples in its students. Integrity, Carneans teach, arises solely from breeding, a bitter refrain in le Carré's fiction that summarizes his satiric view of self-possessed societies. These public school assumptions metaphorically equate honor with deception and infiltrate the society. The tenured faculty vary only in the degree to which they presume themselves aristocrats, and hence they secure the system and their positions by commending titles gained through desultory lineage over abilities. Hired teachers, particularly grammar school graduates like the slightly vulgar Stanley Rode, are by definition coarse, uneducated, and vulgar – adjectives more suitably applied to Carneans. But they perpetuate the system by confirming it. The boys intuit lessons beyond their classroom lectures from what their elders manifest: emotionalism portends social distinction as clearly as one's clothing or speech. Ambitious pretenders, even when their increasing economic power threatens the conservative old school allegiances, never achieve social acceptance because their heritage cannot warrant it. Reforming the strict castes is unthinkable, a subject suitable only to unctuous mockery and criticism.

Carne's hypocritical nature is best exemplified by three of the novel's satirically drawn characters: Shane Hecht, Carne's unofficial spokesperson; Felix D'Arcy, Carne's morally dubious protector; and Terence R. Fielding, Carne's temporary senior housemaster, who suffers the society's distorted benevolence. Mirroring her community, Shane Hecht is a facile caricature. "Massive and enveloping," with dark hair, an aged ermine stole, contrived mannerisms, and "the slow rotten smile of a whore," Shane is a "faded Valkyrie" who venomously holds Stanley's murdered wife, Stella, a "busy little creature" with "such simple taste" that her greatest accomplishment is decorating the wall in her home with china ducks: "Big ones at the front and little ones at the back. Charming, don't you think?" (*Murder*, 11). When she meets Smiley, Shane presses her dominance through ridicule. His expensive clothing and educated speech should confirm his suitable breeding, but to Shane, who knows nothing of his lineage and everything about his unsuitable match to Ann, he's merely another laughable object. She condescendingly goads him: "The only Smiley I ever heard of married Lady Ann Sercombe at the end of the war. She left him soon afterwards, of course. . . . So tragic. One doesn't talk about it at the Castle" (*Murder*, 111). Smiley has no adequate defense, for Shane's remarks go directly to his secret fears.

Felix D'Arcy justifies his hypocritical behavior by identifying himself completely with the institution he serves. An effeminate, dedicated senior French tutor, D'Arcy's smooth, unlined yet expressive face, high-pitched voice, and permanently fixed smile give him a Dorian Gray image that intrigues Smiley. A "bachelor by profession, sublimated pansy by inclination" (*Murder*, 60), D'Arcy protects Fielding's reputation after Fielding discredits himself and his family through a homosexual affair with an RAF officer during the war. D'Arcy learns of the affair when it goes to trial before Samuel Glaston (Stella's father). For concealing his knowledge of the scandal, D'Arcy exacts private torture by forcing his onetime friend to beg annually for a renewal of his lecturer's contract.

D'Arcy pressures Fielding further when he reasons that Fielding murdered Stella. His concern is with appearances, not with the suffering he causes or the justice he should uphold. To him, Stella – "a thoroughly mischievous woman" (*Murder*, 74) – deserved her fate, for she intentionally derided Carne. D'Arcy construes her death as a product of her working-class past and an indelicacy that will fade from Carne's collective memory. Reveling in the increased power this hidden intelligence brings him, D'Arcy nonetheless shields Fielding from the law. By D'Arcy's accepted system, his class protects its own because institutions, no matter how skewed their values, survive to shield their incompetents.

Shane Hecht and Felix D'Arcy are Carne's survivors. As members of a tarnished elite, they exist to manipulate others for derision, power, amusement, or their own dubious benefit. Terence Fielding's motives, however, are more complex. Fielding represents his class as willingly as he is victimized by it. He avoids contact with his talented, public-spirited brother because he is a fraud who "can't afford to be seen beside the genuine article" (*Murder*, 59). He joins in Shane Hecht's brutal degradation of Stella Rode, all the while fearing the power her knowledge has over him. When faced with opportunities to know himself, he lacks the requisite strength of character and so retreats into the patronizing duplicity that defines him. He remains at Carne without full citizenship and faces without any sense of direction a desultory retirement after 25 years.

Fielding endlessly rehearses his role as Carne's consummately hollow philosopher. He poses theatrically as the tortured, decadent aesthete but is known more correctly as "the Vampire of Carne," who sucks life from a dead class to sustain his life of living death. When dining with Shane and Charles Hecht, an appropriate if unimpressed audience, Fielding flails theatrically at the impiety the school represents, giving wizened evaluations of Carne and his colleagues while sidestepping his claims to membership. His most impressive performance is in response to Smiley's interrogation. He melodramatically sobs "in great uncontrollable gulps, holding his hand across his brow" (*Murder*, 152). He haughtily interprets the clues he planted to indict Stanley Rode. He assumes newcomer Smiley is ignorant of his depravities, and so he falsely confesses to cheating on Perkins's examination, for Tim is the only being at Carne he loved. After this confession Fielding steadies himself to overcome his stage fright and overwhelm Smiley. But the act is grossly overdone. Smiley leaves him, confident that Fielding is "the most accomplished liar he had met for a long time" (*Murder*, 159). Fielding's pretenses are amusing, but Smiley, who suspects Fielding is the murderer long before Tim Perkins's death, chastises himself. Had he acted rather than suffered the masquerade, a second life might have been spared.

Hypocrisy at Carne School is a game any denizen can play, but betrayal is reserved exclusively for insiders who choose to trifle. Le Carré portrays outsider Stanley Rode in relief against Smiley and his own thwarted dreams. Smiley's marital connection to Carne parallels his educational connection to Britain's aristocracy and his professional connection to the Circus. He is a familiar who can confidently reject Carne's social distinctions for his own intellectually derived standards. Rode, however, is trapped by his working-class background and his wife's malevolence, and can at best try to redefine himself by the superficialities Carne represents. Hired at the last minute as a science teacher, Rode tries to conform to Carne's vision and Stella's aspirations. He abandons soccer, which he does not play, for rugby, a game not played in grammar schools; he changes his style of speech, religion, and clothing preferences to fit in. Nonetheless, his walk, bearing, and preferred dress alienate him from Carne's hierarchy. Barred admission by the shadow of doubt Carne imposes on uncultivated outsiders, Rode cannot be betrayed by Carne's society, because he never belongs to it. He can only betray himself by adopting their deceits. He all too willingly prostitutes himself for Carne's false riches but succeeds only in corroborating Carne's elitism by confirming the vestments of that system and affronting the court he seeks to influence. Thus by mirroring their morally empty style, Rode unwittingly disgusts the people from whom he seeks sanction.

For Stanley's wife, however, Carne's duplicity is classless and familiar. Stella Rode presents herself as a plain, forthright "good worker." As her sordid past merges with her present manipulation, Stella loses her sympathetic victim role. Her presumably commendable work shipping clothing for a Carne's socially correct charity, the International Refugee Year, is motivated by base desires: she wants to outdo her energetic neighbor, D'Arcy's sister Dorothy, and to collect gossip about Carneans along with discarded clothes. She indiscriminately blackmails a local tradesman, Mr. Mulligan, not for money but for her amusement. She befriends Mad Jane Lyn so she can control another human being totally. She destroys the family dog because Stanley forbids her to beat it anymore. She further victimizes Stanley by accusing him, surreptitiously to her minister and in writing to Ailsa Brimley, of plotting her murder. She discovers Fielding's past indiscretions and humiliates him by calling him to meetings "at absurd times and places" (*Murder*, 152). Her payment is control of Fielding's will, the same fee D'Arcy demands, and eventually the cost is too great.

The Rodes are characters in conflict with each other and with their surroundings, and their interactions replay the doubling motifs prominent in *Call for the Dead*. Whereas Stanley (like Fennan and Smiley) seeks acceptance and stability, Stella actively circumvents the goal. Stanley dreams of a life much like Smiley once imagined, but Stella corrupts those dreams, subjecting her husband to a betrayal equivalent to Else Fennan's. Rode marries Stella deluding himself into believing her innocent and gentlehearted; he takes a position at Carne only in part to pursue his academic interests. His concern for his obdurate wife affects him more. He ignores others' warnings about his spouse more resolutely than Smiley fails to recognize Ann's penchants. Stella's father cautions Stanley to be wary. His daughter's treacherousness leads people on "till they'd told her everything, then she'd hurt them, saying wicked, wicked things, half true, half lies" (*Murder*, 171). Naively sentimental, Stanley ignores history to pursue illusion. He chooses Stella and her aspirations over his father-in-law's counsel and his own experiences with her. Irritatingly, he blinds himself to her betrayals as he does to Carne's messages and turns himself into a buffoon. Others lay out the bait, and Stanley, lacking Smiley's protective intellect, rises to it.

Smiley's intervention into Carne's society rectifies nothing. Fielding exposed, now as much Smiley's victim as were Else Fennan and Dieter Frey, is dragged away screaming in terror, "They'll hang me," while Smiley looks on helplessly (*Murder*, 189). He has again confirmed that "we just don't know what people are like, we can never tell" (*Murder*, 186). Stanley's prospects replay Fielding's: either incessant temporary employment and ostracism at Carne or a like fate elsewhere. Shane Hecht and Felix D'Arcy will thrive as parasites.

Throughout both *Call for the Dead* and *A Murder of Quality* Smiley searches for sane motives in claustrophobic worlds but finds none. The themes le Carré establishes in these two novels through Smiley's interactions with adversaries and compatriots and his reflections on his own and their catalysts reverberate throughout his fiction. Whether it's London, Cambridge Circus, Bonn, Berlin, Vienna, or the Middle East, combatants disrupt systems to defeat individuals; order, like justice, is difficult if not impossible to define. Those who deny love cannot reestablish society's order, because such harmony is illusionary, yet those who love – and le Carré consistently argues that honorable characters must love – risk personal annihilation. Introspective characters select humanity over causes, but only by acting on this choice can they exercise a limited degree of control over their world and its players. The bitter irony, however, is that their actions lead inexorably to tragedy.

Chapter Three

Cold War Fiction

> Like war, spying is a dirty business. Shed of its alleged glory, a soldier's job is
> to kill. Peel away the claptrap of espionage and the spy's job is to betray trust.
> The only justification a soldier or a spy can have is the moral worth of the
> cause he represents.
>
> — William Hood, *Mole* (1982)

Little Deeds and Great Illusions

When he flees to Sweden in Joseph Heller's *Catch-22* (1961), Captain
John Yossarian opposes personal ethics to collective absurdity. War,
as Heller sees it, epitomizes senseless violence and waste: Milo
Minderbinder manages to make a tidy profit in the egg trade by buying them for 7¢ and selling them for 5¢; Major Major entertains
visitors only when he's absent; the Mediterranean theater is com-
manded by a mail clerk, former private first class Wintergreen; the
war, rather than a legitimate means of ensuring justice, is an excuse
for aggressive imperialism. Heller distinguishes heroes and combatants like Yossarian not for their courage or ability but for their rea-
sonableness and willingness to abandon discredited institutions. The
bureaucracies in *Catch-22* subsume individuals nonchalantly and
keep military operations bizarrely disorganized and ultimately dehumanizing. Heller describes the "hot war," World War II, in terms that
make the horrors of unreasoned military actions contemporary and
bitterly absurd. Readers laugh, and at the same time they are disturbed by *Catch-22*'s implications.

Whereas Heller uses the outlines of a hot war as the context for
analyzing ethical behavior, le Carré uses the cold war to define the
philosophically divided worlds. *The Spy Who Came in from the Cold*,
The Looking-glass War, and *A Small Town in Germany* use different
stories to probe the same themes: the limitations individuals wel-

come when they hide from painful realities, the betrayal that is a necessary part of any form of affection, the decay guaranteed when institutions become self-defining, the inevitable destruction that arises from losing touch with human nature, and the inescapable conflicts provoked when personal and political interests collide.

At the close of World War II, a cold war settled over Europe that pitted the United States and its allies against the Soviet Union and its Eastern Bloc nations. British and American leaders equated Stalinist Russia with Hitlerite Germany: both were antidemocratic, anti-individualist, anticapitalist, irrational, untrustworthy, and unrelentingly imperialistic. Soviet leaders, conditioned by two world wars, suspected their former allies. In the ensuing ideological confrontation, the West was at a philosophical disadvantage: it denigrated communism and decried human rights violations but had no appealing affirmative doctrine to counter Soviet ideology. For their part, Stalinists justified terrorism as serving the goals of history.

The cold war changed the nature of spying and the significance of espionage.[1] In the 1940s the mostly amateurish intelligence agencies became professional, bureaucratic combatants. Secret agencies not only vied with their enemy counterparts but squabbled among themselves. Citing national defense, interdepartmental rivalries caused branches to withhold strategic information from one another to augment their puissance. Bureaucratic growth supplanted political ideology as a diplomatic goal.

News of betrayal and conspiracy captured the public's interest and fed its demand for realistic espionage literature. Whereas pre-cold war spy fiction glamorized intelligence agencies and spies, much cold war espionage literature detailed the daily tedium and distasteful immorality of spying. Unlike Edwardian gentlemen agents, cold war operatives – workaday stiffs caught in intrigues beyond their all-too-human capabilities – were not permitted to rely on patriotism. If they reflected at all, they struggled to justify the impure results guaranteed by covert operations and to endorse their governments' questionable moral premises. Naive boyhood adventures matured into deadly adult drudgeries.

At the height of cold war tensions, le Carré turned from sleuthing motifs to espionage, finding in the genre a ready vehicle for his interpretation of contemporary political debate and responsible humanism. Popular in the West, his novels were predictably received in the Soviet Union. In 1965 critic V. Voinov reviewed *The Spy Who Came in from the Cold* and *The Looking-glass War* for the Moscow *Literary Gazette*. Granting the Western novelist talent and an urbane patriotism, Voinov censured le Carré as "an apologist for the cold war" who, in presenting fictional spies and contemporary heroes, "fans the flames" of East-West distrust (Lewis, 60).

Seven months later le Carré rebuked Voinov harshly in an ironically titled letter, "To Russia, with Greetings." Acidly, he points out that Voinov "is marching out of step [with his government] in objecting to the image of the spy hero" because Soviet leaders exploited this counterfeit notion with equal mastery. The spy-as-patriot image had waned but not disappeared at the public disclosure of failed espionage operations or traitors like Igor Gouzenko, Vladimir Petrov, Donald Maclean, and Kim Philby (see discussion in Chapter 5). Rather than clean their secret houses, diplomats on both sides perpetuated childish fantasies by acting out to one another lies "they had long ceased to pass off on the people" ("To Russia," 5). Western readers seek escape from the cold war's nightmarish menaces by reclaiming the "gilded dream of James Bond" – an option denied Russian audiences. For their part, Eastern intelligence agencies, in proclaiming covert operations nationalistic and spies like Richard Sorge heroes, validate "the Bond Image." Such a view implies that the Soviets consider espionage an extension of diplomacy, a position le Carré deprecates.

Voinov, however, is not le Carré's primary audience. Le Carré's criticism, like his cold war novels, is sharper for his own government's espousal of its enemies' tactics. Communist ideology mocks the late-nineteenth-century utilitarians: the collective good supersedes the individual good. Communist dogma, unlike Western credos, should have been able "to reconcile the loss of innocent life with the progress of the proletarian revolution." Basic to Communist totalitarianism is the tenet that the uncommitted are necessary sacrifices to history.

Western ideology, on the other hand, springs "from the Christian and humanistic ethic that the individual is worth more than the collective" and should thus reject as antithetical Soviet ideology and practices. Yet all too easily "Western man sacrifices the individual to defend the individual's right against the collective" and blurs the goals and actions that should separate the two political systems ("To

Russia," 4). Westerners, le Carré argues, must gauge whether their democratic systems can justify totalitarian methods and remain societies worth defending.

Le Carré's bitter argument in "To Russia" underlies *The Spy Who Came in from the Cold, The Looking-glass War, A Small Town in Germany*, and, most critics argue, all his fiction.[2] These three novels shun Flemingesque superheroes who, like Stalinists, exalt a morally facile "short answer in the perfectly-made world" as surely as they question reluctant team players like Smiley who variously bear the multiple paradoxes of their profession in the name of national security and a privately defined morality.[3] The novels instead offer ordinary professionals who, in pledging themselves to their compromising societies, live in organized chaos without pat solutions or logically justifiable convictions that could resolve prevailing ambiguities.

If le Carré, as Voinov claims, manipulates espionage and spies as metaphors for contemporary history and ethics, then his fiction is rich with the natural irony such maneuvering offers. Le Carré's protagonists are clearly "grunts," operatives rather than strategists – people without extraordinary abilities, special insights, or consistent philosophical creeds. By actively refusing to question or shape ethical ideologies, they define themselves as good soldiers who do a dirty job because someone has to do it. They are promised personal reward but never professional renown. They are used by zealots convinced that cause legitimizes means. And they set the boundaries for the novelist's art as surely as they foreshadow Smiley's inevitable defeat in *The Quest for Karla* or Ned's cynical resolution in *The Secret Pilgrim*.

The Unreflective Professional

The Spy Who Came in from the Cold opens and closes at night, in the bitter cold, with a nervous Circus agent waiting vainly for a defector at the most poignant, hostile boundary of the Allied-Soviet frontier, the Berlin Wall. Built to quarantine West Berlin and seal desperate East Germans from freedom and torn down at the economic collapse of communism, the Wall became an instant symbol of institutional repression and competing East-West ideologies, partic-

ularly in mid-1960s espionage fiction. Le Carré's characters extend
the metaphor when, as a result of accepting institutional values as
gauges of personal morality, they erect formidable barriers to self-
evaluation. Further, a character's willingness to cross psychologically
hostile frontiers or barriers can spell destruction. He risks exchang-
ing one bleak, fabricated reality for another, hoping to understand
loyalty and betrayal in a chaotic, contemporary world. Rejecting self-
imposed ignorance is, in le Carré's vision, the measure of integrity.

While le Carré reiterates this journey motif throughout his fiction, *Spy* features its consequences in particular on Alec Leamas.
Leamas is the novelist's first "dogsbody" (British slang for drudge) to
posture without apology as an honorable patriot-warrior. Leamas
believes that time and his blown German networks have hardened
his professionalism into justified cynicism. This quality causes him to
substitute studied disregard for close personal relationships and self-
appraisal. His loss of personal closeness allows Control, and a pas-
sively acquiescent Smiley, to brutally manipulate him into orches-
trating his own betrayal.

Control's stratagem, implied in the book's title, is richly
ambiguous.[4] Maston's Circus successor wants Leamas, the model
subordinate, to complete one more mission, to put *Call's* betrayer
Hans-Dieter Mundt "on ice." Control has to use Leamas up before
he retires from the cold anonymity of a distasteful occupation to the
warmth of private life and his country's quiet gratitude. The
betrayal's intrinsic themes are quintessential le Carré. For Control's
plan to work, Leamas must willfully refrain from analyzing his or
Control's motives and prefer artifice to substance; he must abdicate
his humanity to serve the system. Leamas complies, but love forces
him to doubt his shallow decision. He eventually chooses honor
through suicide rather than sustaining his profession's rampant
amorality.

A troubled Leamas waits at the Berlin Wall for doomed agent
Karl Riemeck (codenamed "Mayfair"), the last survivor of Leamas's
East German (GDR) network, to escape Mundt's vengeance. The
events leading up to this night extend, somewhat unconvincingly, the
loose threads that end *Call for the Dead*. Control seized Samuel and
Else Fennan's murderer, Hans-Dieter Mundt, and through undis-
closed inducements lured him to Circus allegiance and implanted
him in his homeland's service, where he rises to deputy director of

operations for Abteilung, the East German intelligence service. To solidify his powerful position and to advance Control's intrigues, Mundt slowly, remorselessly eliminates Leamas's agents – first a naive female courier, then "a discarded agent from Peter Guillam's network," then "two members of another network under Leamas's control," and finally Riemeck (*Spy*, 14).

Superficially, Riemeck's assassination by the East German border guards fits genre standards: he is murdered to authenticate Leamas's cover. Tellingly, Riemeck's demise foreshadows the novel's didactic means-ends argument. An official in the presidium for the East German Communist party (SED), Riemeck is a double agent ostensibly feeding Leamas information while secretly doing Control's and Mundt's bidding. When Riemeck draws the attention of East German intelligence, Control and Mundt contrive his death as the linchpin in a scheme to eliminate Mundt's chief accuser, Jens Fiedler. They orchestrate their loyalties and conspire in Riemeck's death – as they will in Leamas's. In this type of society no individual, motive, or consequence escapes le Carré's censure.

Because they resemble each other personally and professionally, Leamas's fate replays Riemeck's. Like Riemeck, Leamas is a divorced parent who craves the loving comfort of family but spurns commitment and, like "agents the world over," dismisses love as an occupational hazard, a professional betrayal, and a stupid compromise (*Spy*, 10). Nonetheless, he lies to Control "by omission" about his lover, Liz Gold, as Riemeck does to Leamas about his mistress, Elvira. Riemeck dies, as Leamas will, in a volley of machine-gun fire, believing, wrongly, that he has both served Leamas and Control and saved Elvira. Leamas, however, eventually chooses loyalty and love over professional standards, and by this act he affirms individualism over institutional tyranny. His suicide does not reform the status quo but, as an act of moral protest, eloquently condemns his controllers and affirms his own humanity.

Because *Spy*'s narrative and doubling imagery reinterpret events and characters from *Call*, Leamas invites comparisons with another Circus agent, George Smiley. Like Smiley, Leamas was educated in Europe, was familiar with several foreign languages, was recruited by Fielding and Steed-Aspry, served as a fieldman in Europe during World War II, and left the Service only to return to duty in Berlin.

These superficial similarities, however, mask the agents' enormous differences. Unlike the sagacious, angst-ridden academic, Leamas's brutish appearance informs the man. Short, burly, with stubby fingers and hands, "close, iron-grey hair," steel-rimmed glasses, a strong neck, and "a stubborn line to his thin mouth," Leamas is a sexually appealing antihero who cannot be mistaken for a privileged, toadish Smiley. His rugged good looks suggest "a man who could make trouble, . . . who was not quite a gentleman" (*Spy*, 15). He capably replaces Smiley's scrutiny of ideological details with illusions born of limited access to information.

Thought paralyzes action for Smiley, but for Leamas action deadens thought. He performs rather than evaluates, swaggers rather than ponders, competes rather than questions. Reminiscent of American hard-boiled detectives, Leamas stands aloof from his contemporaries in his cynical resentment and directness. He fancies himself an arrogant, "stubborn, wilful" loner, "contemptuous of instruction," and deludes himself that no one, not even Control, could run an operation on his turf without his knowledge. In truth he's a second-rate, melodramatic actor lost in a tragicomedy. He is not as hard-boiled or cynical as he is war-weary; he is far less enigmatic than philosophically passive. Moreover, Leamas's theatrics are usually performed for an unappreciative or sometimes absent audience. He fills his small, private world – a small, squalid apartment – with images of decay and death: "flower pattern curtains, not lined or hemmed" and "fraying brown carpets and the clumsy darkwood furniture" reminiscent of cheap brothels or funeral homes. The "foul stench of decaying fish oil" permeates his clothing and hair, "lingering in his nostrils like the smell of death" that no amount of cleaning can remove (*Spy*, 26-27). Callers are always repulsed, passers-by avoid him, and fearful shopkeepers oust him.

In professional terms, Leamas's maintaining his personae even when alone is sensible: successful agents prepare cover stories that are deliberately close to the truth in order to defend themselves, fool opponents, and maintain plausible deniability for their controllers. By maintaining these fictions, however, Leamas intentionally blinds himself to the operation's ethical inconsistencies. He originally agrees to Control's plan because he's appalled by Mundt's perfidy and his own deficiencies at playing the game. He fails to face the inherent conflicts between his fictions and others' reality. His defense is professional: "intelligence work has one moral law – it is justified by results" (*Spy*, 13). Yet he refuses to apply that law to his assignment and eventually dies a moral victor to the law's caustic ironies.

Le Carré plays this paradox out across the novel in a series of confrontations that force Leamas to question his convictions and their justifications. Control, Leamas's first confrontation, argues smoothly for expediency. Jens Fiedler, his second confrontation, fuses Control's arguments with Leamas's professional admiration into a coldly logical consistency. Childlike Liz Gold, his final confrontation, argues through her passion for Leamas for the superiority of selfless love.

After Riemeck's assassination, Control, a Svengali for unsuspecting agents, debriefs Leamas in his Circus office, where the arid heat from a coal fire counters the cold without warmth. Control nurtures Leamas's romanticism and machismo by diverting his questions and playing on his injured professional pride and desire for revenge for his compromised Berlin network. He manipulates Leamas into believing that, despite his awkwardness in his superior's presence, Leamas belongs to Control's privileged caste. Both can command agents like a child's toy soldiers. The lengthy interrogation (chapter 2) is permeated with ironic symbolism. Dressed in a shabby brown "cardigan under his black jacket" and affecting a duplicitous fatherly concern for his demoralized "son," Control detaches himself through his "same donnish conceits; the same horror of draughts . . . same milk-and-water smile, the same elaborate diffidence, the same apologetic adherence to a code of behaviour which he pretended to find ridiculous. The same banality" (*Spy*, 17). Repetition of a key word (here, *same*), a stylistic commonplace for le Carré, focuses Control's defining trait. As director of the Cambridge Circus, Control embodies his community's standards as surely as he extends them to its opponents.

Abteilung officials, Control warrants, are pitiless ideologues devoid of ethical standards; they hold fundamentally different values, he says, even though he cannot substantiate this claim. Yet he freely admits to Leamas that the Circus's practices are indistinguishable from Abteilung's. He cynically avoids the contention that disreputable means discredit honorable ends. It's "their" stratagems that force us to do disagreeable, sometimes "very wicked things," but we only act so that Western ideals prevail and so "that ordinary people here and elsewhere can sleep safely in their beds at night." It would be, Control concludes for Leamas, simplistic to believe that one side can be "less ruthless than the opposition simply because your government's policy is benevolent" (*Spy*, 19).

Control wants Leamas to replace instinct, pleasure, and love with professional discipline, denial, and obedience – an easy transfer for one with Leamas's proficiencies. Control hides his motives and Operation Rolling Stone's details from Leamas, but he cannot from Smiley. Smiley's flaw is that, while he deplores the operation's means, his professional silence and conflicting overtures to save Liz Gold condone its principles.

Leamas's flaw is his contentment: he willingly believes the snippets of reasoning and incomplete directions Control offers because these hints give him conspiratorial status. In this confrontation Control wins. He deftly turns their conversation to their allegedly common interests, superficially acquits a means-over-ends argument, sugarcoats his chicanery, and waits for his agent to accept and obey. The scene ends with Control offering Leamas the condemned man's last cigarette; the symbol is later repeated when Liz, fleeing toward the Berlin Wall, lights Leamas's cigarette. Whether Leamas as a character warrants this subtlety is immaterial; he's operationally important to Control. To succeed in Control's terms, Leamas must believe his parts both as a wronged agent and as Control's worthy partner. And to believe, Leamas abdicates his humanity.

Leamas rejects the same argument from Jens Fiedler, a Jewish survivor of Nazi atrocities turned head of Abteilung's counterintelligence. Orderly, short, "sleek and slightly animal" in appearance, Fiedler is a loner whose abilities as a lawyer and whose remorseless dedication to his service have spared him from Abteilung's political machinations and earned him respect from others in his trade. Framed as Control's counterpart, Fiedler's characterization perfects *Call*'s sketchily drawn Dieter Frey and anticipates *Quest*'s Karla. Like his Circus opponents, Fiedler weds utilitarian absolutism with scrupulous honor and capably "banishes perplexity with action, morality with duty" ("To Russia," 6). He further enriches this union with his articulate interest in Communist ideology and its comparative value to Christian dogmas.

A true patriot, Fiedler sees his duty as purging his country of its betrayer, Mundt. Fiedler's battle with Mundt turns the novel into a tightly structured political allegory in which integrity is the ensured casualty.[5] After securing Leamas in a prison camp behind East Germany's borders, Fiedler routinely frees him for brisk walks and private interrogations. Fiedler wants the names on Circus subscriptions lists, locations for meetings and drops, the colors of operational files, even the Circus preference for pins or clips to attach papers. Dissecting his witness's cover for any inconsistencies and finding it sound, Fiedler accepts Leamas as a reputable professional and, implicitly, as a worthy intellectual adversary. His approbation lets Leamas relax, as he never could with Control, and concede their unstated kinship.

Fiedler confronts his doppelgänger with their societies' comparable goals and philosophical underpinnings. His positions echo those in "To Russia, with Greetings" as well as mock Control's insinuated case. Because they are rational beliefs rather than shams for intrigue, they are even more difficult for Leamas to refute. Politicians in Christian societies, Fiedler contends, profess humanism as their bureaucratic impetus but tender no consistent belief in either theory or religion and thus cannot defend their actions. Only through the actions of agents like Leamas and Fiedler do Western societies exhibit a functional doctrine Fiedler can respect: "All our work – yours and mine – is rooted in the theory that the whole is more important than the individual" (*Spy*, 113). In light of this dictum, debates rooted "in the sanctity of human life . . . [in] a soul which can be saved . . . in sacrifice" (*Spy*, 124) fail to recommend Western political ideology over Stalinism.

Personally disdaining murder outside duty, Fiedler gives philosophical voice to the prison commissar's blunt statement to Liz that "You cannot plan a great building [i.e., a Communist state] if some swine is building his sty on your site" (*Spy*, 202). Fiedler can accept that Mundt practices "the deterrent principle" and Control an amoral manipulation because for him their actions advance the concerns of their communities.

Fiedler's consistent ideology and personal decency validate his arguments as Control's appeal to class status cannot. Le Carré sets Fielder's blend of philosophical certainty with ironically judicious methodology against both Leamas's cynical myopia and Control's preference for strategic victories over ethical debate. Callous and unflinching, Fiedler remains true to his institutions until he comprehends Mundt's manipulation and Control's betrayal. For his part in their debates, Leamas can only growl at Fiedler that "the whole lot of you are bastards" (*Spy*, 123). Leamas is too uninformed about both political philosophy and operational reality to respond sensibly to Fiedler's Socratic arguments.

Their one-sided contest nonetheless forces Leamas closer to defining his uncertain positions and questioning others' facile resolutions. When Fiedler recognizes Control's plot and acts decently to a fellow professional, Leamas is forced to starkly compare their two systems. Finding both wanting, Leamas openly repudiates their implied ethics. Leamas is slower than Fielder to concede betrayal: he adamantly refuses to blame his service because such an acknowledgment forces him to introspection. When he can no longer deny it, Leamas is nauseated by his system's hypocrisy. Fiedler and Leamas can break out from their self-imposed prisons only when they substitute individual morals for institutional methods.

If Leamas invites comparison with *Call*'s protagonist and *Spy*'s honorable operative, then Liz Gold, his third and most compelling challenge, invites comparison with *Call*'s Else Fennan. As Jews, both women suffered from the Nazi wartime atrocities, Else being imprisoned and Liz losing her father. Both women align themselves with their former enemies, Else as a spy and Liz as the party's dedicated branch secretary. Both betray and are betrayed by the men they love, Else by choice and Liz by stupidity. Superficial likenesses, however, give way to substantive differences. Else is frail, older than her 43 years, possessing an intense self-control and dedication to the cause. Liz is strong, younger than her 23 years, possessing vacillating convictions and a soppy romantic outlook. A shortsighted liberal, Liz loves intimate, candlelight dinners and the warmth companionship promises rather than the sacrifices demanded by party ideology. Her naïveté borders on stupidity. She hates the Germans but only timidly questions why she's chosen for an exchange program in East Germany. She accepts party officials' vagaries as answers and ignores communism's moral ambiguities, preferring to be in the center stage of a quixotic world.

Liz's puerile dedication to ideals stands in sharp relief to that of her fellow Communists. Ashe, Leamas's initial contact, is a mercenary. Kiever, Leamas's traveling companion to Holland, professes socialist commitment but appreciates captialism's sullied fruits. To pitch the defection, Kiever takes Leamas to a tawdry nightclub that fits Leamas's role as potential defector as clearly as it fits Kiever's libidinous preoccupations. But the club's main attraction serves as an obvious sexual contrast for Liz. A "young, drab girl with a dark bruise on her thigh" stares at them "with the precocious interest of a child in adult company" as she performs a lifeless striptease, an explicit image of the fraudulent sensuality Liz gives lie to (*Spy*, 61-62). Kiever delivers Leamas to Peters, the paid toady who initiates Leamas's interrogation. Of the three typecast GDR agents, Peters is the most distant and therefore a transparent, aloof contrast to Liz. Kiever's impassive commitment to communism, like the commissar's mindless dedication, demands of him no explanation.

Liz's nebulous political commitment provides her with little more than an outlet for turning sentimentality into passionless action. To maintain her party affiliation, she consciously lies to herself by filling her apartment with unread classics and her life with untested ideologies. She deceives only herself by prattling one doctrine while indiscreetly living a life that manifestly violates its credo. Callow and uncultured, she giggles behind the book stacks at Miss Crail, the supervisor at the Bayswater Library for Psychic Research, and cries when her own footsteps kill thousands of minute creatures on the pavement. Ironically, these unseen victims would have died without her intervention, just as Fiedler and Leamas will.

When faced at the tribunal with the party's brutal truths and her lover's sure collusion, Liz ineptly equivocates. The East Germans could not hold her in a prison reserved for traitors, spies, reactionary intellectuals, and "brain workers"; she cannot be one who must be destroyed for the good of the revolution. She is convinced honesty cannot condemn rather than save those she loves. She blinds herself to how her naive truthfulness ensures her continued manipulation. She has, to her credit, tenaciously sacrificed for individuals, unselfishly nursing Leamas when he's been ill and vowing to protect him during Mundt's trial, even if doing so means lying. This mockery, orchestrated through London, leaves her confused, remorseful, and persuaded that she is the cause of Fiedler's and Leamas's convictions. Le Carré insists that if Else's cynicism will not secure individuality, neither will Liz's childish innocence.

Liz's inability to balance sentiment with reality distorts her perceptions and degrades her motivations. Her challenge and redeeming merit in *Spy*'s melancholy landscape are her desire to love. Even here she stumbles. She wants romantic commitment with a man who dismisses her with nihilistic rebukes, labeling her political targets (i.e., Americans, public schools, "military parades and people who play soldiers" [*Spy*, 35]) shallow and her love artless.

Liz persists, pointing Leamas unwillingly toward his hidden contradiction. He does not "want to think," because thought challenges his script. For an instant she intuits that Leamas holds "some poison in [his] mind, some hate" that makes him a "fanatic" (*Spy*, 35). But true to her shortsightedness she replaces this momentary insight with her quiet fantasies. Nevertheless, her ardor changes Leamas's outlook. She becomes for him a secret part of his expected private warmth; hence he refuses to see how her incredulity replays his.

Although nearly a caricature, Liz is neither a facile representation of socialist doctrine nor a cliché for infantile awareness. Instead, she illustrates a liberal impulse stumbling about for humanitarian outlets only to end up smashed between opposing ideologies. Liz is able through love to move Leamas from being "permanently isolated in deceit" toward having a "faith in ordinary life" and a "respect for triviality which he had never been allowed to possess" (*Spy*, 93). Her love disproves his profession's "great lie" as vividly as his choice to die with her does. This change enriches the image of innocents caught between competing ideologies that le Carré threads through the novel. In one telling scene – a near collision on the Autobahn with a car holding four "waving and laughing" children – Leamas finds himself "unprofessionally" shaken and curses the father's irresponsibility. For no obvious reason he sees himself crushed between two giant trucks, "pounded and smashed, until there was nothing left" (*Spy*, 104-5). This poignant image of victims crushed between opposing forces reappears to Leamas as he falls, gunned down by Mundt's henchmen at the Berlin Wall.

Le Carré's relentless examination of collectivism versus individualism and of love betrayed culminates in the tribunal, Mundt's trial. The disparate images of death, sentimentality, naïveté, paternal protection, and East-West conflict merge with the metaphor of crossing hostile frontiers as Fiedler, Leamas, and Liz are convicted by their truths. Leamas pridefully insists on his autonomous role as fieldman.

Fiedler corrects Leamas's truth with reality: Riemeck was Mundt's unwitting channel to Control; Mundt eliminated Leamas's Berlin network for the Circus's expediency. Mundt's attorney, Comrade Karden, uses Liz's admission of love and the help she accepted from Smiley to expose Leamas. Trapped, Leamas reacts by protectively claiming that Control's plot is inconceivably insane. Smiley's "wretched little conscience," he thinks, must have driven him to sabotage the operation.

To save Liz, Leamas confesses Control's plan to the tribunal. Still, Leamas fights seeing his truth for himself. His explanation defends Fiedler and accuses Mundt correctly, but it is Mundt's slight hesitation, his single lapse of professional expertise, that finally enlightens Leamas. "Suddenly, with the terrible clarity of a man too long deceived," Leamas comprehends "the whole ghastly trick" (*Spy*, 200). The tribunal turns on him and condemns Fiedler, rightly refusing to believe an enemy agent over its highly successful director of covert operations.

Mundt surreptitiously releases the lovers as reparation for his cover, although he labels Leamas "a fool" and Liz "trash, like Fiedler" (*Spy*, 207). Fleeing East German guards, the lovers argue, and a spiritually demoralized Leamas vainly critiques Control's script. Espionage implies only false romanticism because spies are not "priests, saints and martyrs. . . . They're a squalid procession of vain fools, traitors too, yes; pansies, sadists and drunkards, people who play cowboys and Indians to brighten their rotten lives" (*Spy*, 213). Liz argues for moral consequences, but Leamas counters that they have saved a murderer "so that the great moronic mass that you admire can sleep soundly in their beds at night" (*Spy*, 213). Both arguments can fit the facts; neither carries the day.

Leamas's heroism is confirmed by his choice to die with Liz. With only seconds to scale the Berlin Wall, he pulls Liz up toward him as she is assassinated by Mundt's lackeys to protect the network. Smiley calls to him, but, in an act that affirms his humanity, Leamas returns to Liz, forcing Abteilung's murderers to kill him. His espionage compatriots' lies and manipulation served the conspiracy well until Leamas acts from his sense of decency. His death eloquently condemns his controllers and, at least momentarily, silences their deceits.

The Uninitiated Professional

The success of *Spy* is attributable to its taut structure and suggestive characterizations. Paring down action, philosophical debate, and dialogue, le Carré dissected betrayal in institutions and in personal and professional relationships. The novel's financial success allowed le Carré to leave the Foreign Office to write about instead of work in espionage. His next two novels, *The Looking-glass War* and *A Small Town in Germany*, are longer and less satisfying examinations of cold war ethical and political betrayal in the innermost circles of British intelligence. In *The Looking-glass War* le Carré replaces the "ideological deadlock which provided the background for *The Spy Who Came in from the Cold*" with "the psychological deadlock of men whose emotional experiences are drawn from an old war. The piping has stopped but they still dance" ("To Russia," 6). In *A Small Town in Germany* myopic people who search for truth end up questioning its value. Truth may enlighten, but when used as an absolute it also defeats. Artistically, both novels show le Carré's attempts to stretch his talents, in the former for dramatic tension deriving from psychological interplay rather than action and in the latter for dialogue and indirect characterization.

The Looking-glass War, suggested by British interagency rivalry, retells three failed missions undertaken by an all-but-defunct intelligence agency, probably modeled on an RAF intelligence organization from World War II. The agency, never named, had its glory days during the war, when its leaders were young Oxonians, much like the brave young men pictured in the fading military photos on the walls in its current head administrator's (Leclerc's) office. They trained pilots as agents, dropped operatives behind enemy lines and rescued them, and sabotaged enemy outposts. Their days were those of boyhood adventure ennobled by unquestioned patriotism.

But wartime esprit de corps does not wear well in the cold war years. Time, rather than inconstant alliances or operational expediencies, mandates that adversaries hold reflective, nearly indistinguishable principles. Some 20 years after the war, the Foreign Office and Ministry allow this moribund agency, called the Department, to continue to exist without purpose or charter. Nostalgic for the days of battle and confrontation, the Department's aging, bureaucratic spies seek the glory they imagined from the world wars – and the intrigue from the cold war – by perpetuating the agency and its importance to British defense. To preserve their childhood, they must enlist adults who do not want to grow up (new Peter Pans) and initiate a mission more appropriate to 1945 than to 1965. Their stated enemy is, of course, their World War II enemy, Germany; however, the adversary they continually envision is the Circus.

Through unexplained shreds of information, the agency believes it has discovered a missile site at Rostock on the border between the two Germanys. Director Leclerc authorizes an overflight by a commercial airliner to photograph the site, but the airliner comes dangerously close to being shot down by Russian MIGs.[6] Leclerc ignores obvious warnings and sends Taylor, an inexperienced-courier-hastily-turned-operative, to retrieve the film. Taylor is given a covername he cannot spell ("Malherbe" – a sentimental homage to a dead World War II pilot), too much money to spend, and no cover instructions. Drunk, he is killed while thrashing through the snow, perhaps accidentally but more likely on purpose, and the precious canister of film rolls "gently with the camber to lodge for a moment against the frozen bank, then to continue wearily down the slope."[7] From its inception Taylor's "run" is a exercise in boyish bravado. His lack of experience and preparation, coupled with his childish belief in his superiors and the rightness of the cause, dooms him and foreshadows the remaining two runs.

John Avery, Leclerc's latest convert, makes the second abortive run as proof of his conversion to Leclerc's faith. Avery, a young man with neither a war nor political interests, swore allegiance to Leclerc's cause when he became a part of the game. His views are youthful, untainted versions of Alec Leamas's belief in the silent glory and necessity of his work. Both Leamas and Avery need to belong. Avery's need, however, is callow, born of icons rather than reality. The novel's images of false religion and psychological gamesmanship replacing painful reality and individual commitment converge in the so-called vows Leclerc insists true Department agents embrace. When Avery silently repeats his superior's first vow, a promise of loyalty and secrecy, he is admitted to Leclerc's inner circle. When he willingly accepts the second vow, an acknowledgment of his complicity despite his ethical reservations, he trades his scruples for acceptance.[8]

Although Avery accepts Leclerc's interpretation of relationships and consequently betrays his wife, Sarah, and son, Anthony, he does not join Leclerc's fantasies unknowingly. Smiley warns him, gently and repeatedly, to separate the Department's delusions from unpleasant but operational reality; he encourages Avery to use his own intelligence and sense of ethics and sharply censures Avery's illusions, but to no avail. Leclerc – not Smiley – is Avery's master. Serving his novitiate, Avery willfully believes Leclerc's description of Smiley and the Circus as a curious crowd that cheats and, though better financed and trained, probably does no better job than the Department.

Avery is sent to claim Taylor's effects and, Leclerc hopes, the canister of film. He returns from his abortive run determined to resign. He calls Sarah, however, only to learn that people identifying themselves as the police have questioned her about him. Sarah, in her fear, told them about Taylor, a breach of security Avery initiated. Sarah cries in pain and fear for his understanding, but Avery belongs to the Department now. He is furious at her interferences with his adventures and savagely strikes out at her,"You may have wrecked the whole thing" (*Looking-glass*, 97). He rejects her by lying that his mission is "terribly big. More important than you can possibly understand. I'm sorry Sarah, I just can't leave the office" (*Looking-glass*, 97). Unlike Sarah, Avery replaces the crumbling dream of their marriage and her sensuality with the Department's illusion and sterility. Sarah's fear and love only push him further into Leclerc's delusion.

Avery attempts to confront Leclerc and Adrian Haldane, Smiley's overly class-conscious former colleague, but is scolded into waiting until his "elders" can be interrupted. Avery lamely protests their incompetence, but his words sound impertinent to the professionals. In a moment of rare insight, Avery grasps that the Department is a dream factory, chasing live agents to train and insert behind "enemy" lines to best its bureaucratic rivals. Avery realizes it is a dead dream, but it is so powerful and seductive that he ignores reality and participates willingly in the abortive third run.

For this fiasco Leclerc recruits Fred Leiser, a self-exiled Danzig Pole who, since the war, has run the King of Hearts garage in London. With "a face which at first sight recorded nothing but loneliness" (*Looking-glass*, 144), Leiser has quietly grown fat, unsuccessfully trying to fit into British society. By Department criteria, he is touted as a perfect spy because of his wartime experience; he is, in fact, Leclerc and Haldane's choice because his sense of himself as an outsider makes him an overly willing puppet. Haldane, a flagrant bigot, symbolizes the Department's callous betrayal of Leiser. Leclerc's public-school education and subsequent military intelligence career taught him to prostitute his sense of humanity. Now he faces Leiser – a man he despises because he is a foreigner, a second-class citizen, and is capable of unselfish love – and chauvinistically uses the Pole's desperate need for acceptance to convince him to undertake the Department's reckless operation. Haldane sees Leiser as little more than one of the masses who should suffer for his moral impotence.

For Leclerc, Leiser is the Department's toy, a former agent who, if successful on this run, will play his small part in drawing attention to the Department's competence. Leiser, Leclerc argues, is little more than a disagreeable laborer who can be easily sacrificed as a pawn in the Department's chess game with the Circus.[9] Playing expertly on Leiser's futile desire to be seen as a gentleman, Leclerc gathers outdated equipment and borrowed money for his whimsically code-named "Operation Mayfly." He presents his booty to Leiser as the best gear for the mission. With Avery's help, Leclerc secrets Leiser in the Department's outmoded Oxford safe house, where the inexperienced Avery, schooled in liberal arts rather than espionage, savors the suicidal conspiracy as he "trains" Leiser. After decades of inactivity Leiser has 30 days to learn ciphers, equipment, routes, and radio techniques as well as get himself into physical shape for possible unarmed combat with much younger, more agile opponents. At moments when Leiser turns fainthearted, Avery stays his resolve by cultivating Leiser's fatherly affection. It is Leiser's passion to be one of them, and his attachment to the younger man, that makes Avery's betrayal of him all the simpler and more insidious.

Following this grievously inadequate training, Leiser is dropped into East Germany. He senselessly kills a young border guard and seeks refuge with a passionate local woman. He is discovered by the East Germans in Kalkstadt as he is broadcasting radio signals that even the East Germans find amateurish and outdated. Leclerc, true to character, publicly disavows Leiser, completing the circle of betrayal.

Throughout the novel Smiley and Control observe the Department's movements as a chorus would in Greek tragedy. Several times Smiley steps away from this role and tries to stop the farce by gently warning Avery or by questioning Control's motives in allowing the obviously ill-fated operation to continue. Smiley's actions serve to blur his character and intentions. Other Circus insiders assume that the senior agent seeks the complete dismantling of the Department. If true, then Smiley's silence is treacherous, not humanitarian. More likely, Smiley cannot predict Leclerc's psychopathic schemes and, therefore, acts in the only way he can: he warns the errant agency's operatives. When they ignore his conscientious protests and indulge in even grander delusions, he secures his superior's orders to close the Department permanently.

The Looking-glass War illuminates two themes: burned-out professionals seeking a return to glory and the destructive effect their schemes have on genuine human emotions and individual lives. Leclerc's and Haldane's manipulation of Avery and Leiser replays Control's manipulation of Leamas and reminds the unschooled of the dubious prizes won by institutional methods. Avery serves as Leclerc's and Haldane's reflection of their youth, and sacrificing him opens their way back into their looking glass.

John Avery is, however, neither an unsullied nor ennobled victim; he conspires childishly to gain his supervisors' approbation. He begins his search for acceptance by willingly becoming Leclerc's recruit, faithful to a possibly insane supervisor. Avery shuns marital, personal, and professional dilemmas. Real love, common sense, and individualism die while he chases formless submission. His friendship with Leiser and the Pole's capture open Avery to the real nature of Leclerc's fantasy world, but the knowledge is insufficient to mature Avery. Begging his superiors to listen to Leiser's futile radio transmissions, Avery seethes petulantly at Leclerc and Haldane for making him love "Peter Pan's last victim" (*Looking-glass*, 311). Yet he only incompletely realizes what Leiser's sacrifice has cost him.

Because the details of the operation overtake character development, readers are left understanding the lifeless nature of espionage but uncertain of whether Avery will mature into a man of scruples or become a younger version of Leclerc, devoid of career, home, respect, and love. Avery's anger at Leiser's betrayal holds out hope that the character will learn self-awareness. But the promise is faint as le Carré ends the novel with Leclerc jovially admitting that the Department-Circus rivalry is dead and inviting Smiley, Control, and Haldane to toast the game over dinner with him at his club. Unheeded by colleagues, Avery sits "sobbing like a child" while Jack Johnson, the Department's radio trainer, winds up the aerial wire "as an old woman spins her thread" (*Looking-glass*, 312). Le Carré's message is categorical: if Avery – or any individual – continues to ignore the qualities Leclerc and Haldane evince, he can never reach the awareness required to look at the past without nostalgia or to best the afflictions that deteriorating institutions exact.

The Distrusted Professional

A Small Town in Germany, le Carré's darkest cold war novel, was suggested by Britain's petitions to enter the European Economic Community (the Common Market). In this romance Alan Turner, "a big, lumbering man, fair-haired, plain-faced and pale," is sent by London as a troubleshooter, not spy, to investigate the disappearance of German national Leo Harting and his probable security breach in the British embassy in Bonn, West Germany, before any missing information ruins Britain's chances of joining the EEC.[10] Turner has none of Avery's misguided emotionalism or unfortunate loquaciousness. Rather, he is a divorced, occasionally violent, working-class "tired schoolboy" cut from the same cloth as Alec Leamas. Walking "with the thrusting slowness of a barge" (*Town*, 37), Turner enters the dream factory of British diplomacy and, though never finding Harting alive, changes from suspecting to admiring the Bonn embassy lackey and from respectfully approving to hostility opposing his own country's diplomats.

Turner finds the British Chancery a hothouse beset by the international political strategies of wartime-enemies-turned-economic-allies. Foremost among the cronies is career civil servant Rawley Bradfield, a member of the British upper class who has been educated in the public schools to rule the empire and who has, over his professional lifetime, sought transfer from one insulated community to another. "A hard-built, self-denying man, thin-boned and well-preserved, of that age and generation which can do with very little sleep" (*Town*, 55-56), Bradfield, like other le Carré sycophants, abuses subordinates – particularly women like his secretary, Jenny Pargiter – when he notices them at all, and cultivates diplomacy, "the art of the possible" (*Town*, 279). Of Turner's world, Bradfield hypocritically complains that "secrets are an absolute standard" (*Town*, 57), yet it is his desire to repress information that sets the search for Harting into action and the embassy's double standards into satirical relief.

Bradfield's foreign home, Bonn, also becomes a major player in the novel. Bonn is a "stained and secret" capital village, a "state within a village" that "is permanently committed to the conditions of impermanence" (*Town*, vii, 58, 9). Bradfield's Embassy deputy, Peter de Lisle, feels comfortable in this distorted death-house where "dreams have quite replaced reality" (*Town*, 54, 63) because de Lisle and other embassy staff are inseparable parts of Bonn's impermanence. As attachés, Bradfield and de Lisle consciously ignore Bonn's "cold, friendless and deserted" streets, its "houses soiled like old uniforms" (*Town*, 214), and, more important, its Nazi past and possible neo-Nazi future. These nightmarish images central to Bonn's identity signal the empty morality that Bradfield and his ilk recommend.

Professing a diplomatic certainty strikingly reminiscent of Leclerc's operational certainty, Bradfield and his colleagues trap themselves in Bonn's unreal world. They fail to comprehend how contemporary events are fed not by German metaphysics but by a Gestapo past. The pale world they desire is encoded in faded gray embassy offices and impotent protests and carried over into their spiritual lives. Bradfield, "theoretically a Roman Catholic" (*Town*, 30), attends embassy chapel for show, as Rode attended chapel in *A Murder of Quality*. Rode acted on the false assumption that actions equal acceptance; Bradfield acts to create inequality. The embassy church and the Bonn consulate demand such service, and Bradfield, the man who warns Turner not "to disturb, annoy or offend," professes such service for England. Even in the diplomats' ordered procession into embassy meetings and chapel, Bradfield and his cronies preserve both an extinct empire's hierarchy and the local pecking order.

Bradfield is all the more understandable and detestable because he can clearly and meticulously articulate the results of Britain's failed empire. To impress on the coarse, working-class Turner the delicacy of Britain's disadvantaged negotiating position, Bradfield carefully selects the metaphor of a poker game played by ill-matched conspirators. The Britons are gambling, he says, but without credit or resources: "That smile is all we have. . . . Our situation is as delicate as that; and as mysterious. And as critical" (*Town*, 58). For Turner's search for truth, Bradfield substitutes the effort to obscure facts and embrace expedient political reality. While Turner's idealistic absolute is ethically preferable, Bradfield's is supportable. A failed empire needs disguise, and Bradfield's articulate nature adequately obfuscates diplomatic reality.

Denied information by Bradfield, Turner pursues his quarry as Inspector Mendel does: collecting clues, questioning principles, suspecting everyone silently. He does not uncover a minor German official's defection or the theft of supposedly sensitive documents. He does, though, find the British officials consumed with fears of disclosure: they do not want the disdainful way they use and discard people to be made public; nor will they abandon these actions. Turner's investigation uncovers Bradfield's misguided effort to ingratiate the British with Bonn's chief of police and German government spy, Ludwig Siebkron, and with a political faction of young radical Germans in order to secure, Bradfield hopes, more influence and a better economic future for Britain.

Turner's real search is for absolutes, for black-and-white truths that will unify his tortured soul. Devoid of family, love, and status, he presents himself as "a cynic in search of God" (*Town*, 259), but his attitude is immediately suspect. Working not from cynicism but from his versions of class bigotry and morality, Turner condemns institutions and, even more, their representatives, because they exact retribution through evasion and fear, tactics Turner also uses. Yet he does not question the embassy's condemnation of Harting as a traitor. Slowly, he confirms that his ethical judgment, although skewed by his prejudices, is unquestionably preferable to Bradfield's expediency. He doggedly pursues the embassy's designated antagonist, Harting, only to discover that, because they share an unfounded idealism and unrewarded patriotism, he and Harting are imperfect mirror images. Turner's investigation forces him to admit to himself his own intolerance and to plea – belatedly and somewhat unprofessionally – with embassy cronies to save Harting's honor and life.

If Turner unconsciously fears a collapse of his chimerical world, Bradfield consciously fears the disintegration of his. Bradfield's nemesis is Dr. Klaus Karfeld, a charismatic demagogue who leads a loosely organized movement of anti-British political dissidents and who currently wields power over Britain's foreign interests as West Germany's chancellor. Ostensibly, the Karfeld movement's goal is to force a political confrontation that will benefit Germany. Karfeld's bigger plan, however, is reuniting the Federal Republic of Germany with German Democratic Republic under Soviet rule. Karfeld threatens to speak out against British entry into the EEC; his speech could sway FRG votes away from Britain, thus defeating its chances for entry. Both Bradfield and Turner incorrectly assess the movement's actions as a sort of effort at détente popularized by politicians. Moreover, Turner initially discounts the totalitarian movement as an interference with his investigation. But the more he stalks Harting, the more clearly he understands Karfeld's character and the more he realizes why all should fear Karfeld's designs.

Leo Harting, the object of the manhunt, fascinates readers because his character is more suggested than defined. Like Prideaux in *Tinker, Tailor*, he is considered a handy outsider who serves both the institution's public needs and a few wives' private needs yet can never belong. A German national with a questionable family, he is ironically dubbed an "unpromotable, unpostable, unpensionable" embassy eunuch (*Town*, 46).[11] When interrogating embassy officials, Turner senses the embassy staff's insensitivity and obtuseness to Harting's plight. Through long interviews Turner learns from what the staff does not say how Harting is his employers' natural moral superior. Only Harting has vigorously defended British values, and only he attempts to halt Karfeld's neo-Nazism. Harting had stolen documents to punish Karfeld for atrocities that now fall outside Germany's 25-year statute of limitations but not outside his own moral outrage. Vaguely aware of his thefts, embassy officials shun Harting, preferring their appearance to his probes into past and present fictions. Harting, Turner discovers, was left with Leamas's choice of moral apathy or death. With little support for his sacrifice, Harting chose death.

Turner's success as a detective comes from his sharply intuitive nature and his identification with Harting. When he reacts from his training rather than to his social superiors, he becomes one with his

quarry. He reconstructs Harting's actions and motivations and gar-
ners more information from the slight glances and innuendoes his
informants provide than from official documents. When their versions of the facts do not add up, Turner's hard-boiled individualism
separates him from their fraudulent superiority and rightly prompts
him to doubt their veracity and sincerity. In Graham Greene's par-
lance, the hunter becomes the hunted.

Close to finding Harting, Turner is fired because Bradfield
believes Turner's unpleasant insights can disrupt the embassy's delicate negotiations; Bradfield, not Harting, becomes Turner's adversary. Bradfield attacks Turner and dismisses him as a disagreeable,
uncouth functionary rather than a professional. Turner, however,
stays unofficially on the case, perceiving now why silence is not
preferable to truth. Ferreting out Harting and his secrets becomes a
statement of personal faith for Turner. His final confrontation with
Bradfield, when Turner publicly announces Harting's monstrous discovery, climaxes the novel: Karfeld's recently completed doctoral
thesis traces the effects of poisonous gases on 31 concentration-
camp inmates that Karfeld himself incarcerated and murdered during
the world war. Bradfield and Siebkron have shielded Karfeld's
hideous secret all along for dubious political gain. Furthermore, they
helped Siebkron – on a tip from Harting's best friend, master spy
Harry Praschko – to lure Harting out of hiding so that Karfeld's thugs
could murder him. Expediency and Turner's outrage no longer allow
Bradfield to overlook Karfeld's guilt. EEC or not, some truths
demand public condemnation.

For *A Small Town in Germany* le Carré tacitly accepts a Marxist-
Hegelian dialectic that history controls events. Appropriate to le
Carré's artistic technique, historical events define the characters and
guide the novel's plot. Wartime winners seek support from the losers
to bolster their sagging economies. But 1968 is not 1938, and contemporary political crises are not well served by a British WWII
elitism. Instead of learning from its past, Britain tries to negotiate
with a radical faction in the West German government, an ill-defined
movement of post-Hitler youth who seem to blame "their parents for
losing the damn war, not for starting it" (*Town*, 333). Ethical realities
for the self-proclaimed leaders of Western democracy have become
"all doubt . . . [a]ll mist. There are no distinctions" (*Town*, 323). Le
Carré paints a by-now-familiar landscape. In a world that forgets

individuals and the history they create, that uses people and their pasts for private, institutional ends, no absolutes are possible other than deceit.

The Spy Who Came in from the Cold, *The Looking-glass War*, and *A Small Town in Germany* weave together viewpoints le Carré introduced in "To Russian, with Greetings" with major themes and motifs of a realistic fiction heavily dependent upon visual details. Whereas *Spy* succeeds as a taut, espionage novel, *Looking-glass War* and *Small Town* disappoint. *Spy* limits the action to that necessary to trace one main character. Leamas begins wedded to his insecurities and changes substantially through his discovery of love. On the other hand, because *Looking-glass War* shifts its focus from Avery to other characters, its narrative structure unravels. By the middle of the novel, the convoluted action required for Leiser's run replaces the interplay of characters. Whereas Leamas in *Spy* finds himself caught in an unstable labyrinth he helped to create and chooses to take heroic action based on his greater understanding of a means-ends argument, Avery gets lost in minutia. He cannot overcome others' questionable ethics, recognize love or manipulation, or evaluate the interrelationships of morality, justice, and love because he cannot effectively assess events or motivations.

A Small Town in Germany, which ends le Carré's didactic interpretation of the cold war, borders on tedium. Turner's character initially suggests various complexities sketched in Alec Leamas, but these features are subordinated late in *Small Town* to the adventure demands of an espionage plot. Critics argue that *Small Town*'s somewhat tacked-on denouement reflects the novelist's growing frustration with espionage as a genre and impatience with himself to produce, as he calls it, truly great works of fiction. A more plausible explanation is that *Looking-glass War* and *Small Town* are early and, though lengthy, somewhat unseasoned explorations of covert operations, of Western historical events and political philosophy, of characters whose personal and political ambitions clash, and of nearly unresolvable factional and emotional tensions. As such, they should be seen as ambitious, sometimes overplayed experiments in genre fiction rather than anomalous preludes to the work of a postmodernist fiction writer.

Chapter Four

David and Jonathan

Private faces in public places
Are nicer and wiser
Than public faces in private places
    – W. H. Auden, "Shorts" (1931)

Despite le Carré's early success at espionage fiction, he also wanted to write credible, nongenre literature. His resolve to accomplish this goal was so strong that, following the phenomenal reception and sales of *The Spy Who Came in from the Cold* and *A Small Town in Germany*, he declared, "I'm not going to plod like an old athlete around the same track just because it makes money."[1] His short prose, however, has been mostly ignored, and his one venture into mainstream fiction, *The Naive and Sentimental Lover* (1971), was briskly discredited by most critics as maudlin and overwritten.[2]

Le Carré's short stories and nonespionage novel are, however, more than curiosities or footnotes to his more popular fiction. The stories evince the black comedy and irony that arise when reluctant actors catch themselves in discordant actions. Likewise, his nongenre novel exemplifies his artistic strengths as clearly as it lays out his weaknesses. *Lover* shows how le Carré plays narrative techniques that confuse chronological sequences against the betrayal and perversity possible with familial and sexual love. But the book rejects political intrigue, a stock in trade of espionage fiction that explicitly complements le Carré's preferred stylistic and thematic interests. Hence, when le Carré blends resources from genre and mainstream fiction, he succeeds in creating intricate best-sellers like *Spy* or *Small Town*. But when he abandons espionage fiction's recognizable contexts, as he does in *Lover*, his technical prowess and philosophical allusions overcome story and characterization. Page after page, readers may marvel at the novelist's verbal agility, but they remain largely unsatisfied with the author's visions.

"You Can't Sack a College Boy" (1964),[3] le Carré's first attempt to mix verbal and situational ironies, humorously sketches the protagonist's stories of himself as a young man at his first job, working as a seasonal employee at Stain's department store. He remembers how he unwittingly managed to disrupt sales in each department he was sent to but kept his job because, as Rick Pym (*A Perfect Spy*) might illogically opine, "He's a college boy. . . . [Y]ou can't sack a college boy." The story's situational humor depends on incongruity: although he bungled his assignments, this nostalgic hero deftly shielded an elderly shoplifter. No longer a stockboy, he now mischievously hopes his shoplifter is "still around, pinching things."

"Dare I Weep, Dare I Mourn" (1967)[4] and "What Ritual Is Being Observed Tonight?" (1968)[5] are experiments in, respectively, black comedy and melodramatic romance. "Dare I Weep" retells a typical le Carré conflict: the ironic yet tragic victory a son achieves over his troublesome father. Traveling to East Germany to recover his father's body, successful West German shopkeeper Dietrich Koorp discovers that his father has contrived his "death" to escape political repression.[6] One man's freedom spells the other's oppression. Distressed that his cantankerous father will dominate him, Koorp suffocates his father in the coffin, ironically making his father's scam credible. Emotionally impotent and mouthing the values of self-determination in a desperate attempt to justify patricide, Koorp weeps, but his tears are tears of relief, for he imagines that his morally bankrupt soul is victorious.

"What Ritual Is Being Observed Tonight?," a question Aldo Cassidy ironically poses in *The Naive and Sentimental Lover*, anticipates the latter novel by mixing a romantic plot with philosophical debates and erotic allusions. Believing his love, Marie-Louise, does not return his affection, the self-conscious narrator undertakes to exclude passion from his life. He embraces a narrow study of German philosophy and letters, particularly Friedrich Schiller's dichotomous philosophy of the naive and the sentimental. He dismisses Marie-Louise's generosity as matronly concern and cuts himself off from natural beauty and affection. Years later, when invited to lecture on Schiller, he finds her again, married to a Schillerian scholar, Du Chêne. Du Chêne is a caricature of the scornful, barren academic (i.e., the ultimate sentimental poet) the narrator could have become without Marie-Louise. The narrator and true love triumph, a successful union le Carré only hints at in *The Little Drummer Girl* and *The Russia House*.

In "What Ritual" and "Dare I Weep" le Carré indulges in long, detailed descriptions of his English and European countrysides and reveals his love of German life and letters. He intertwines plots and symbols in the repetition of key props (i.e., a type of wine in "What Ritual"). He explores personal anguish (i.e., Koorp's inner dialogues) and melodrama mixed with sentimentality (i.e., the lover's anguished ruminations). He pits emotion and intellect against each other and hints at his view of sensuality and sexual love.

The stories also attest to le Carré's habit of layering characters and plots. Nothing in a le Carré romance is simple: relationships are incessantly complicated by interpersonal clashes, and characters' idiosyncrasies attract and repel. Moreover, the action arises from the characters' efforts to reconcile conflicting demands on their allegiances. A penchant for intellectual certainty blinds the protagonist of "Ritual" to Marie-Louise's love, much as Aldo Cassidy of *Lover* misses his wife's messages and Smiley misinterprets Ann. Devoted more to self-defining institutions than personal relationships, Koorp narrows his vision of familial harmony, as do Cassidy, Smiley, Charlie (*The Little Drummer Girl*), and Magnus Pym (*A Perfect Spy*).

Finally, themes that overlay and motivate espionage operations reverberate in le Carré's nongenre fiction – for instance, a son holds on to an untenable relationship with his father or the precision of dichotomous philosophy belies a man's suppressed sensuality and eroticism. Koorp's anguish is as common to John Avery (*The Looking-glass War*), Gadi Becker (*The Little Drummer Girl*), young Magnus Pym (*A Perfect Spy*), and Ned (*The Secret Pilgrim*) as the lover's submerged passion in "What Ritual" is to diverse characters in *The Quest for Karla* and Barley Blair in *The Russia House*. "Dare I Weep," by counterexample, and "What Ritual," by direct statement, reaffirm le Carré's belief that stability, even limited happiness, is achieved by securing love through a balance of intellect and emotion, or, in Schillerian terms, by attempting to merge the real and the transcendental.

Those motifs find diffuse expression in *The Naive and Sentimental Lover* and won the novel critical condemnation as "an unhappy

venture into the metaphysics of love."[7] The plot loosely retells David
Cornwell's turbulent relationships with James Kennaway and his
long-suffering wife, Susan. James Kennaway (1928-69), a Scottish
novelist, screenwriter, and self-centered bohemian, was a man "who
lived his life at an orgiastic pace."[8] To Cornwell, respected writer
and family man, James Kennaway was a romantic antihero trapped by
his own violent love, speech, actions, and thoughts. He intrigued
Cornwell because of his similarities to a character type Cornwell as
John le Carré variously and sympathetically explores with George
Smiley, Alec Leamas, Jerry Westerby, Magnus Pym, and company
lawyer Harry dePalfrey. Like these protagonists, James Kennaway was
a divided man, dependent on his family's and friends' affection yet
unable to avoid destroying that affection.[9]

Kennaway and Cornwell's friendship, affairs, and dramatic confrontations fed British scandalmongers long before either writer fic-
tionalized them or Susan Kennaway divulged them. They met and
became quick friends in 1963, Kennaway attracted to Cornwell's
intellect and conscious artistry ("the head is strong and the heart a
much hunted one" [Kennaway and Kennaway, 17]), and Cornwell to
Kennaway's freedom and romanticism that did "more for me in a
week than I have done for anyone else in a lifetime" (Kennaway and
Kennaway, 18). Cornwell found in Kennaway the paradox that
allegedly drives Shamus, the antagonist of *Lover*: a man insistent on
creativity, often courting titillating experiences, but bound tightly to
mundane values he publicly abhors. So great was Kennaway's attraction that Cornwell, now internationally recognized by his literary
pseudonym, dedicated *The Looking-glass War*, another novel
reflecting reality through distorted fantasies and mirror images, to his
friend.

During the preliminary discussions of the screenplay for *The
Looking-glass War*, le Carré insisted – over director Karl Reisz's
objections – that Kennaway accompany him to Paris. There,
according to Susan Kennaway, the two spent many late nights
carousing (see *Lover*, chapters 10-19). But on his return to London,
le Carré found himself attracted to his friend's wife. Susan's nonfictional description of their liaison and of James's retribution for
it – *The Kennaway Papers* – recounts how neither she nor James
thought "that I would actually fall in love with David. To complicate
matters further I still loved James. I believe also that David fell in love

with me and I know now that James and David loved each other in the way that David and Jonathan were brothers." Susan and le Carré "had arrived at the same point at the same time," and the torturous union that followed "was inevitable" (Kennaway and Kennaway, 24).

Like Link in James Kennaway's version of this triangular affair, *Some Gorgeous Accident* (1971), and Shamus in le Carré's version, *The Naive and Sentimental Lover*, James reacted hysterically to his wife's affair. Susan recounts that the affair and James's rage ended in a bizarre episode on an uneasy holiday at Haus am Berg, a skiing lodge in Zell-am-See, Switzerland. There James, raving and threatening injury to himself and others, renounced Susan to le Carré. Susan reports that the three found themselves "shouting and screaming in the lobby of the frozen station, creating an appalling scene. James had one of my arms and David had the other and they pulled in opposite directions; God knows why, because neither really wanted me by this time" (Kennaway and Kennaway, 55-57). The tirade ended with James and le Carré, drunk and confessional, ignoring Susan, falling into one another's arms, "comforting and swearing and laughing and crying all at once" (Kennaway and Kennaway, 56). In James Kennaway's hands, the tragicomic event deepens Link's understanding of himself. In le Carré's hands, it epitomizes the destructive potential inherent when shallow characters betray themselves and their infatuations.

Beyond a literary interest in how three writers reinterpret their common, psychologically wrenching experience, these biographical elements have fueled speculation about the influence of Cornwell's personal life on his fiction. Many critics acknowledge that le Carré's fiction has moved from minimally personal (*The Spy Who Came in from the Cold*) to highly autobiographical (*A Perfect Spy*) and back to impersonality (*The Secret Pilgrim*). Le Carré finds this literary evolution natural. He contends in numerous interviews that writers, like spies, learn their tradecraft by watching, recording, and eventually interpreting those around them through their actions and motivations. Both create "legends" (fictional histories) and, when sufficiently talented, will abandon factual reporting and interpret sources' lives ostensibly in their own words. Hence, le Carré's relationship with the Kennaways, like his relationship with his father, is best viewed as a backdrop whose accuracy is less important than the novelist's search for his characters' hearts of darkness.

Moreover, le Carré's connection to the Kennaways provides only one facet of *Lover*'s complexity. Equally important is his academic view of nature and the artist. *The Naive and Sentimental Lover* gets its name and metaphoric framework from le Carré's study of the aesthetic theories of German playwright and philosopher Friedrich Schiller (1759-1805).[10] An enthusiast of Kant's aestheticism and Goethe's creative genius, Schiller sought an explanation of how art can possess universal significance. By positing an antithesis between the rational and the creative, the ideal and the mundane, art and nature, Schiller extended Kant's dichotomy between *noumena* (items in themselves) and *phenomena* (items perceived through the filter of human cognition) and claimed a central role for art in human life and culture. In his letters and in the *Brief uber die asthetische Erziehung des Menschen* (1794-95) Schiller initially separated the naive viewpoint from the sentimental one, giving precedence to the naive as the more direct, commonsense perception of nature. The naive person believes that he perceives nature spontaneously and without self-awareness, whereas the sentimental person intentionally imposes notions of reality and rational evaluations on his perceptions of nature. The naive person claims that his re-creation of nature mirrors reality; the sentimental one claims only skewed perception. The dichotomy between the naive and the sentimental, Schiller contended, established necessary criteria for an objective concept of beauty.

In *Uber naive und sentimentalische Dichtung* (1795) Schiller extended this general theory of human nature into specifics by developing a topology of poets that maintains that writers with different modes of perception share equal importance in interpreting nature. By his earlier view the naive poet, exemplified by Goethe, transcends the sentimental poet because the former instinctively transmutes nature into poetry. The naive poet "lives life and doesn't imitate it. Feeling is knowledge" (*Lover*, 62). By contrast, the sentimental poet, exemplified by Keats, discredits naïveté. The sentimental poet "seeks nature" but, having lost touch with it, projects it as a sophisticated ideal – something the naive poet cannot do.[11] The sentimental poet cultivates "the natural state [left] behind" (*Lover*, 62). Conditioned by education and civilized institutions, the sentimental poet accepts that nature is only rarely idyllic. More often, nature disappoints his ideals or turns repugnant, and he poetically responds with lyricism, satire, or sorrowful verse. Discovering that Goethe unconsciously imposed his prejudices on his perceptions, Schiller revised his aesthetic philosophy. Now, because nature can be known only through the perceiver's image of it, naive and sentimental poets merely provide contrasting representations of nature. One writer's image cannot eclipse the other's. The ideal poet therefore merged the naive and the sentimental to convey a total vision of nature and beauty. Barred from the ideal, Schiller advocated the quest: to aspire to an art beyond human capacity was preferable to any actual work of art, an essential concept for the romantic poets.

With Schillerian philosophy to embellish each dialogue in *The Naive and Sentimental Lover*, le Carré sets out to explore the multiple sides of pram manufacturer Aldo Cassidy, who serves as both the novelist's satiric self-portrait and the fictional realization of Schiller's quest for a union of the naive and sentimental.[12] Cassidy immerses himself in the personal and professional lives of Shamus and Helen, le Carré's fictional depictions of James and Susan Kennaway. Cassidy and Shamus are doppelgängers. Approximately the same height, age, and build, each is handsome; each is married to a wife who reflects his aesthetic ideas; and each takes intellectual delight in mimicking different ethnic speakers. Each achieved status early, Cassidy through his virtually accidental invention and Shamus through his only novel, *The Moon by Day*. Each disreputably journeys toward artistic achievement and a union of passion with life, but each fails when measured against le Carré's well-practiced means-ends argument.

Aldo Cassidy is le Carrésque: a 38-year-old Englishman and respected professional who avows control over his life. To casual acquaintances he's an inventive man, "the architectural prototype for the middle class Englishman privately educated between the wars; one who had felt the wind of battle but never the fire of it" (*Lover*, 5). Intimates, however, sense the weaknesses that dominate him. Called the nickname "Doubtful" at Sherborne School and one of Oxford's "lesser colleges," Cassidy is a conservative by choice, one who hides in his club, the Nondescripts, and prefers "a selection of Frank Sinatra's music on the theme of male solitude" (*Lover*, 28). A henpecked husband, estranged parent, and failed first novelist ("the spy vogue was high at that time, and he thought he might get in on the market" [*Lover*, 453]), Cassidy aspires only "to make people happy." That sentiment, common to Cornwell's father, Ronnie, and to sundry le Carré protagonists, warrants immediate suspicion. Like his espionage counterparts, Cassidy maintains a public nobility that camouflages his artifice. He passes off a love of ancient mansions, "fine silver and old Worcester," titles, ancestry, and the finest British sterling as the sophistication of an educated entrepreneur. But his clichés bespeak a man searching for a secure but illusory history.

Under this studied facade Cassidy is a shallow man whose childhood left him an emotionally displaced adult unable to cope with his impending midlife crisis. His mother, Ella, abandoned him when he was six. His father, Hugo, a sketchily drawn manipulator, prospers from his short-lived liaisons and considerable abilities to exaggerate. Hugo's world, like Rick Pym's in *A Perfect Spy*, is filled with "food and waiters, the fragrance of angels and of heavenly flowers" (*Lover*, 191), paid for by sizable loans that he extracts from Aldo through his guilt-ridden recriminations and that he never repays. Hugo's influence shapes Cassidy's character, outlooks, and approaches. To set things right between them, Hugo offers up prayers for Aldo, negotiating for guidance with "his Divine Employer" so that God, not Hugo, can repair the damage: "*Look down in your goodness on young Aldo here. . . . He is very much confused between sin and virtue just at the moment. My view, for what it is worth, Lord, is that he has put his hand into a snake's nest, but only Thou, oh Lord, in Thy wisdom can give a final ruling on this one; and so be it*" (*Lover*, 329-30). Although he never hears Hugo's prayer for him, Aldo echoes his father's commercial appeals to God in his own prayers for life.

Hugo's legacy predisposes Aldo to failed family relationships. Sandra, Cassidy's prosaic mate, makes jam, sleeps 12 hours a day, and operates a failing clinic with her mother, Mrs. Groat, herself a shrewish caricature. A minimally talented pianist, Sandra extends her artistic world by trivializing every part of Aldo's. She calls him "Pailthorpe the Bear," "*Pitiful* Cassidy," and "*Abject* Toad," each nickname manifesting the derision and animosity it substitutes for love. She demeans his literary dreams by choosing "a *straight* book suitable to a tired Pailthorpe of little fantasy" for a business trip to Bristol he fabricates to get away from her and his responsibilities.

Sandra's nicknames and taunts, like Hugo's recriminations, revive Aldo's seditious childhood memories. What marriage they have exists through aggravated separations and contentious exchanges; no warmth or stability sustains either partner. Together, they fight like "two cats who had till then slept peacefully in each other's arms" but "woke and began spitting" (*Lover*, 116). Apart, she is his sparring partner, a nagging voice on the telephone, or a vexing competitor across the tennis net.

Cassidy chooses to separate himself from his sons, Mark and young Hugo; le Carré hints that Cassidy's emotional withdrawal and his sons' physical impairments concretely manifest the family's dysfunctions. Mark, recently cured of peritonitis, attends Sherborne to learn "virtue and patriotism" despite Aldo's pain-filled memories of the school and Mark's abhorrence of its repressiveness. Cassidy constantly writes Mark letters he never mails. In one long, confessional letter (a literary technique le Carré cultivates in *A Perfect Spy*), Cassidy explains, more to himself than to Mark, how "animal energy," not love, forced him to marry. Aldo casts himself as the martyr in this myopic allegory and Sandra, Hugo, and Mrs. Groat as his persecutors. As a suitor, Cassidy, "naturally a very polite person," dissembled because Sandra "might disapprove" of his aspirations. Now he sees himself and Sandra as "child martyrs to a grown-up world." He wants things "to be *better*" for Mark and young Hugo, but with superficiality and fear he excuses himself. He cannot repair lost loyalties, prevent future perfidies, or "really spread much love around" (*Lover*, 130), because he is incapable of such attachments.

Lacking courage, Cassidy acquiesces to Sandra's puissance, takes his revenge in secret, and further jeopardizes stability in his life. When Shamus dubs Sandra "bosscow," Cassidy seldom refers to her again by another name. Sandra eventually discovers Aldo is supporting Shamus and Helen. Facing his wife's rage and lacking emotional reserves, Cassidy shrinks and silently agrees with Sandra when she says he is a latent homosexual and has not a "scrap of decency or moral fiber or human compassion" (*Lover*, 166). Given to childish, insincere diffidence, he acts to ensure emotional outbursts in others and consequently guarantees confrontation and betrayal.

Cassidy blames his home life and his experiences with Shamus and Helen for his spiritual death, but he never exemplifies this passing. Rather, the more he bargains clichés and money for love, the less affection anyone extends to him and the more his children repeat his obdurate past. In relationships built on bullying, separation, and rejection, Aldo's family *and* Shamus and Helen hold absolute power: their glances or casual innuendos transform him from a middle-aged businessman into an abused child. His complicity is equally obvious. He blinds himself to his own platitudes and subsequently extends Hugo's bankrupt legacy by estranging himself from his sons and family. Selfishly, Sandra degrades Cassidy's psychic journey and, "for the children's sake," overlooks his alleged spiritual death (*Lover*, 452). He betrays Sandra in secret by bedding her friend Heather Ast and joking with his mistress about his wife's idiosyncrasies and deficiencies.

Cassidy charges his business with corrupting and then denying him an attachment to Mark and his father, as well as his search for artistic fulfillment, with estranging him from young Hugo. By age seven Hugo can bully his father with questions, insist that he play roles (i.e., the cowboy Sturrock) for his amusement, and embarrass him before visitors. The child learns his lessons from his grandfather and his mother, who badgers Cassidy, "How on *earth* you have the *nerve* to *pretend* you *care* about your *children* when all you do is get *drunk* in front of them and *swear* and make *filthy-imputations-against-people-they-respect*" (*Lover*, 151). A frustrated Cassidy flees to Paris rather than act when Sandra refuses to take Hugo to a specialist for a broken leg. These events typify Cassidy's nature: whatever the crisis, Cassidy supplants his attachment to his family with a quest for excitement and romance.

If his own childhood leaves him uncentered and searching for emotional stability and self-esteem, Cassidy purportedly compensates through his success as a businessman.[13] Yet he believes his company restricts him by denying him the emotional security he wants. Cassidy's fortune comes from a safety-brake system he unintentionally designed for baby carriages. Though the safety brake, his only invention, revolutionizes the industry and promises to save future generations, Cassidy wants only overblown titles ("Founder, Chairman, Managing Director, and principal shareholder of Cassidy's General Fastenings" [*Lover*, 451]). Viewed as metaphor, the brake should reverse his unstable childhood, but the fortune it brings him leaves him unable to affect the direction of his adulthood or halt his disastrous fate.

Cassidy, however, never portrays his business acumen and inge-
nuity, giving rise to critical suspicion about le Carré's control of this
character. If success breeds self-confidence, even in those who lack
it initially, why does Cassidy remain weak-willed?[14] Other characters
report that Cassidy is a "gentle troubleshooter" called "deft . . . in
the *Times Business News* during a recent take-over battle" (*Lover*,
17) and that he soothes angry trade unionists, deprived competitors,
and surly employees. Yet nowhere does Cassidy act with the self-confidence expected of a successful inventor and entrepreneur. He
turns his holdings over to minions who increase the company's
wealth despite him, and his doubts permit these subordinates to
intimidate him. Cassidy alternately postures absurdly and whimpers
helplessly while he conforms to his audience's expectations.

When he addresses financial gatherings, he mouths platitudes
("Ideals are like the stars" [*Lover*, 158]), not progressive innova-
tions. In the novel he never chairs a board meeting, composes a
company document, negotiates a profitable transaction, or bests a
business antagonist. He steadfastly avoids confrontation by overtip-
ping service attendants and silencing himself when verbally challenged. Vicarious fantasies combined with images of sterility and
death circumscribe Cassidy's professional life. He spends his days
hiding in his "sweet deep casket" of an office and prays for his
release in terms of old Hugo's negotiated separation (*"Dear Lord
this is Aldo Cassidy. . . . I specifically asked you for a quick, useful
death against appalling odds. I should now like to revise my
request. I don't want death any more; I want life, and only Thou,
oh Lord, can provide it. So please don't let me wait too long,
Amen"* [*Lover*, 123]). Nonetheless, his two-year affair with Shamus
ended, he retires to an even more directionless and vulnerable life.

Cassidy, le Carré insinuates, could be not only a public success
but also a secretive one. After all, his childhood of watching his
beguiler father and adapting to inconstant circumstances leaves him
an able dissembler. Lies always suit the circumstances. As a child he
lies easily to a music teacher, Mrs. Harabee, about his father's
"death"; as an adult he avoids a speeding ticket by lying about his
mother's death. Aliases come as easily. He is Viscount Cassidy of Mull
at his Bohemia hotel; during their Paris debauch, he chooses
[Donald] Maclean and [Guy] Burgess as his and Shamus's cover-
names. He keeps safe houses (his decaying Haverdown mansion,

Shamus's London apartment) and searches for new ones. In all his
dealings, whether business or personal, Cassidy lives his lies completely because they are his personae. Silently, he acknowledges that
he lies because Sandra does not *"know how to deal with* [the truth]
any more than I do" and because he is *"beginning to discover the
truth and the truth, my angel, is outside us"* (*Lover,* 166). Like le
Carré's discredited agents, Cassidy embraces obsequious treason by
refusing to question his incongruities.

Bored with his wealth and impatient with his civilized marriage
and tedious family and friends, Cassidy dreams of experiencing
romance by escaping from deadening institutional allegiances. *What*
Cassidy is diametrically opposes *who* he desires to be, and his means
to self awareness cast doubt on his quest. Searching for illusion, he
travels to Haverdown, an "elegant wreck of a dozen English generations" (*Lover,* 14). From the womblike safety of his company-bought
Bentley ("a hearse for a Nondescript" [*Lover,* 21]) he indulges his
vanity and pedestrian daydreams. He puzzles over the pronunciation
of Haverdown ("Was the *a* long or short? To have or to haver?"
[*Lover,* 8]), dismisses a local farmer as illiterate and possibly drunk,
and fantasizes the status Haverdown will spontaneously confer: "You
know young Cassidy of Haverdown? Remarkable fellow. Flourishing
business in London, gave it all up, came down here. Locals adore
him of course. Generous to a fault" (*Lover,* 9).

The mansion, rebuilt by a bankrupt Lord Alfred de Waldeberre,
promises an emotionally starved Cassidy release from his oppressing
obligations but symbolizes hopeless subjugation. Its name echoes le
Carré's disaffection with British gentry and their decaying standards,
for *havers* (Scottish for "nonsense") connotes unstable hovering
and wavering.[15] Dreaming himself a wifeless, childless, freewheeling
country squire, Cassidy wanders into the mansion. His resolute concern "with exteriors" casts the mansion's cold symbols as sentimental visions. He disregards how its "disintegrating griffins, glumly
clutching armorial shields . . . their feet manacled to the plinth and
their shoulders hunched from fatigue" (*Lover,* 9) suggest repression.
He pretends that the ill-tended, deciduous trees surrounding the
mansion have a "fatherly gentleness" – a particularly ironic image,
given Cassidy's family. The images reiterate Cassidy's shallowness.
Defined by convention, he lacks the inner resources, defiance, and
endurance to be a tragic figure.

Haverdown introduces Cassidy to Shamus and Helen, squatters who break into empty houses, deplete the owners' resources, and flee, leaving the homes impoverished. Shamus has no surname and apparently no childhood or literary progenitors; hence he is tinged with a disconcerting unreality meant to lure artistically naive Cassidy.[16] Shamus (slang for "policeman") emerges as the artistic outlet that the jejune Aldo requires: "Where Cassidy was weak, his examiner was resolute; where concessive, zealous; where Cassidy was fluid, the other was rock, and where he was pale and fair, his examiner was dark and sudden and eager" (*Lover*, 20). The novel initially suggests that Cassidy's psychic merger with Shamus will infuse Cassidy with artistic and personal integrity and fulfill his self-defined quest. But the psychic and artistic union le Carré sets up can never produce an ideal, because the means and ends are absurdly flawed: neither participant meets the individual criteria for naive and sentimental.

A wild, protean writer, Shamus quotes Dylan Thomas, is compared to Brendan Behan, and believes himself a romantic bohemian à la Goethe's young Werther. But he proves himself a morally bankrupt charlatan determined to control others by policing their reactions. His posturing, fetid wit, and puerile epithets (i.e., "bosscow," "the Few," "the Many-too-Many") show his artistry as pretense.[17] He's a caricatured iconoclast, married passionately and replenishing his creativity through perversity ("if he didn't make hell he wouldn't make books" [*Lover*, 314]). Whereas Cassidy lamely protests the superficiality of his institutions, Shamus challenges "convention, morals, manners, life, God" (*Lover*, 63), the images he prefers to perpetuate rather than destroy. Shamus couldn't exist without a conventionalized world to rebel against, but his protests pervert artistry into eccentricity. He defames the middle class ("the fucking bourgeoisie") because it replaces creative passion and an artist's requisite spiritual pain with creature comfort. Yet he wantonly squanders Cassidy's money on liquor and prostitutes and abandons arts for a "romantic," deeply felt life (*Lover*, 193). He shuns the stability and quiet that would allow him to write and prefers to excuse his literary impotence by condemning the reading public ("the proles"). They, not he, are an undifferentiated collective too stupid to appreciate his "art."

Shamus's prosaic churlishness is best exemplified in his treatment of women. He dismisses "bosscow" Sandra yet lusts after her more crudely than Cassidy lusts after his secretary, Angie Mawdray. He verbally and physically debases all women: only prostitutes, he tells Cassidy, have hands sensitive enough to iron the wrinkles from passports. Should Helen, his "fifth-rate concubine," disobey him, he publicly rejects her and secretly beats her, "with his right hand, a hook probably; a hard wide one from the side. . . . [S]he tasted just a little of blood, as if she had had a tooth out" (*Lover*, 413). Shamus lives through raw emotions solely, drinking himself into stupors and violating only those too weak to offer resistance.

Shamus's impotent rebellion, brutalization of Helen, drunkenness, and artistic pretense make his attraction to Cassidy incredible.[18] As explanation le Carré proffers Helen's beauty. Through Haverdown's cold Cassidy sees Helen naked, "a towel over one arm and a small transistor radio in her hand." Her appearance, "fractional hesitation," and "double glance" flash on his "heightened consciousness," impressing her as an "apparition . . . upon Cassidy's beleaguered fantasy." Her vision dismantles "his ever-ready apparatus of disbelief," arouses him to epiphany (*Lover*, 28), and liberates him momentarily from wife, family, and business obligations. Helen's role as archetypal artist's mate and abused wife lets her unabashedly magnify Shamus's inventiveness while willfully absenting herself from his brutality. She knows he's not "even Irish, he just has funny voices and a theory that God is living in County Cork disguised as a forty-three-year-old taxi driver [Flaherty]." But she fantasizes that he's "a marvellous, wonderful writer" who's "altering the course of world literature" (*Lover*, 46). This chimera sustains her dysfunctional love.

Caught in his illusion of her, Cassidy accepts Helen's image of Shamus as a true (i.e., naive) artist because her explanation vividly imprints itself on him. Shamus, Helen explains "as if remembering a hard-learned lesson," typifies theories propounded by Schiller, "a terrifically famous German dramatist actually but of course the English being so insular had never heard of him" (*Lover*, 62). Shamus is the life force, Schiller's naive poet, and Cassidy the sentimental because he would "long to be *like* Shamus" but, having left a natural state behind, has become "sort of . . . corrupt." Whimsically, Helen posits that "It's the attraction of opposites. He's natural, you're corrupt. That's why he loves you" (*Lover*, 62-63). Lacking the acumen Kennaway gives *Some Gorgeous Accident*'s heroine, Helen demurely accepts Shamus's molestation and Cassidy's munificence. Her attraction to Shamus is pathological; her attraction to any man who reveres rather than beats her is understandable. Cassidy's attraction to a woman who gratifies his whims without argument is equally obvious within the confines of sentimental fiction.

Yet Shamus and Helen have moments of insight when they acknowledge their fraud. Faced with Cassidy's unbridled love for him, Shamus quietly confesses that "You've got me wrong, lover." He is imprisoned by the same private, stultifying vices: "I'm just a failed businessman" (*Lover*, 196). Likewise, with Shamus in yet another abusive, drunken stupor, Helen can judge her husband assiduously as a reactionary, "a drooling old Victorian fuddy-duddy" who cons Aldo and Helen. There's "one law for him, another for us. . . . Shamus *hates* convention. That's the message. But we mustn't. Oh no. We've got to love it" (*Lover*, 318). These phatic utterances seldom affect the characters' insight. Each clings tenaciously to a distorted reality, and each forfeits compassion for the effort.

Their menage à trois climaxes, bizarrely, at a Swiss chalet. Following a vicious confrontation with Sandra over his affair with Helen, Cassidy searches in somber images for his forfeited institutional security. Along the way he unsuccessfully seeks shelter ("I need a bed") with his father, his secretary, and, finally, a male Swiss business colleague who, presuming Cassidy's homosexuality, propositions him. At Sainte-Angèle Shamus, brandishing Hugo's gun, forces Cassidy back to the chalet to confront Helen. Shamus, learning of the affair, has beaten her again. Cassidy briefly glimpses Shamus as he is, with "no physical constancy, no shape or profile" (*Lover*, 421), but Aldo disregards the telling apparition. Still raging and irrational, Shamus "marries" Cassidy and Helen and sends them away. But Cassidy procrastinates leaving, intentionally missing the last train. Imagining Shamus will attempt suicide, Cassidy returns to the chalet and finds his now-ex-lover wearing his dressing gown and screeching for a whore.

Artistically, the climax defeats the novel. With no emerging self-awareness, Cassidy can't learn from the confrontation. Now little more than figments, Shamus and Helen desert him, disappearing in his tears "like two pedestrians in the rain, before the hood of his rich

man's car" (*Lover*, 450). His ill-conceived journey toward enlighten-
ment, art, and passion leaves him barren and more unloved than
before.

The *Naive and Sentimental Lover*'s concept is daunting but its
execution unfortunate. Le Carré tries to animate unsavory characters
with romanticism. He instead succeeds in arranging lush portraits of
three lost souls whose complex interplay rivals any of Smiley's
cross/double-cross exchanges. He casts Shamus and Cassidy as
mirror images revealing the other's desires and hates and exemplify-
ing Schiller's artistic dichotomy. Although Schiller's words are cited,
his concepts are disguised at best. *The Naive and Sentimental Lover*
doesn't illustrate Schiller's merged dichotomy, because it skirts the
debate of what defines a true artist: Shamus never approaches
Schiller's naive poet, and Cassidy confuses love with sentimentality
and the metaphysical definition of "nature" with nature as the phenomena of the material world. Because the characters lack dramatic
angst, the novel comes closer to being an erotic caricature of Robert
Louis Stevenson's *Dr. Jekyll and Mr. Hyde* than an investigation into
the nature of the divided soul or a nonespionage exposé of betrayal.

Schiller's theories promise a simpler life, one lived naturally, as
Shamus allegedly does. But the journey as reinterpreted in *The Naive
and Sentimental Lover* develops as an internal, costly trip strewn
with betrayal and discarded ideals. In transit characters sacrifice
their innocence and consequently any pretense to naturalness.
Bound by choice to institutions, Cassidy destroys his hope for naturalness, his image of family, Shamus and Helen, and his adolescent
idealization of the writer. Shamus perpetuates his emotional immatu-
rity as a means of preserving his sham artistry. And Helen fawns over
her capricious abuser.

The novel is more successful when viewed as another example of
a standard le Carré theme: the search for ethical, moral, personal,
and aesthetic values that leads a willing character to fantasy (i.e., Did
Shamus and Helen exist?), betrayal, and spiritual death. Cassidy's
tragedy is premised on a cheapened desire for instant self-knowledge
and direct experience of love and life. His flaws thwart his dreams,
and his shallowness leaves his search undefined ("A quest for *what*?
. . . A quest *towards*, or a quest *from*?" [*Lover*, 7]). Cassidy's haste
arises from his fear of the pain spiritual reevaluation exacts. To

shortcut it, he voyeuristically embraces intellectual and sexual unions with Shamus and Helen.

This overly philosophical, sentimental, and often artistically confused novel closes with a now-common warning. In "whatever there was left of [his world] to inhabit," Cassidy dares not remember love. This one element, le Carré consistently argues, makes any quest bearable and, as Smiley tirelessly professes, defines whatever you can still betray.

Chapter Five

The Quest for Karla

All things merge into one another – good into evil, generosity into justice, religion into politics.

– Graham Greene, *The Honorary Consul* (1983)

While a few reviewers found it a "splendid romantic fantasy," most attacked *The Naive and Sentimental Lover* as "a disastrously pretentious book" of "turgid prose and menopausal romanticism," born of "self-indulgence and intellectual laziness, often descending into whimsy."[1] They urged le Carré to go back into the cold to rediscover his "appropriate genre" and reactivate the dark storyteller within him. Venturing into mainstream fiction, they argued, squandered his considerable talent and jeopardized his place as one of Britain's foremost espionage novelists.

Le Carré's reaction to the criticism was harsh. He bristled at interviewers' questions and dryly remarked that their critiques were proof of "what a good writer I am not" (Abley 1983b, 51).[2] Disgruntled, le Carré returned to espionage fiction and wrote a trilogy of stylistically individual novels. In *Tinker, Tailor, Soldier, Spy* (1974), *The Honourable Schoolboy* (1977), and *Smiley's People* (1980) he reiterated his familiar themes of loyalty/betrayal, love/duty, past/present, and institutions/individualism.. The novels recount George Smiley's pursuit of and eventual union with his supposedly darker half, Soviet spymaster Karla. When these works were completed, le Carré vowed to "hang up Smiley's boots, at least for a while."[3] This trilogy, reissued in 1982 as *The Quest for Karla*, both answered le Carré's critics and further confused them about the novelist's place in the larger tradition of postmodern fiction.

In the trilogy le Carré reshaped medieval quests into a code of chivalry appropriate to contemporary dilemmas. The medieval quest begins when a treasure is taken from its rightful owners by an evil force that, because it is surrounded by secrets and power, appears absolute. A heroic St. George or Sir Gawain journeys, often against his will, across hostile borders to reach the evil, defeat it, and reestablish his community's status quo.[4] The hero, a man of extraordinary abilities, must separate himself from his community in order to defend it. But separation traps the hero between the evil he must defeat and the community he serves. Resolution of the quest always changes the hero. If he obliterates evil (i.e., slays the dragon), he can rejoin his community through a union with the princess (his anima, or soul), but this union will preclude his self-awareness. If he recognizes his kinship with the evil force, no victor emerges. Consequently, the quest becomes incomplete and ends in uncertainty.

Romance archetypes such as the quest motif allow le Carré to treat Smiley's public and private inquiries as studies of the metaphysics of deceit. Principle among these studies, *The Quest for Karla* chronicles the exposure of a mole in the Circus by its knight-errant, George Smiley; his reconstruction of the destroyed intelligence agency; and his part in the eventual downfall of the Soviet head of the Thirteenth Directorate, the man who orchestrated the Circus's humiliation. Smiley eventually combines this public quest for his "Black Grail" with his private search for his lost Ann. But his society's pervasive paranoia and betrayal irreparably damage Smiley's spirit and preclude his forgiving or reconciling with Ann. At this point Smiley as a person and as le Carré's creation comes to a quietus.[5]

The trilogy resonates with quest and adventure motifs. Recalled by his service from his Bywater Street Avalon, Smiley pursues Karla with increasing monomania. Smiley is now the tired ruler of his Round Table of agents perpetually locked in battle with an illusive Mordred. Ann appears as "the woman," Smiley's lascivious Guinevere, drawn into indiscretions with lesser men including the Round Table's charming Lancelot, Bill Haydon. Secondary knights, such as Jim Prideaux, Jerry Westerby, Toby Esterhase, and Peter Guillam (Smiley's "tight-mouthed cupbearer"), assist Smiley in unearthing his enigmatic adversary, but their service destroys the order they intend to save.

Moreover, Smiley is faithfully served by a series of almost-stereotyped romance familiars. The haggish, unquestionably loyal Connie Sachs, whose "fairy-tale smile" reappears as she reminds Smiley that

Haydon is "rebuilding Camelot" (*Tinker, Tailor,* 108), reiterates her encyclopedic knowledge, "the abracadabra of the obsessive bur-rower's trade" (*Schoolboy,* 60). Karla's misinformation is fed to the Circus through Source Merlin in an operation codenamed "Witchcraft." Jerry Westerby, Smiley's yeoman knight, thinks of him-self as Galahad rescuing the fair but disreputable Lizzie Worthington. The wise mother Maria Andreyvna Ostrakova bestows the token that secures Karla's defection to her "magician," Otto Leipzig, a man sporting curved eyebrows and black hair brushed into horns, who cures her pain as he soothes her paranoia. With such characters' help, Smiley journeys to restore Camelot; his archetypal crusade takes him, through his knights, across Europe to Russia, Hong Kong, and Southeast Asia. Yet nothing can return Smiley or the Circus to the virtues of the past. His Round Table is destroyed from within by agents who break their vows of loyalty and obedience. Union with his anima, the faithless Ann, repulses Smiley, and defeat of his neme-sis, Karla, leaves him an uncertain victor and his quest inconsequential.

Throughout the trilogy le Carré's knights are filled with the exis-tential anxieties common to ordinary men caught in philosophical and emotional labyrinths of their own making. These contemporary knight-errants battle not with fire-breathing dragons but with life's moral ambiguities. They find that the standard demarcation line between good and evil disappears; thus symbolic representations of righteousness and hypocrisy, common to romance and adventure lit-erature, are confused.

In earlier novels a more idealistic Smiley could fuel his search for meaning with his intense compassion for decency, patriotism, and humanity. But the trilogy's repeated betrayals force Smiley to admit the futility of the institutions he has revered for a lifetime, while those around him learn that they must condemn the value of the Great Game itself. Smiley's and Karla's worlds coalesce. No longer able to identify the enemy clearly, Smiley wearily reconciles himself "to interpret the whole of life in terms of conspiracy."[6]

Smiley's quest replicates, in a political sense, Britain's patriotic search for past glory sacrificed by the Cambridge spies: Anthony Blunt (1907-83), Guy Burgess (1911-63), Donald Maclean (1913-83), and particularly Harold Adrian Russell (Kim) Philby (1912-88).[7] Philby, apparently nicknamed for Kipling's boy hero, was the son of author-explorer Harry St. John Philby (1885-1960). As a child Philby (like David Cornwell and his perfect spy, Magnus Pym) watched bewitched as his father postured eccentrically and finagled his fortunes. Educated (on credit) at Trinity College, Cambridge, Philby publicly advocated Marxism. With his degree in economics, schoolboy's allegiance to communism, and flimsy cover as a *Times* correspondent, Philby was recruited by the Secret Intelligence Service (SIS).[8] His organizational skills and dedication to duty advanced his career, but communism sustained his revolutionary faith even when "the aberration of individuals" threatened it (Philby, 13).

By the late 1940s Philby, as head of SIS's anti-Soviet section, was posted to the United States, where, with Maclean, he passed American atom bomb secrets to the Soviets. Eventually exposed as a Comintern (Communist International) agent, Philby defected to the Soviet Union, where, 25 years later, he died a Soviet hero and a world enigma. While Philby and his fellow Cambridge spies unraveled networks, breached security, and demoralized British and American intelligences services, their more intriguing legacy for novelists is their complex motivations for betrayal.[9]

Philby's inconstant youth and his adult disloyalty complement le Carré's literary preoccupation with betrayal, but le Carré defers his scrutiny of familial influence for *A Perfect Spy*. As he had done in earlier novels, le Carré in the trilogy implicitly censures the British ruling class for creating Philby (he "was of our blood and hunted with our pack") and argues that Philby-like characters expose Britain's political morality for public scrutiny ("Introduction," 5). The secret services, "microcosms of the British condition, of our social attitudes and vanities" ("Introduction," 7), further degrade the philosophical status of Western democracy, first by refusing to reform themselves and second by reducing their standard-bearers to liars, deceivers, and murderers. Traitors like Philby create stasis, not progress, and the espionage services' superficiality encourages questioning individuals to betray their countries, their services, and themselves. The trilogy fictionalizes this stasis and presents, without substantive evaluation, various rationalizations for betrayal, ranging from Haydon's ideological excuses in *Tinker, Tailor, Soldier, Spy* to Westerby's misguided sentimentality in *The Honourable Schoolboy* and Smiley's increasingly cynical apologies in *Smiley's People*.

Le Carré fuses this view of society's culpability with the afore-
mentioned romance motifs. The Circus steals its treasure from itself
but blames others for its appropriation. Salvation must come from an
exiled knight who would redeem his society by ridding the community of both external and internal decay, a process that inevitably
defeats him. This synthesis of reprobation and myth reinforces Conrad's "hearts of darkness" theme as it poses the question common to
all le Carré's work, How can a society hold itself as ethical when the
methods of its agents are no better than those of its adversaries?

Additionally, quest literature provides le Carré with a ready symbolism, chiefly one that shows how psychological travail champions
experience as besieged operations search for self-understanding. In
striving to recognize, confront, and defeat inner monsters (their own
conditioned anxieties), individuals jeopardize their emotional security. Viewed allegorically, the hero's pursuit of his community's treasure signifies his private search to create stability and existential
meaning for himself by gaining control over his chaotic existence.

Smiley typifies this psychic conflict in his futile appeals to reason
and to muted patriotism, abortive reconciliations with Ann, and final
identification with his doppelgänger, Karla. Struggling with the self-
awareness that these conflicts bring, Smiley discovers to his dismay
that while he can defend his values as ethical, he cannot distinguish
his methods from his adversary's. He pawnbrokers Karla's Ann,
Tatiana, as indifferently as Karla beds Haydon and Ann. Cold war
conflicts in an age of détente blur his colleagues' absolute political
values and confound their private ethics; caught in the crossfire,
Smiley loses his intellectual aloofness and ability to discriminate
between his own goals and those of his masters and adversaries. Like
King Arthur, Smiley pays for resolution with his spiritual life. His resurrection, while as hoped-for as Arthur's, never happens. The Round
Table regains no glory, for its glory was always illusionary.

The Quest for Smiley, Ann, and Karla

Three presences – George Smiley, Ann Smiley, and Karla – dominate
the trilogy even though the last two appear only once. Smiley animates *Quest* as a more operationally skilled character but one little
changed from the earlier cold war novels. Presumably now in his

seventies, Smiley is beyond active fieldwork but not yet formally displaced as the Circus's distinguished senior statesman. More obviously than in previous novels, Smiley reads people, surmises their intentions, and projects himself into their minds. Accustomed to tedious research, he assimilates outwardly insignificant details that he then uses to sharpen his skills as an interrogator and master his style of indirection and subterfuge. Yet Scotch tape still defeats him; he casually polishes his glasses with his tie, awkwardly dismisses himself from unpleasant social gatherings, and, though uncomfortable with its ambiguous ethic, continues to hold himself out as his profession's proponent.[10]

Once described as having "the cunning of Satan and the conscience of a virgin" (*Murder*, 74), Smiley seeks stability in a world made chaotic by institutional, not personal, allegiances. Incapable of reordering his Service's value system, he degenerates across the trilogy as he loses his own moral sense. Weakened by unending betrayal, the man who cried for Dieter Frey surrenders his humanity and embraces abhorrent means. He fails to prevent Bill Haydon's death and then shields the murderer with his silence. He dismisses blackmailer Frost's brutal murder as an operational necessity because it "advanced the case" (*Schoolboy*, 319). He forces Karla's defection even though contemporaries warn him and his oft-noted instinct confirms that defection cannot reestablish stability. He wants yet coldly rejects Ann, precluding any reconciliation. He shrugs off Oliver Lacon's unusually perceptive insight that Britain's "future was with the collective" but its survival, like that of Western democracy, "was with the individual"; this paradox no longer threatens him.[11] As Smiley merges with the institution he seeks to reform, his questions become more desperate and his justifications more cynical. In the end he accepts that democracies and love affairs will be compromised as surely as means will perpetually sully ends. He recognizes that the mind and the romantic spirit will seldom appeal as strongly as pledging loyalty to a self-defining clique and that love redeems only when it is defeated.

His Lady Ann haunts Smiley throughout the trilogy, but she is sketched ambiguously through others' reports of her and hence never becomes a well-developed character. Connie Sachs deems her a vicious "she-devil," and Saul Enderby dismisses her as Smiley's "bitch goddess." To those of her decaying Set, Ann's natural sociability is attractive and her irreverence titillating. Tall, with "a Celtic look" befitting a queen, Ann acts for the moment. She takes lovers as her means to avoid boredom and, when confronted, falls back on epigrams of unmistakable artificiality.

From Smiley's myopic view Ann's directness checks his liberal angst, while her independence attracts and repulses him. In truth he has little idea of what she's made of or what gives her satisfaction. She recommends action over contemplation and, he thinks, infuses life in his bloodless, professional world. Responding to his anger about his profession's disregard and his research's ineffectualness, Ann counsels Smiley to act rather than accept facile arguments, to press for what he believes in rather than sanction others' expectations. When he rejects this advice, she flip-flops and instead urges him to "burn the lot" of Circus memories and rid himself of the irritant, just "don't rot" (*Tinker, Tailor*, 72). Ann expects unquestioned forgiveness for her infidelities, yet her capriciousness is antithetical to Smiley's pensiveness. Hence, while her absence ensures his emptiness, her presence more often silences him.

Despite the vivacity she brings to his life, Ann's independence complicates Smiley's ruminations and threatens to reveal the sterility of his increasingly claustrophobic worlds. Constantly seeking novelty, she refuses to enter or approve of either the masculine world of spies and the impotent world of dusty books on dead philosophers and poets that distracts Smiley from espionage. Yet her professed love for Smiley fails to redeem her.

In the end her flippant independence and refusal to abandon her superficiality make her Karla's ideal means of discrediting Smiley and inflicting profound wounds. Smiley construes her affair with Bill Haydon as insidious and agonizes because Karla, not Ann, contrived the liaison. Moreover, the indiscretion makes her the central player she never wanted to be, feeding Smiley's pathological pursuit of Karla. Her independence, for all its attractiveness, serves primarily to emphasize the threat an unbridled emotional commitment poses.

Smiley tries to surrender his illusion of Ann long before their single meeting in the eight novels in which she is a presence. Seeing her as "permanently stained for him by Karla's cunning and Haydon's scheming embrace" (*Smiley's*, 371) permits him, like all secret sharers, to abandon first what he loves most. With "lines of age and pains" marring her beauty, Ann entreats Smiley to reconcile, but to him she is now only a memory "of someone he had once known a long time ago" (*Smiley's*, 286). Metaphorically, he killed their love long before this meeting by revering a derelict collective over her individuality, his own form of betrayal.

Even though he suffers for his faithlessness, Smiley rebuffs Ann to pursue his alter ego, Karla, the third mysterious presence in the trilogy. Moscow Centre's spymaster received his codename "Karla" for his first network and the "Sandman" because (like the demonic character in the Baltic fairy tale) he puts even tenacious adversaries to sleep.[12] But his feminine codename ironically recalls women's impotence in espionage operations. "The proverbial cold-war orphan," Karla is described as a "shabby, gnomic" priest to Smiley's "vicar," "tough schoolmaster," and sagacious researcher operating "within the limits of his experience" (*Tinker, Tailor*, 197). This small, old man with a "body a fraction too long for his legs" (*Smiley's*, 370) remains an abstraction, but the paucity of his written characterization makes Karla the trilogy's most diverse character. Karla is seen through Smiley's eyes as Smiley's darker side, a totalitarian rather than a liberal humanist. Additionally, the shadowy hints and undefined motives that constitute Karla encourage freer speculation as to what makes Karla the man he is. That "what he is" is as much a part of what readers imagine as it is what le Carré or any of his characters say about Karla. His speculative portrayal, imaginatively exceeding Smiley's concreteness, enriches their only meeting in the Delhi prison, a scene le Carré found important enough to repeat in each volume of the trilogy.

Besides quest literature's mysterious evil, Karla's shadowy character is reminiscent of a medieval personification of death. Seen through a glass, darkly, Karla lacks substance to an adversary who assumes him to be the personification of evil. Smiley knows him only in fragmentary glimpses and endows the few small gestures he sees with importance. Karla alone receives this portrayal, and this uniqueness adds a dimension to Smiley's obscure world not possible in any other fashion.

Tinker, Tailor, Soldier, Spy

Tinker, Tailor, Soldier, Spy opens with the Cambridge Circus under-going reorganization according to the prevailing attitude of "lateralism" – that is, central control of regional operations. Jim Prideaux, "the Circus' Number One Leper" (*Tinker, Tailor,* 291), is replaced as senior scalphunter/assassin by Peter Guillam; Smiley and Connie Sachs are sacked; and the ambitious and inept Percy Alleline is appointed to direct the service. Against this backdrop the novel blends Smiley's principal quest for the Circus's double agent with Prideaux's hunt to discover his betrayer. Smiley's search for personal release and professional vindication is presented as less significant. Control, sick and secretive, rightly suspects that a Soviet mole (codenamed "Gerald") compromised the Circus through Alleine's Operation Witchcraft, a rich but mysterious vein of Soviet intelligence. Unable to reveal his suspicions, Control devises Operation Testify to obtain the mole's name from a disillusioned Czechoslovakian general, Stevcek, and dispatchs Prideaux, his skilled and loyal fieldman, to intercept Stevcek. For security Control codenames Operation Testify's suspects for a children's elimination game (a source of the novel's title): Alleline is "the Tinker"; the privileged dandy Bill Haydon, "the Tailor"; Alleline's "cupbearer" Roy Bland, "the Soldier"; head lamplighter/surveillance operator Toby Esterhase, "the Poorman"; and George Smiley, ironically, "the Beggerman."

Operation Testify, "launched by an old man for his dying glory," fails when Haydon, hidden behind his patriotic, "slightly Dorian Gray look" (*Tinker, Tailor,* 86), sabotages Prideaux's mission. Haydon destroys Prideaux's Czech networks Plato and Aggravate, and forces a discredited Control to resign. Haydon, now London station chief, turns his former lover and protégé Prideaux over to Circus interrogators at Sarratt, the Circus's training and debriefing center, who brutalize him; then Haydon dismisses him. The Circus, scrambling for bureaucratic gratuities, indebts itself to Merlin's unverified source (Aleksey Aleksandrovich Polyakov) and compromises itself for Operation Witchcraft.

Control's suspicions and warnings from Prideaux, Ricki Tarr, and occasional agent Jerry Westerby force Cabinet Minister Oliver Lacon to unofficially recall the "Sir Perceival," George Smiley, to "clean the stables" (*Tinker, Tailor*, 71). Chagrined by his failure to heed Smiley's earlier warnings, Lacon ruefully attributes the Circus's suspected mole to Smiley's generation. Who better, then, than Smiley, "out of date, but loyal to his own time," to "spy on the spies"? (*Tinker, Tailor*, 25). Painstakingly studying documents purloined by Guillam, interrogating dismissed Circus associates, and matching dates with suppressed initiatives and operations, Smiley retraces Control's steps and discovers the mole he already knew. But before Haydon can be exchanged for captured British agents, Prideaux easily penetrates Sarratt and snaps Haydon's neck, exacting a revenge Haydon's contemporaries are too judicious to demand. Alleline is removed; Smiley returns to Ann, "essentially another man's woman" (*Tinker, Tailor*, 354); and Prideaux retreats to his safe house, the Dip, possibly to suffer Karla's revenge.

Smiley's task focuses attention on the Circus professionals' "tacitly shared . . . unexpressed half-knowledge which [is] like an illness they hoped would go away if it was never owned to, never diagnosed" (*Tinker, Tailor*, 332). The Circus's claustrophobia feeds its patriotic nostalgia; consequently, its traitors are shielded. Haydon's approbation is the mole's perfect disguise, and his exposure falls hard on the younger generation of spies who swallow their elders' naive myths. Peter Guillam, a perpetually immature yeoman, doggedly resists regarding his model "of a certain kind of antiquated romanticism" "with much other than affection" (*Tinker, Tailor*, 334, 338). Only Smiley struggles with the human consequences of the act. Listening to Haydon's coldly egotistic rationalizations, Smiley recasts the Forsterian question into terms familiar to his private hell: Why betray with disillusion and spent passion? He rationalizes Haydon's treachery as arising from the disappointment a man of vision realizes when his reality is "a poor island with scarcely a voice that would carry across the water" (*Tinker, Tailor*, 332). In his last analysis Smiley, this "fat, barefooted spy . . . deceived in love and impotent in hate" (*Tinker, Tailor*, 333) envisions his friend's treason by imaging Haydon as a wooden Russian doll hidden inside another doll. Smiley laments that it was Karla, not he, who saw the last doll. Foreshadowing imagery dominates as "the unyielding face of Karla replaced Bill Haydon's crooked death mask" (*Tinker, Tailor*, 354), and Smiley, stunned by Karla's first assault, retreats into remorseful evaluation of his allegiances.

Smiley's quest depends equally on the subplots tracing his own and Jim Prideaux's psychic journeys. Smiley shuffles between his public and private worlds attempting to excise the inevitable loneliness and pervasive melancholy brought on by Ann's abandonment and his profession's disregard. The Circus's mission rekindles his emotional intensity as he searches through discarded histories of finer days. Yet at every juncture lost loves reappear. Former colleagues open wounds by offhandedly asking after Ann, forgetting what younger lover she's eloped with, or linking her with her cousin Haydon. Smiley remembers Ann walking on the Cornish cliffs, dreaming, he supposes, of Haydon, while his thoughts are lost "to Control, to Jim Prideaux and Testify, and the whole mess he had left behind him on retirement" (*Tinker, Tailor*, 140).

Ann's suggested reappearances amplify Smiley's loyalty to his service, but the Circus, an equally unfaithful mistress, confounds him. His private disharmony redefines itself in his service's disaffection with its own past. Each path he retraces toward Gerald merges past and present forces until "there was no longer any difference between the two: forwards or backwards" (*Tinker, Tailor*, 122). His profession robs him of comfort in his quest to revive the status quo. By the close of *Tinker*, Smiley vainly searches Haydon's hypocritical heart for legitimate answers to the web of lies plaguing him: "Bill was a man, after all, who had had something to say . . . a romantic and a snob. He wanted to . . . lead the masses out of darkness . . . [to stand] at the middle of a secret stage" (*Tinker, Tailor*, 353). But disillusioned by battle, Smiley can only shrug paradoxically, still unable to secure stability from his chaotic, inhumane milieu.

Prideaux's subplot borrows from *Kim* the lessons a teacher (Prideaux) and his student (Bill Roach) share. The novel opens at Thursgood Preparatory School, whose namesake headmaster has hired linguist Prideaux, despite his inexperience, as a last-minute replacement. Decidedly more humorous than their geographic neighbors at Carne (*Murder of Quality*), Thursgood's eccentrics puzzle over the unexplained gaps in the curriculum vitae of this "very patriotic bloke." They accept him as one of them, "a poor white of the teaching community," not one of those "bogus Oxford men" (*Tinker, Tailor*, 3, 14). Nonetheless, Headmaster Thursgood, to retain his school's unwarranted privilege, promises himself that this odd humpback will "do us very well till July" only (*Tinker, Tailor*, 3).

Hiding from his Circus past, Prideaux rumbles into the Dip, an abandoned-swimming-pool-project-qua-mythological-fantasy, "on a Friday afternoon in a rainstorm . . . driving an old red Alvis and towing a second-hand trailer that had once been blue" (*Tinker, Tailor*, 4). The isolated location and aged vehicle are deliberate tradecraft affording Jim a protected safe house. His mysterious arrival is watched by Bill Roach, le Carré's image of Smiley as a child. Nicknamed "Jumbo," Roach is Jim's secret sharer and Thursgood's number-one leper, a fat, asthmatic child "graded dull, if not actually deficient" by the staff (*Tinker, Tailor*, 4). Thursgood's staff misjudge Roach, however, as surely as the Circus does Haydon.[13]

Roach's broken home and public school indoctrination produce a "natural watcher," desperate for special attention and thus ripe for espionage. His family's wealth, coupled with his unappealing physique and name, handicap him as an outsider. Prideaux, an outsider by choice, smartly encourages Roach's watchfulness, telling him with le Carré-esque irony that he has "known a lot of Bills. They've all been good'uns" (*Tinker, Tailor*, 7). The praise swells Roach's precarious self-esteem and gives him purpose: in an act of pathetic devotion that starkly contrasts adult betrayal, he appoints himself a stand-in for the other Bill that he intuits has betrayed Jim. The duty perpetuates his misunderstanding of adult love but provides him with a surrogate parent whose outward deformity embodies his psychic one.

Prideaux's school retreat parallels Smiley's retreat into German love poetry. Both want to replace their emotional pain with the loyal, uncomplicated love they enjoyed as children. But the past intrudes on Prideaux as on Smiley and judges him harshly. Discovered by *Call*'s Inspector Mendel and questioned by Smiley, Prideaux begins his own reconstruction of his and the Circus's betrayal. A "tall crooked figure in a dark coat" (*Tinker, Tailor*, 314), he tails Smiley, pieces together the enigma from Smiley's leftovers, and exacts revenge. He steals back to Thursgood even further isolated.

With Ann's and Haydon's betrayals, Smiley ponders whether all love and each of his sacrosanct philosophies aren't visions built on self-delusions that others (here Prideaux) can easily molest and murder. Neither the Circus's defender nor Roach's unworthy savior triumphs personally; time reinterprets their quests as dreams, which, like the world of espionage, have only the trappings of reality. The novel opens sarcastically with "The truth is" (*Tinker, Tailor*, 3) and concludes quietly that it was "after all, a dream" (*Tinker, Tailor*, 355). Le Carré hints that Roach's childlike loyalty implies hope for adults like a Prideaux or a Smiley but concedes that that fragile hope is probably illusionary.

The Honourable Schoolboy

Critically regarded as the trilogy's least successful novel, *The Honourable Schoolboy* sprawls travelogue style across much of Southeast Asia, le Carré's first novelistic sojourn outside Europe and Smiley's only offensive mission as Circus chief.[14] A cast of familiar characters moves through a relatively straightforward counterespionage operation complicated by emotional betrayals of lovers, colleagues, and family.[15] In mid-1974 Circus director Smiley launches Operation Dolphin to trap Karla's Chinese mole and possibly destroy Karla's standing in Moscow Centre. He is surrounded by his court: his Telemachus Peter Guillam, Circus research sorceress Connie Sachs, China expert Doc di Salis, and former scalphunter Fawn. Poring over the devastation left in Haydon's wake (known biblically by insiders as "After the Fall"), Connie, Smiley's librarian, discovers that Hong Kong is the final destination of an unexplained goldseam – that is, a route through banks for laundered money. Smiley directs the remnants of the Circus's Southeast Asian network, run by Australian agent Bill Craw, to trace the funds to the mole and, if possible, unearth Karla's vulnerability. Operation Dolphin succeeds when the mole Nelson Ko, and his gangster brother, Drake, are captured.

In the familiar le Carré labyrinth, the British victory, however, is hollow. Their ungentlemanly Cousins (the CIA) and the agents of the Drug Enforcement Agency rob the Circus of its momentary glory by seizing mole Nelson Ko. Smiley's field agent Jerry Westerby is soured by the operation. Infatuated with Drake's round-eyed mistress, Lizzie Worthington, and seduced by the Kos' familial ties, Westerby opts for love as Alec Leamas did and pays the same consequence. Fawn (Westerby's murderer), the gentle-giant-qua-psychotic-killer, acts out

Smiley's openly expressed frustrations and Britain's openly thwarted ambitions. The novel's notions of honor and love for country and family reveal themselves as empty platitudes. Like his quest, Smiley is again shelved from the Circus, this time replaced by fatuous Saul Enderby.

Clive Gerald Westerby, the novel's titular character, is a womanizing journalist, a goodhearted eccentric, a failed novelist, and a zealous part-time field operative; he is, for obvious and spiritually wrong reasons, more enticed by spying than by journalism. Westerby's involvement resembles – with a significant twist – Leamas's questionable relationship with and ultimate betrayal by his service and its leader. Whereas Leamas falls victim because he knows neither parents nor viable love, Westerby falls because he knows, through his father, only bankrupt love.

Westerby is the son of Sir Samuel ("Sambo") Westerby, an insolvent newspaper tycoon, racehorse owner, and notorious philanderer. Left emotionally adrift and isolated by this shiftless father, young Westerby cannot sustain himself. His oxymoronic nickname, "Honourable Schoolboy," suits him better than his journalist's sobriquet, "Voltaire," because it implies a chivalric romance hero coupled with a naive schoolboy. Westerby fits this bill. He grins his way past adult challenges and introspection, learning little about failed idealism from his early homelife, from liaisons, or from the Joseph Conrad, Ford Madox Ford, Graham Greene, and T. E. Lawrence novels that fill his schoolboy's backpack.

Westerby's love life is unusually well detailed for le Carré's espionage fiction. The Schoolboy has many brief, intense, immature attachments with women – appropriate to a character given to loneliness and self-destructive allegiances. His Tuscan mistress, although some 25 years his junior, promotes commitment based on honesty. Jerry blinds himself to the value of her offer; like Smiley, he abandons her for the inconstant Circus. Moreover, Westerby isolates himself from his daughter Catherine, the product of one of his several failed marriages; in this act he follows Sambo's example as a father. An Englishwoman's dismissal, "Oh, the Westerbys are *always* changing their women" (*Schoolboy*, 31) ironically sums up Jerry's failed relationships in flippant terms Westerby would himself use. Jerry's affairs, like all his emotional bonds, are little more than momentary gratifications that Jerry quips about with his fellows to advance his playboy image in their eyes.

Desperate to belong, Westerby is both a familial and a professional Occasional.[16] Whereas newspaper acquaintances see him as freewheeling and rebellious, Westerby views himself as a skilled writer and a worldly-wise professional spy, loyal and deeply patriotic. Intimates know him as puerile. Haydon dismisses him from the Circus, but Jerry hangs around and joins Circus regulars' ranks – not as a skeptical careerist but as Smiley's loyal footsoldier, an adult Kim flawed by romantic idealism. The "pillar of his uncomplicated philosophy" (*Schoolboy*, 446) is action, encapsulated in le Carré's refrain throughout all his novels that "*In the beginning was the deed.*" Westerby submits to Smiley's control, trusting that conformity equals acceptance. In a scene that echoes Control's interview with Leamas, Jerry bypasses Smiley's questions by agreeing to act without reflection: "You point me [George] and I'll march. Okay? You're the owl, not me" (*Schoolboy*, 105). Clearly his value to his superiors rests in his childishness: he is Sarratt's ungraduated schoolboy, obediently reviewing Circus training lectures and following Smiley's orders without question.

Le Carré portrays honor through love in the piece's fallen noblewoman, Lizzie Worthington, and in her Asian consort, Drake Ko. Lizzie, thinly drawn as a woman of questionable morality, advances the complexities of the novel's narrative as she exposes the chauvinistic character of the men around her.[17] The daughter of ambitious but shortsighted parents, Lizzie deserts her insensitive schoolmaster husband, Peter Worthington, and son, Ian, for an illusory existence in Vientiane, Laos, as a courier, a whiskey runner, a prostitute, and, finally, as Drake Ko's mistress. Her father's chimera advance his, not Lizzie's, desire for recognition; Worthington tries to mold her into his ideal wife and mother; Ko wrongly idealizes her. Brutalized by most, Lizzie defines herself by unworthy men as willingly as le Carré's agents define themselves by objectionable institutions.

To Drake Ko, the only man who treats her decently, Lizzie is not the prostitute whom drug pilot Tiny Ricardo willingly trades for his life but Liese Worthy, the symbolic reincarnation of his beloved adoptive mother, Liese Hibbert. Ko's vision of her as a good, loving individual comes closest to Lizzie's buried self. He rewards her bargain to save Ricardo with physical comforts and wealth; she rewards his ironic humanism with loyalty. Hers is Liz Gold's lesson, sans naïveté: the greatest loyalty grows from an ability to find the human-ity in people; the greatest betrayal comes from the manipulation that turns humanity into a weapon.

Ko's devotion and uncomplicated code of ethics result from the loss of family and the restored honor that directed values make pos-sible.[18] Professionally, Ko is a ruthless gangster who exacts revenge on his enemies worse than "your Christian Baptist hell" (*Schoolboy*, 523). Yet he elevates family over commerce or politics; for Ko, the loss of a family member is devastating to all. Thus Ko's goal of reunion with Nelson at any cost ennobles him in le Carré's ethic. Those who come closest to understanding Ko respect his adherence to a code that demands that one "hold fast to that which is good" (*Schoolboy*, 513) even when respect ensures defeat (i.e., Lizzie faces prison, Westerby dies, Nelson becomes a CIA prisoner). Ko's quest implies that all honorable individuals and actions are debased when systems ignore a consistent moral code. Ko, then, despite his other-wise morally reprehensible character, represents loyalty; he alone honors the loving commitment to family.

Unreflective and lacking a similar background, Westerby accepts others' values without question. Westerby does not evaluate his pro-fession's myths; hence, he fails to obtain the mythical stature of tragic hero. He ends neither an able combatant like Prideaux nor an enlightened cynic like Leamas but as an adventure hero flawed by dubious commitment and a misguided, immature honor. He disap-points; le Carré gives him opportunities for growth, only to have Jerry sidestep them. For instance, when the Ko brothers are reunited, Westerby glimpses real love, but he barely grasps the value of Drake Ko's faith and loyalty to family over cause. He tries to secure a similar faith by idolizing Lizzie. Acting from his newfound sense of unselfish love, he betrays Smiley in order to rescue Lizzie, thereby precipitating his character's central crisis. But his momen-tary self-awareness, presented in a style befitting myth creation, is insufficient to ennoble him. The Kos, safe in the CIA's hands, are beyond Jerry's intervention. Lizzie sees her unnecessary rescuer "not as her Sir Galahad but as just another part of a hostile world that encircled her" (*Schoolboy*, 478). And Jerry, for all his efforts, dies ignominiously.

Westerby and his actions invite comparison with the protagonists of Graham Greene's thematically similar Southeast Asian novel, *The Quiet American* (1955).[19] Akin to Fowler and Pyle, journalist Westerby laces his cynicism with literary references, spouts moralistic aphorisms, and acts fatally in the name of a love he cannot comprehend. Time and writing styles, however, differentiate these characters. In 1955 Greene consciously subordinated his condemnation of America's abuses of power in Southeast Asia to highlight the conflict engendered by Fowler's personal betrayal and Pyle's unabashed naïveté. Thé young American's foolish support for General The and innocent understanding of Phong and her country's condition are appealing but disastrous. Both force the older, questioning Fowler to embrace self-interest over commitments to country, colleagues, and family.

Le Carré conflates Pyle and Fowler into Westerby. Jerry has Pyle's appealing enthusiasm and stupefying ignorance of people but asks himself Fowler's sophisticated questions. Unfortunately, Jerry responds with the platitudes that compromise *Schoolboy*'s themes. The novel becomes a mock-bildungsroman, centered on a problematic hero who fails to learn and on caricatures who variously illustrate how institutions define individuals and how betrayal degrades the human spirit.

Westerby's quest kills him. Smiley's quest overtakes his sensibilities and compromises his humanity. Against East Asia's grand landscapes and the pressing contemporary political backdrop of the Sino-Soviet split, the American defeat in Vietnam, and the question of Chinese control of Hong Kong, Smiley's covert attempts to rebuild his Round Table complement rather than reform unsavory political realities. Karla's image in a grainy picture, purposefully hung over Smiley's Circus desk, leers down on Smiley throughout, and the increasingly tarnished idealist responds by sacrificing one of his beloved, faithful knights to achieve an irresolute goal. Smiley becomes Westerby's executioner as he takes on the role of the uncaring bureaucrat who steals people's anima and exploits their humaneness.

Smiley's People

Smiley's quest for Karla ends much as it began, with Smiley unofficially recalled to the Circus to clean up a Moscow "hit." As in previous novels, a convincingly drawn minor character – here Maria Andreyvna Ostrakova – unites the novel's disparate narratives. Smiley at last unearths the means to merge with Karla, but their union fails to relieve the sordidness and pervasive paranoia of their profession or to reform the system that nurtures such corruption.

With the Labour government's "Wise Men" forcing détente on his espionage bureaucracy, Oliver Lacon again calls on Smiley – this time to cover up the gruesome murder of a former Circus stringer and exiled Estonian freedom fighter known as General Vladimir Miller. Solving Vladimir's murder means discovering why the general sought official contact with his former vicar, Smiley.

Smiley's search leads him to Maria Ostrakova, a Russian émigrée living in Paris whom Vladimir was attempting to save from certain assassination. Ostrakova has been approached by Soviet agent Oleg ("Kirov") Kursky – Connie Sachs's "Ginger Pig" – with an offer to reunite her with her illegitimate daughter, Alexandra. Guilt-ridden for abandoning the child but suspicious of Kursky's ploy, Ostrakova writes the aged general for help in identifying Kursky. Operating unofficially, Vladimir sends his emissary, the patriotic Leipzig, to Ostrakova to confirm Kursky as Karla's plant and his runner to Hamburg to gather evidence against Kursky. But fellow Estonia Mikhel betrays Vladimir's interest to the Soviets, and, before his inexperienced Circus handler Mostyn can meet him, Vladimir is murdered by Karla's thugs.

Gathering fragments together, Smiley intercepts Ostrakova's second desperate letter to the general. He finds a film negative concealed by Vladimir in a discarded package of cigarettes and secures from Leipzig's loyal friend Kretzschmar Ostrakova's first letter – along with "honey-trap" photographs and tapes of Kursky – laying out Karla's duplicity. Smiley then backtracks and finds that Karla has manipulated Moscow Centre's system to create a legend (false history) for a young agent codenamed "Komet." As the consummate interrogator Smiley blackmails Grigoriev, a frustrated diplomat trapped in a loveless marriage, into admitting that a mysterious young woman now confined in a private Swiss psychiatric

clinic is Karla's illegitimate daughter Tatiana. Smiley correctly surmises that Karla has misappropriated his agency's funds for Tatiana's
treatment by fraudulently crediting the expenses to the nonexistent
mole Komet.

Empowered with secret information, Smiley sets Karla the same
terms he proposed at their first meeting, 20 years earlier in a Dehli
prison cell. At that meeting – which he recounts in each book of the
trilogy – Smiley offered the Russian a chance to defect to the West
and to save the love Smiley assumed "Gerstmann" (Karla's alias) had.
Smiley's humanity overcame his dedication to service, a flaw Karla
later exploited by seducing Haydon and Ann. Smiley, projecting himself into Karla's silence, tried to confirm in Karla's unresponsive face
that they, as individuals, were superior to any ideology. But Karla's
absolutism prevailed. In an image that haunts Smiley because it symbolizes Karla's victory, the chain-smoker Karla refuses Smiley's
cigarettes but pockets his lighter, a gift "To George from Ann with all
my love" (*Tinker, Tailor*, 202).

Years later absolutist Smiley impassively watches not a maniacal
evil but a Riemeck-like agent, "one little man, hatless, with a satchel
. . . his face aged and weary and travelled" cross Berlin's
Werschauerbrucke Bridge (*Smiley's*, 372). While surveying a
defection that holds "the very reaches of his own long life"
(*Smiley's*, 369), Smiley alone notices Karla drop Ann's lighter on the
icy cobble. The vindictive act metaphorically consigns Smiley to the
same defeat Karla faces. Accepting "the curse of Karla's fanaticism"
destroys Smiley's last illusion of love; Karla, a victim of "the curse of
Smiley's compassion," clings to his illusion of constancy and
ironically bests Smiley (*Smiley's*, 391). As Guillam quietly responds,
"George, you won," Smiley offhandedly dismisses him: "Did I? . . .
Yes. Yes, well I suppose I did" (*Smiley's*, 374). Smiley, the rational
man, realizes that his final victory has lost him more than it won. The
anticlimactic surrender places Smiley in a Sisyphean struggle with the
ethical contradictions of his dubious victory.

Doubling imagery permeates *Smiley's People*, each instance
effectively completing le Carré's aged hero. Smiley operates between
two worlds as a researcher/detective and agent at risk, yet both
worlds collide with Smiley's desperate quest for any human instinct
he can understand. In his researcher's world he seeks constancy
through literature; in his nonacademic world he finds himself an

obsessed cuckold. As a detective he defeats himself by separating his analytic mind from his sense of decency. Dividing himself among London's intrigues and bureaucrats, his bitter memories, and Europe's dangers, Smiley agonizes over Ann's recent "half breed" lover as he pursues "half awake," "half aware," with "half a network" Vladimir's twin proofs and Karla's schizophrenic daughter Tatiana/Alexandra. Connie Sachs, the Circus's "Mother Russia," casts Smiley and Karla as "twin cities, . . . two halves of the same apple" (*Smiley's*, 205). Smiley laces his characterization of his correspondent with mirrored self-irony. Even Karla in Smiley's eyes is twins: one a flawed father with a "stoic face, . . . patient eyes, . . . wiry body waiting philosophically upon its own destruction" and the other "so self-possessed that he could allow, if need be, ten years for an operation to bear fruit" (*Smiley's*, 245).

Splitting wholes into halves confuses, and confusion is at the heart of *Smiley's People*. Instead of thriller fiction's chronological narrative, the novel joins past with contemporary events.[20] The past (Vladimir) calls on the present (Lacon's professional but insensitive Circus) to reach the past (Smiley's pursuit of Karla) for answers. Karla threatens to fox Smiley "all ends up" as a fool of his own time. Smiley pores over nonsequential fragments made more puzzling by his emotional reactions to them. Personal and professional confusion make his mission "grey. Half-angels fighting half devils. No one knows where the lines are" (*Smiley's*, 202).

Confusion born of duality also defines Tatiana. Obsessed with sex and God, Tatiana poses trouble for those unsure whether she is a sane dissident or a genuinely disturbed psychotic.[21] Her mental instability in fact originates in a repressive Soviet system and is fueled by an insecure father unwilling to acknowledge her publicly. These elements effect her dual identity: as the putative Alexandra Borisovna Ostrakova and as "the daughter of a man who is too important to exist" (*Smiley's*, 360), Tatiana has a fractured nature that makes her see too much. She recognizes Smiley as a kind but "extremely dangerous man" (*Smiley's*, 359). Her two Russian-speaking guardians, Dr. Ruedi and Mother Felicity (called Felicity-Felicity by Tatiana), make good their promise of her continued instability by repressing her further. An imprisoned princess, Tatiana is the perpetual victim, a dual symbol of Karla's inhumanity and Smiley's meaningless victory.

The search for an order regardless of the consequences changes Smiley into a driven "caseman" unable to delegate authority. Weariness with his profession rather than commitment fuses his bond to Karla. Recalling Conrad's images of the doppelgänger, Smiley sees Karla as "the one hollowed face that, like a secret sharer, seemed to have swum out of the little contact photograph to board his faltering consciousness" (*Smiley's*, 147). The image fits Smiley aptly.

Later, watching Karla defect, Smiley merges another Conradian image, the idealist-turned-monster, with T. S. Eliot's paralyzed hollow men. The betrayal he has fought against defeats the humanity he has striven to save, and the realization overwhelms Smiley. "An unholy vertigo" seizes him as Karla, "the very evil he had fought," possesses him. Smiley has destroyed Karla "with the weapons I abhorred, and they are his." They have crossed each other's frontiers, "the no-men of this no-man's-land" (*Smiley's*, 370-71). These now-indistinguishable adversaries are left hopeless old men, at last defeated by each other.

The termination of Smiley's close association with Connie Sachs and his union with Lady Ann adumbrate his final personal defeat. He seeks out each woman, but their meetings expose to Smiley more of his vulnerability than key evidence. Exactly midway through the novel, Smiley travels to Connie's witchlike dacha in the forest outside Oxford. The daughter and sister of Oxford dons, Connie was recruited by Control, defined by her Circus service, and expelled by Haydon. Now crippled and gradually escaping into a timeless self-deceit, Connie has found love with the much younger Hilary, whose tenuous hold on sanity parallels Connie's equally tenuous hold on life.

The lure of institutional service destroyed Connie. As Smiley interrogates her, Connie, smelling the hunt but too infirm to join, tries his patience. She fills her futile, often unrealistic appeals for attention with militaristic and chivalric images. Impatient for information, Smiley turns on her, shouting at her when she reminisces, pressing her for details instead of fragmented philosophy, even threatening violence for her coyness. His betrayed conviction and emotion frighten her. Smiley's pathetic divorce from Connie, the researcher who so expertly served him in *Tinker, Tailor* and *Schoolboy*, emphasizes his increasing monomania. A combination of age, a remarkable memory, eccentricity, and booze permits Connie to dis-

criminate between Smiley's vision and Karla's absolutism simultaneously, while implicitly recognizing their union. But Smiley, now cor-
rupted by the quest, attacks her truisms, barely capable of restraining
his viciousness.

Smiley's impassioned rejection of Connie foreshadows his passionless dismissal of Lady Ann.[22] When Ann seeks reconciliation,
Smiley first shuns her and later punishes her, unable to separate
their love from their betrayals. She contacts him repeatedly, trying to
reach his passion for her, but when they talk "they began their conversation as strangers, much as they began their love-making"
(*Smiley's*, 142). Smiley refuses to be beguiled away from his quest by
this alluring yet forbidden lady. Over the impersonal phone Ann
pleads, but Smiley will not forgive. His mind reviews the list of her
betrayals, and, frozen in pain, he sees Haydon's shadow falling
across her face each time he wants to reach for her.

Their one meeting, immediately preceding Smiley's blackmail of
Karla, confirms how the pair have lost whatever affection was possible. Ann's ancestral home, "Harry's Cornish heap" (*Smiley's*, 283), is
an image of a committed relationship now decayed beyond resurrection. The crumbling granite house, the Sercombes' Haverdown, is
surrounded by "a coppice of bare elms still waiting for the blight";
"a crowd of gables" cluster "like torn black rents above the tree-
tops"; and "stubs of felled trees lay like yellow tombstones either
side" (*Smiley's*, 283).

But this symbol only partly captures the ambiguity of their relationship and deflects attention from their confrontation. Le Carré
casts Ann and Smiley as believers in the trade aphorism that love is
the most important aspect of the human spirit that can be betrayed.
Uncharacteristically, Smiley seeks Ann out to warn her of danger at
the Bywater Street flat. The warning, a breach of his, Leamas's, and
Westerby's professional code, is understandable given his past emotion for her but novel given his sense of duty. Ann genuinely wel-
comes her husband for one last attempt at reconciliation. Mis-
matched, each accepts and assigns blame, yet, because Smiley's
character remains evasive and pivotal, no reconciliation occurs.

The Quest for Karla opens new narrative avenues for le Carré; it
unites Smiley's halves and terminates him. Through eight novels
Smiley professes an undying belief in the power of Western democracy, in the superiority of moral means over questionable ends, in

the permanency of intellectual ideals, and in the salvation possible
through love. Yet at every step he fears these decencies are illusions.
In the trilogy Smiley searches for certainties that will resurrect lost
illusions and loves. In a typically Conradian dilemma, Smiley's isolation from his society as a result of his profession and his avocation
forces him to come to terms with himself. But whereas Conrad's
heroes gain victory through self-knowledge, le Carré's do not. By
succumbing to Karla's methods, Smiley damages (if not defeats) the
beliefs he seeks to ratify. He rejects Ann, openly in *Smiley's People*
but covertly in every Smiley novel; he is responsible for the deaths of
many admirable men, including his well-loved agent Jerry Westerby;
and he forces Karla's defection even though their union concludes
ambiguously. Nowhere in the trilogy does le Carré admit serious
political or emotional evaluation, yet in the end he has Smiley accept
that democracies will be compromised as surely as ends will perpetually degrade means, that exercising the mind will seldom appeal as
strongly as exercising the romantic spirit, that ideals become quickly
tarnished, and that love redeems only when it is defeated.

Chapter Six

The Story within the Story within the Story

It will raise people's opinion of our character to say, for instance, "We ought not to follow the saying that bids us treat our friends as future enemies: much better to treat our enemies as future friends."

— Aristotle, *Rhetoric*

The dissimilarities among *The Little Drummer Girl*, *A Perfect Spy*, *The Russia House*, and *The Secret Pilgrim* imply a novelist taking radically different stylistic turns with his fiction, only to return to his cold war advocates and themes. *Drummer Girl* is set in the eternal Middle East conflict between Israel and its Arab neighbors. Events sweep across continents, and the central character moves from relative safety in superficial theatrical productions to extreme danger in the real terrorist theater. The humor is black, and *Drummer Girl* is almost as didactic as it is captivating. War's daily atrocities, such as bombs killing civilians, are condemned even as le Carré characteristically exposes the duplicities of manipulators plotting these terrorist raids.

The second novel abandons historical backdrops and turns inward to canvass the psychological motivations of a British traitor, Magnus Pym, who pays indiscriminate allegiance to immediate companions rather than to ideology. The protagonist's lifetime "anchor" is his businessman-carny father, a character capable of outmaneuvering the comparatively inept Mr. Micawber. While few contemporary political references intrude on the narrative, the novel, through detailed descriptions of locations and characters, imitates a Dickensian landscape populated with eccentrics. *A Perfect Spy* exorcises David Cornwell's familial ghosts through its pessimistic humor and sympathetic explanations for betrayal; it marks a change in the nov-

elist's approach but not in his thematic concerns. This novel con-
solidates le Carré's humor and unites it with his preoccupations with
human foibles, betrayal, its motivations, and its dispiriting effects.

The third novel excels in merciless characterizations yet is sometimes encumbered by mawkishness and airy flirtatiousness. Characters adjust uncomfortably to the advent of *perestroika* and *glasnost*
in Karla's homeland. *The Russia House* asks whether the Soviets can
amend their society and Western intelligence professionals their ideology. Moments of almost-slapstick humor briefly invade the subter-
ranean life preferred by espiocrats. The world is not saved, love does
not triumph, and the cold war adherents stubbornly resist adopting
new rules. This time, however, an ordinary man's seduction into
espionage and betrayal fails to defeat him.

The Secret Pilgrim returns to a melancholy George Smiley, now
the Circus's superstatesman as well as its near-mythical spymaster,
and to *Russia House*'s Ned, now on the verge of a well-earned
retirement. Smiley entertains Sarratt's graduating class with Circus
lore from his past, while a cynical Ned reminiscences on his own victories and defeats. The enemies are the same, and the heroes continue their personal compromises for the sake of their institutions.

The Secret Pilgrim is a loosely knit collection of cold war tales
told from a post-cold war vantage; its numerous characters are as
eccentric as ever, and betrayals are predictable. The book also serves
as a recapitulation of le Carré's use of the espionage game as a
touchstone for history, morality, and culture. New graduates pick
Smiley's brain, and his responses trigger Ned's recollections, which
in turn give context to Ned's last assignment and its supposed legacy.
New, more insidious enemies have replaced cold war antagonists.
Decent, honorable Ned ponders these adversaries' originality, but le
Carré seemingly accepts that they, like older betrayers, can be challenged only by vigilant questioning and bona fide integrity.

The Little Drummer Girl

In le Carré's milieu families are often sources of perversion. They
perpetuate themselves through painful relationships, destructive
psychological games, or intimate betrayal. Much of le Carré's mature

fiction reflects the inner dynamics of the family and the characters' unrealized potential for nurturing.

The Little Drummer Girl traces the spiritual denigration of an unreflective amateur searching for a mythical security defined as family. Its protagonist, Charlie – significantly, without a family name – comes from a dysfunctional family and grows up in a markedly similar way to David Cornwell through his Oxford days. Chronically dislocated by and from her questionable family, Charlie matures in instability and develops an inconstant ethical code. To escape Charlie clouds her thinking with "generous and idealistic impulses," replaces real commitments with "some passing enthusiasm," and dramatizes herself through tall tales about her dissembling father. Her childhood education taught her how to avoid totalitarian philosophies. As an adult she is cynical enough to distrust but naive enough to rely on counterfeit families.

Le Carré's characterization of Charlie echoes that of Arthur Koestler's Hydie in *The Age of Longing* almost to his word choice. Hydie is a "political chameleon" who has "no core, no faith, no fixed values."[1] Charlie is one of the "rich English suburban kids from Nowheresville," with "no tradition, no faith, no self-awareness, no nothing."[2] Unlike Hydie, Charlie strikes out against authority while acting roles that simulate stability. Rebellion against British middle-class life primes Charlie before the Israelis recruit her. Theatrical make-believe is as dysfunctional as her natural family and her adopted Israeli spy and Palestinian guerrilla families, but the theater's artifice affords her some comfort.

Charlie's rebellion masks her weaknesses and vulnerability. Feminine, caring, and inconsistent, Charlie mothers everyone in her repertory group, even her abusive lover, Alastair. Because she is wise and has a sense of social duty, she keeps the group's accounts and knows "where the anti-sting [is], and the sticking plaster for cut feet" (*Drummer*, 49).

She interchanges this role with another, public persona: the carnal hypercynic oblivious to others' pain. In this role Charlie substitutes indiscriminate sex for affection and becomes, despite physical beatings, Alastair's "body slave." She rebels from her theater family and pursues her "demon lover" Gadi Becker (codenamed "Joseph"), but he refuses her sexual advances and leads her, despite the emotional beatings, to his Israeli controllers. She rebels against

his remoteness and tries desperately to attract his attention by joining the Israelis' theater and working to deceive the Palestinian cause
she publicly espouses. She terrorizes Israeli regulars by defiantly
flirting with their betrayal: they are not sure she will not turn to the
Palestinians as a means of abandoning the family security Israeli
spymaster Kurtz offers and the constant love Joseph intimates. Yet
her cynicism, like her sense of honor, is an unexamined role that
makes any action she chooses dishonorable.

Primed by her homelife for duplicity, Charlie's vocation serves
her manipulators' well. An actor "so trained to pretend, how can
one believe anything?" (*Drummer*, 276), Charlie is a perfect agent:
she can lie with ease and quickly display different personae. Her theatrical adeptness produces one of the novel's sources of tension in
an operation as cleanly managed by Kurtz as Control's operation of
Leamas was. With her childhood lessons enriching her professional
career, Charlie is easily motivated by the Israeli operation to give her
greatest performance in what Kurtz labels the "theatre of the real"
(*Drummer*, 106). Unconsciously, she is also motivated by the vague
hope that she can achieve stability through another person's love.
Neither goal, however, is Kurtz's. Charlie redeems herself only when
she sees how her unreflective choices are the source of enormous
pain to those she loves and to herself. Her revelation destroys her
spirit but changes her from a manipulated object to a sympathetic
character.

Never far from his mainstay techniques, le Carré gives his protagonist a male name (Charlie, short for Charmian), much as he gave
Moscow Centre's enigmatic spymaster a woman's name. This character shares some of the naïveté of such earlier heroines as Liz Gold.
Liz and Charlie exhibit a "natural humanity" that finds expression in
their search for love and their political gullibility. Liz nurtures others
as an outlet for her humanism; Charlie replaces her sense of lost
community with a "caring for the world," "incurable goodwill," and
an overly generous liberalism (*Drummer*, 48-49). Both women lack
religious conviction and self-confidence and prefer unexamined faith
in abstract political creeds. "Charlie the Red," as her friends call her,
finds reprehensible a lock-step world with a "malign sloth of authority" (*Drummer*, 246), but she lacks genuine individuality. Kurtz easily recruits her by using her need for "a better conformity"
(*Drummer*, 108): he offers her a role no insecure actor can refuse,

and she, hollow and waiting to be filled by others, takes on his fraudulent challenge.

Kurtz (alias Schulmann, Gold, Raphael, and Spielberg) seems an Israeli Smiley, complete with national pride and questioning humanism. Physically similar to Smiley, Kurtz is a quiet, older man, somewhere "between forty and ninety," overweight, "squat and Slav and strong . . . with a barrel chest and a wrestler's wide stride" (*Drummer*, 14). His eccentricities recall Smiley's habits: he crams his jacket sleeves back and twists his wrist around to stare at his old steel watch much as Smiley continually hides in his large overcoat or polishes his eyeglasses with his tie. And Kurtz's treatment of his underlings recalls Smiley's darkest moments. Both spymasters abrogate on the trust others place in them, and both leave their faithful charges to annihilation.

Kurtz also shares Smiley's unearthly forbearance and his colleagues' grudging admiration. Held in high esteem by the Mossad, Israel's intelligence service, and his compatriots, Kurtz is from an older generation of spies. His fierce, pragmatic patriotism keeps him mindful of history's lessons and antagonistic toward all governmental leaders. Kurtz justifies spilling Palestinian blood to prevent a greater bloodbath much as Smiley could have justified Control's manipulation of Leamas or his betrayal of Jerry Westerby. Kurtz circumvents his country's intelligence Steering Committee as freely as Smiley did the Wise Men. He gathers his people, including Joseph, to defeat his counterpart as Smiley gathered his knights for his battles with Karla. His skills as an interrogator rival Smiley's, and his outward concern for Charlie during her long interrogation replicates Smiley's masterful inquiries.

As alluring as the resemblance to Smiley seems, it is incomplete. Kurtz lacks Smiley's reflectiveness or angst for individuals. Smiley's redemption arises from his relativism and perpetual doubt. Lacking a family, Smiley relies on his intellectualism to sustain his morality. Securely married and given to pragmatic action, Kurtz never shares in "the elitist background of the kibbutzim" (*Drummer*, 28) and never develops a questioning intellect. Paradoxically, therefore, he has less respect for individuals than Smiley and is willing to exploit Charlie's need for familial security. He offers himself as Charlie's surrogate parent, flattering this adored but rebellious daughter. She willingly lets him convey her through events and emotions. Unlike

Smiley, Kurtz deliberately compromises her by offering to fill her life with an instant, loving family and never suffering any remorse for his lies.

Kurtz is a savvy street fighter who has "wheeled and dealed and lied even in his prayers" (*Drummer*, 27) to redress Israel's past sufferings and promote its ideology. He justifies himself by appealing to the Holocaust and his early experiences in Israel when he was threatened by his British liberators with the same gallows they used to hang his friends and "Arabs galore" (*Drummer*, 302). Kurtz's name and reputation as a god-devil recall Conrad's fallen spirit from *Heart of Darkness*. Unlike Conrad, le Carré never allows Kurtz's conscience to suffer for his actions and hence fails to invest Kurtz with heroic stature.

Kurtz is driven by "a deep and awesome hatred" (*Drummer*, 25) that others see as a glint of hatred. This enmity, so clear to his peers, blinds him to the hatred Israel fosters. Kurtz posits that anyone opposed to Israel is anti-Semitic. He rights wrongs done to Israel and believes he leads his homeland to "more good luck than the Jews had had for two thousand years" (*Drummer*, 27). He never doubts the rightness of his country's goals or its means; he never entertains the idea that the Palestinians could be honest or their cause just. In le Carré's judgment Kurtz's society is philosophically indefensible. By implication, Israel can claim neither honor nor justifiable indignation, because its emissary's choices diminish the country's humanity and poison its claims.

This novel's strength is its effort to present a balanced view of the Israeli-Palestinian conflict. It condemns the human suffering born of that conflict and equalizes the political debates, and it refuses to excuse any one reluctant knight from inhumanity simply because he adheres to preferred metaphysics. In brief, the narrative represents Israeli and Palestinian activists whose motivations and limitations cannot justify their monstrous deeds. Just as Kurtz peels away the layers of Charlie's defenses, the novel peels away similar layers of Israeli and Palestinian rhetoric. The Israelis protect their fragile homeland with dissembling; the Palestinians fight the aggressors with mindless terrorism. The results are always the same: Israeli and Palestinian civilians suffer. Moreover, because Palestinian and Israeli combatants are brutal, neither side warrants sympathy.

The novel's opening presents the Israelis' argument. On a quiet, sunlit day (one of the few in le Carré's canon), the Israeli Labour attaché's home is rocked by a bomb, killing his sickly son, nicknamed "Angel Gabriel." The Palestinian act advances no cause other than terrorism. But the Israelis' retaliation, orchestrated by Kurtz, is no less nihilistic merely because it is clothed in patriotic dedication. When called to the scene, Kurtz cares nothing for the dead child, as he will later care nothing for Charlie's emotional health or Joseph's degenerating spirit. His attention at the bomb site is on retaliation; his focus during the ensuing operation centers on whether Charlie will defect from his scheme, lured by her changing passions away from his control and into sympathy with the Palestinian leader Khalil and his cause. Kurtz wonders whether Joseph, sickened by too much death and enticed by Charlie's vulnerability, will fail to kill on command. The bitter irony behind Kurtz's plan is that his successful but morally dubious mission, like the Palestinians' bombing that opens the novel, disappears as "one of the smaller news items in the foreign pages of the Anglo-Saxon press" (*Drummer*, 422). It fails to ennoble him, to secure his homeland, or even to arrest terrorist bloodshed. Nevertheless, Kurtz returns to Israel and its intelligence service a mythical hero, to be enlisted in future covert operations.

The Palestinian cause, begun in terror, is initially dignified. Later it is tarnished by its adherents' questionable means. Khalil and his sister Fatmeh draw the world's attention to their country's plight by acts of murder. Fatmeh could spend her life swabbing baby's eyes but must instead kill to avoid being killed. The Palestinians discredit their cause not only by their atrocities but also by the mercenaries they hire. Helga (alias Edda alias Maria Brinkhausen), Albert Rossino (alias Luigi alias Mario), and Anton Mesterbein are sadistic caricatures of Europeans who support the Palestinians for money, who justify mining German homes because they claim to hate Jews, and who threaten Charlie with violence because she is an incidental, unimportant victim.[3]

Le Carré points out the two factions' dogmatism through parallel conversion scenes (chapters 6-7, 21). First, the Israelis and then the Palestinians enlist Charlie's cooperation by disguising reality with feigned compassion. Kurtz and his chosen few set up a sophisticated theater of manipulation made more complex by the subtle shades of meaning each exchange reveals.[4] Kurtz knows that the best way to ensure Israel's survival is to eliminate opposition leaders, making Khalil a natural target. But "to catch a lion, you must first tether a goat" (*Drummer*, 36, 307), and Kurtz's first goal is mold Charlie into an actress so taken with his guerrilla theater that she fails to examine the consequences of her performance. Offering her reality disguised as fiction, Kurtz is a father and his operatives a warm, accepting family. Relishing Kurtz's promised "long fatherly hug" (*Drummer*, 246), Charlie lets fiction overtake reality. Kurtz is pleased: "Tonight she lies for herself, tomorrow she lies for us" (*Drummer*, 117). Charlie's predictability confirms his ethical posture.

Kurtz's long interrogation during her conversion exposes Charlie's neuroses. At each juncture he pays greater attention to her defense mechanisms than to her pronouncements. With Charlie he has the optimal combination of a displaced child, a consummate actor, and a passionate woman for whom "lying is a form of virtue" (*Drummer*, 117). His strategy is to lance each self-deception and replace it with his script. He pretends that his sole concern is "to address the natural humanity in [Charlie]" (*Drummer*, 105). Because Charlie never completely discriminates between fact and fiction, she is easily converted, although the interrogation extends her manipulation. His process accelerates as he reshapes arguments tenuously predicated on one another, until her only logic is fictional.

The Israelis give Charlie direction, acceptance of her surreptitious guilt, and action for her hollow words. They complete her life, providing her with "a homeland at last" (*Drummer*, 138). Kurtz appropriates Charlie as an individual and remakes her into an expendable agent, using her search for stability and love as terrorist bait. Kurtz's mission motivates the narrative as it destroys Charlie's personality.

Another lure Kurtz dangles is the promise of the most perfect lover Charlie could desire. For this part Kurtz enlists Gadi Becker, "Joseph" to Charlie, a war-weary, sexually magnetic Mossad professional who reluctantly but zealously participates. Joseph is always Charlie's demon lover José (a shortened version of Joseph), who has come to collect her soul. To those outside the Mossad he is a mysterious, Mephistopholian character known as "the Steppenwolf." Insiders know him as disillusioned, fighting to save what love remains in his life and participating in this last conspiracy because he believes it the least reprehensible alternative. He tells Charlie that in

1956 he fought to be a hero, in 1967 for peace, and, stumbling for understanding, in 1973 for Israel. Years of fighting for his homeland and of betrayal have eroded his rationale for combat and leave him battling psychological demons. He wars now against further moral deterioration, challenging all the participants' motivations but Kurtz's.

Kurtz initially charges Joseph to draw Charlie away from her acting "family" into a dizzyingly complex love triangle in which she must love Joseph as Khalil's terrorist brother Salim ("Michel") Yanuka and love Joseph as Joseph. Suffering from Alastair's beatings and eager to embrace an appealing new lover, Charlie is already half-converted. Speaking to her as if her were Michel, Joseph converts her "ragbag of . . . vague left-wing principles" (*Drummer*, 181) into a superficial conception of the Israeli version of the Palestinian cause. Her sham commitment to the Palestinians must not seem staged, for her success – and her survival – depends on her spontaneous reactions.

For this performance Joseph *becomes* the Palestinian conscience, a reminder of how readily a spy can change allegiances and how unrooted a person can become once acculturated to espionage. He creates for Charlie an imaginary love affair with Michel so passionate that her fictitious Arab lover's cause becomes her cause, his family hers, his physical degradation her pain, and his murder her private grief. Joseph responds to her confusion with certainty and to her coarse eroticism with patient affection. An Israeli Jew capable of staging his divorce from both country and theology, Joseph convincingly advocates the Palestinian cause. He shows Charlie how the cruelest joke in history is that, in just 30 years, the Israelis "have turned the Palestinians into the new Jews of the earth" (*Drummer*, 181). The Zionists, he tells her, described Palestine before they seized it as "a land without a people for a people without a land." They had committed genocide in their minds; "all that remained for them was the fact" (*Drummer*, 181).

His able performance, however, takes its toll on Joseph. His identification with the Palestinians further undermines his private ethical traumas. Confusing his performance in Kurtz's guerrilla theater with reality, he assaults his problematic loyalty and becomes aware of his degraded spirit. Were he a character of secure moral temperament, Joseph could abandon the Mossad, subvert Charlie's indoctrination to rescue her, and expose his superior's faulty rationale. Instead, his uncertainties about Kurtz's purposes, the validity of war, and his responsibility for Charlie blind him to any emotional consequences. His physical scars from battle and emotional ones from divorce, like Charlie's, leave him another hollow, perfect actor.

To speed her second "conversion" (chapter 21), Charlie is offered a third ready-made family with Joseph's mirror image, Michel. Charlie, warned by Joseph that she will find the Palestinians "an easy people to love" (*Drummer*, 327), finds herself powerfully drawn to this family, especially Michel's sister Fatmeh, for their "shyness, their virginity, their discipline, and their authority over her" (*Drummer*, 329). Terrorist leader Khalil, movie-star smooth, commands an audience wherever he goes – an undesirable quality for an anarchist. Fatmeh, who shows no real interest in dissembling, has the caution of an abused child and the loving concern of a mother. Dedicated to one another and to their own extended family of refugees, they destroy other families and justify terrorism by commitment to the collective Palestinian cause. Caution keeps them from fully trusting Charlie but not from manipulating and recruiting her.

Because the Palestinians' abbreviated version of Kurtz's conversion scene appears to succeed with Charlie, it comments on the subtle manipulation in the earlier scene. Khalil's characterization of the Palestinians as a committed, rather than psychopathic, people replays Kurtz's enticement that his people are better than those Charlie is accustomed to. Captain Tayeh, Khalil's lieutenant, questions Charlie's love for Michel as a means of testing the depth of Charlie's lying nature. She passes Khalil's – not Tayeh's – test of lying for the Palestinians as felicitously as she passed Kurtz's. More important, the questions that both the Israelis and the Palestinians ask encapsulate both sides' dehumanizing rhetoric; neither allows inquiries into conscience or ethical doubt. Charlie's successful conversions are merely terrorist attacks necessary to perpetuate the two sides' "holy" war.

Symbolic of the Palestinians' dehumanized condition is their exploitation of women as expendable terrorists. Michel sends his real-life lover aboard a plane carrying a bomb in her luggage. Fatmeh and her court are expected to murder their enemies and clean up after their compatriots' debauches. Khalil expects Charlie to satisfy his sexual appetites after her first kill. Le Carré's characterization of the Israelis is equally repugnant. They bomb the Palestinian training camp while they know Charlie is there training and, at the operation's conclusion, slaughter Palestinian refugees in retaliation for the attack on Israeli athletes at the Munich Olympics. For both sides, conversion means manipulation. Charlie as a woman is expendable in a self-contained, mindless confrontation that swallows up individuals as surely as any collective.

Drummer Girl ends much as *Smiley's People* did. The protagonist is successful in her mission yet spiritually degraded. The play demands too much. Her experiences in moving from relative safety under Israeli watch to utter terror under Israeli vengeance trivialize her other theatrical performances and disorient her. Charlie runs to the Palestinians for safety and solace. They prove inconstant, recommending not retreat but another mission. She comes to love Michel after the Israelis murder him but conflates her Arabian and phantom Israeli lovers. She loses her place in the Israelis' script, causing Kurtz his only terror. In the end she cannot distinguish appalling reality from impossible fiction.

The awareness of Kurtz's manipulation crashes in on Charlie shortly before Joseph bursts in on her to murder Khalil. Khalil has taken Charlie to his bed to celebrate their successful attack. Rather than feeling joy at their union, Charlie cries bitterly as she sees her complicity in Khalil's murder. She shouts, "They're pigs . . . ruthless murderers" (*Drummer*, 414), and Khalil presumes her anger is directed against their recent bombing victims, not the waiting Israelis. She tries desperately to save him from her treason, but her script fails her. His last words to her ("And you are the same English who gave away my country" [*Drummer*, 420]) symbolically recall England's betrayal of Palestine by illegally deeding Khalil's homeland to the Israelis.

With Khalil's death, Kurtz's operation concludes. He offers Charlie Israeli citizenship, an ironic offer to a character now stripped of identity, homeland, and illusions. Charlie instead returns to the British stage in a drawing-room comedy, fully aware of how tenuous the "divide between her inner and outer world" has become (*Drummer*, 429). When she spots Joseph at the back of the audience, she flees the theater's artificiality.[5]

Joseph has come to claim her, "dead or alive," and, disillusioned, she is "dead, José. You shot me, don't you remember?"

(*Drummer*, 430). The ending is ambiguous. Perhaps Charlie and Joseph merely replicate the disillusion that condemns Smiley and Ann. Just as likely, however, is that they may repair the damage their psyches have suffered. Hope faintly appears as the two set off together, "awkwardly along the pavement, though the town was strange to them" (*Drummer*, 430).

Drummer Girl explores conflicting worlds, manipulation, honor and dishonor in means-ends arguments, and alienation and isolation. Sympathy is not expended for the combatants' causes but reserved for the individuals who suffer. Collectives, whether familial or institutional, fail to foster honor or compassion. Charlie's unsure union with Joseph promises but does not ensure a loving context for her development and a humanistic role for Joseph. As individuals seeking self-awareness and rationality on their own terms, the two may survive. But they can prosper only by rejecting manipulators' creeds and committing themselves to their search.

A Perfect Spy

If *The Little Drummer Girl* is le Carré's most sophisticated novel, *A Perfect Spy* is his most ambitious and autobiographical. Its narrative traces the British, Czech, and American secret services' search for double agent Magnus Pym. For different reasons his espionage supervisors, Jack Brotherhood and Axel; his second wife, Mary; and Magnus himself are searching for the real Magnus Pym. The novel opens with Pym, MI-6 station head and long-term Czech mole, silently rejoicing at the news of his father's death; he is at last free. It ends similarly, with, some critics argue, a sense of release and freedom. Pym returns to England for the funeral and mysteriously disappears. As "Mr. Canterbury," he checks into his safe house, a Devon boardinghouse run by a disagreeable spinster, Miss Dubber. Pym needs time to write an extended suicide note that traces for his son, Tom, what compelled him to treason.

Pym's self-serving autobiography shares the narrative stage with Jack Brotherhood's interrogations of anyone who can help him find his errant recruit (and save his own career), with his Czech controller and teacher Axel's sincere but futile attempt to prevent Pym's suicide, and with Mary Pym's attempts to comprehend her husband's betrayals. Throughout this complex series of stories and flashbacks, the narrator sometimes inconsistently condemns all the players. By the time Brotherhood finds Pym in Devon, Pym has completed his labor of love. Rather than the tragic act of a desperate man, Pym's suicide is appropriate for a man who is not an angst-driven intellectual, a committed ideologue, or a Forsterian sentimentalist.

Magnus Pym's straightforward plot line is interwoven with his secret, discursive monologue. Moving between humor and bitterness, Magnus disassembles the causes of his treasonous acts. He unconvincingly warns Tom that his national disloyalties are rebellions against the three parents he loves: his criminal but charismatic father, Richard ("Rick") Thomas Pym; his Czech controller, Axel; and his British recruiter, Brotherhood.[6] Trying to please all, Magnus betrays all. Rick's chaotic life-style threatens to annihilate his son, and so Magnus provides Rick's enemies with secrets that give them power over Rick. Axel proffers a subtle recruitment, but, seduced by Brotherhood's facile patriotic appeals, Magnus betrays him to the Swiss authorities; Magnus then spends the rest of his life trying to right this wrong. Brotherhood initiates him into espionage by encouraging him to spy on his friends, and so Magnus rewards Brotherhood's invention by becoming a perfect spy, a nihilist. Yet nowhere in the recounting of his youth, recruitment, or lifetime of treason does Magnus face his true demon, his own intellectual and spiritual abyss.[7]

Although Magnus is the novel's title character, Rick Pym is its protagonist. Rick shares a devious history, accented by personal and profitable betrayals, with David Cornwell's father, Ronnie. When Ronnie Cornwell died in 1975, his son paid for the funeral but failed to settle his emotional debts. The passing of time permitted le Carré to recognize, somewhat belatedly for his fiction writing, Ronnie's comic potential. His beloved father made him "a princeling in the kingdom of the clandestine," and his surrogate parents, the British educational system and the intelligence community, made him a virtuoso at subterfuge (Schiff, 188). He would free himself of Ronnie by a humorous scrutiny of his father's furiously unconventional appetites while continuing his lifelong dissection of espionage's humanitarian defections.

A gentleman swindler, womanizer, and convicted felon, Rick Pym avoids emotional involvements with his marks – behavior he passes on to his son. In his youth Rick duped his future brother-in-law, Sir Makepeace Watermaster, out of nearly £1,000 from Watermaster's church coffers for an abortive transportation scheme. Magnus notes that any money passing through Rick's hands, like information passing through his, was "subject to a redefinition of the laws of property" (*Perfect*, 34). Rick later profits when, to the Watermaster family horror, he marries Makepeace's sister, Dorothy Godchild Watermaster. Magnus Richard Pym was "born to them not six months later" (*Perfect*, 41).

"The lovelies" (women) and "the court" (cronies) Rick attracts become young Magnus's eccentric family and model his adult values. Volcanic and magnetic, Rick controls his followers by finding resources where none exist; in return he demands of them "the totality of your love" (*Perfect*, 42). Rick's lovelies, especially Lippsie, willingly take the place of Magnus's emotionally absent mother. Rick's business partners, even those he swindles, mesmerize young Magnus. One, Syd Lemon, Rick's right-hand man, goes to prison for his boss, and when Rick cannot avoid incarceration Syd protects "Titch" (Magnus's nickname) as devotedly as he protected Rick. Rick's pride is Magnus, yet he hides his private skeletons from his naturally inquisitive son. Rick keeps an explosive set of documents, hidden away in a battered green filing cabinet. The cabinet, reminiscent of the green files Harting keeps in *A Small Town in Germany*, passes from Syd to a very curious Magnus, but by the time Magnus inherits "that stupid filing cabinet" (*Perfect*, 473) he no longer desires it.

As an adult Magnus can no more separate deceit from reality than his father can. Rick's life is a grand illusion, kept afloat by his empty promises and strategies of pacification. To learn the truth about his father, Magnus must assume all facts are lies, must search all documents, and must betray Rick. Thus, the family Rick foists on Magnus leaves his son hollow, ready for training in subterfuge and tradecraft.

Magnus acquires two other father figures, espionage professionals Jack Brotherhood and Herr Axel, distinguished from each other more by their brand of ideological commitment than by their methods. Both are about the same age, height, and physical condition. Jack lost the use of his arm during World War II; Axel is lame. Both admire Magnus, love "his jokes and his voices," and clamor "to occupy the empty spaces in his heart" (*Perfect*, 214). As doubles they symbolize "a world divided against itself; a world in which men must constantly struggle to discriminate among conflicting loyalties and shifting identities."[8] But the two spymasters differ in the way they command Magnus's loyalty.

Magnus is intellectually attracted by Brotherhood, a senior officer in the brotherhood of the Firm (SIS). He tutors the schoolboy and shapes Magnus's sense of honor by joining his expertise with Rick's early training. Brotherhood becomes Magnus's professional patron, procuring for the younger man a career and a wife guaranteed to advance that career. Opportunistic, efficient, and emotionally distant, Brotherhood is predisposed to destroy what he loves, a habit ironically captured in his destruction of his beloved but aging Labrador bitch. A representative of the most patriotic society Britain can offer, he enmeshes himself in a bureaucracy that supplants emotional involvement. Brotherhood is drawn to institutions that cover up discord for the sake of superficial cohesiveness. The Firm is thus his perfect spiritual home; both can easily destroy individuals to preserve individualism, and Jack readily deceives in the name of patriotism, freedom, and justice. Brotherhood's failure to understand Magnus results from this impassive single-mindedness: for him, Magnus is a budding prospect, not an individual.

Magnus is emotionally drawn to Axel, a Czech refugee who befriends him in Berne at the time Brotherhood, back in London, is setting up to recruit Magnus. Codenamed "Poppy" (for the poppies of Flanders' field), Axel becomes "the steady and wise father" that Charlie believes she found in Kurtz. He stands as confidant, confessor, teacher, and manipulator, that "part of Pym that was not owned by anybody else" (*Perfect*, 456). He enriches his protégé's emotions through humor and friendship. Amused with his pupil's naïveté, Axel introduces Magnus to literature, philosophy, German culture, and socialist ideology. He cautions Pym to read everything and reject afterward. His texts are by Rousseau, Marx, Brecht, and Thomas Mann. Axel gives "For Sir Magnus, who will never be my enemy" his valued copy of Grimmelshausen's *Simplicissimus*, a seventeenth-century account of the Thirty Years War.[9] Ironically, the book later becomes their ciphering codebook.

A betrayer often betrayed, Axel deprecates Magnus's British heritage and justifies his own conversion to communism by implying that treason springs naturally from Pym's floundering empire. Haydon's reasoning rings faintly behind Axel's argument that Pym's privileges, snobbery, heritage, and class systems will be swept away by Western democracy's betrayals. Magnus, unaware of such history, stays mesmerized by this intellectual but tortured émigré.

Magnus betrays Axel, ingratiating himself with Brotherhood but affirming Axel's anti-Western argument. Shortly after they first meet, Magnus, for no reason other than pleasing Brotherhood, turns Axel over to the Swiss authorities, who deport him to Czechoslovakia and sure punishment. Years later when Magnus and Axel meet in Austria, Magnus finds that Axel has reconsidered his ideology and has wedded his country's political theories to his earlier criticisms of Britain. Magnus finds that the love and respect they earlier shared still flourishes. He resolves to conspire with Axel not for ideological reasons or for "the illusion of being a servant of national necessity" but because he owes Axel for his earlier betrayal: "I will bring you gifts as you brought gifts to me" (*Perfect*, 371). Many years and compromises later, when American agent Grant Lederer pieces together Magnus's deception, Axel wants his friend to defect to Czechoslovakia. The offer, made out of Axel's love, is important because it allows Magnus to construe his continued treachery as an elevated form of patriotism.

Afraid for his job and seeking justice for Magnus, Brotherhood methodically interrogates everyone from his protégé's past, setting up the novel's suspense. Brotherhood soon discovers that the Firm cares less about Magnus's sham networks than it fears, as Axel does, that Magnus will write his book. Magnus's candid exposé could threaten the Firm's partnership with America, already weakened by the Cambridge spies' debacle. Unwilling to see the betrayal in human terms, Brotherhood refuses to bend or seek a justification for Magnus's actions; he thereby courts inevitable ridicule. "Bo" Brammel, Jack's sycophantic, dandified superior, further equivocates. If the Americans suspect that Pym has gone the way of Philby, the American pipeline into British intelligence will be shut down. Always ready to compromise patriotism for superficial accord, Brammel prevents Brotherhood from questioning the Firm's sad history or disclosing Magnus's escape.

The CIA's motivations for curbing Brotherhood's investigations are equally suspect. Overall, Firm officials condemn the Americans as "vulgar pleasure-seeking people" whose "frank and clamorous" attitudes are too uninhibited for any British agent's "shielded and involuted life" (*Perfect*, 455). Tenacious, pushy, and suspiciously clever, CIA pointman Grant Lederer epitomizes the Firm's anti-American sentiment. He stalks Magnus so that he can use his knowledge to manipulate his British and American colleagues into promoting him. Despite this unpatriotic motivation, Lederer accurately assesses the Firm's disingenuous complacency and concludes that his chief, Harry E. Wexler, demurs because he is an intellectual buffoon. But the messenger rather than the message creates appearances that become priorities. Lederer's reward for his insight is ignominious demotion to the statistics division.

Magnus complicates the personal dilemmas posed in *Tinker, Tailor, Soldier, Spy*: understanding his motivations depends on who is analyzing the desultory reasons for his betrayals. Magnus's first wife, Belinda, suggests that he is a Daedalus character escaping his father. Magnus, for his part, censures his adored father: "Your mantle has passed to me, leaving you a naked little man, and myself the biggest con I knew" (*Perfect*, 465). Mary briefly suspects a socialist allegiance, but to her Magnus is just the consummate actor, incapable of ideological purity. All his life, she says, "he's been inventing versions of himself that are untrue" (*Perfect*, 120). After meeting Axel, she blames him for teaching Magnus "his style . . . how to be superior to human foibles and how to give a Godlike laugh at himself as a way of fending off morbidity" (*Perfect*, 388). Kate, Brotherhood's mistress, suggests that it is futile to look for any truth with Magnus: "The truth is what we gave him of ourselves" (*Perfect*, 191). Sir Kenneth Sefton Boyd, Magnus's privileged schoolmate, suspects a more probable cause: "Love was all he cared about. Didn't know where to find it. Clown really. Tried too hard" (*Perfect*, 328). Axel comes even closer by suggesting that Pym betrays because he is "entirely put together from other bits of people, poor fellow" (*Perfect*, 392).

Magnus's view of himself, the actual subject of his suicide letter, rings most true; it evinces his composite character. Magnus Pym is nationalistic, claiming the privilege and immunity customary to British subjects. Despite such patriotic grounding, he comes to see that he can only be Magnus Pym through other characters. He writes his autobiography to prevent evasiveness, but each line of the work

frustrates a definition of its author. Lacing his history with aphorisms, he reiterates that "Life is paying," "Secrets are a strain," and
"Betrayal can only happen if you love" (*Perfect*, 370, 175, 276).
Magnus the first-person writer shifts to Pym the third-person
observer as he creates a legend for "Tom's father."

For Magnus, duplicity befitting one person at another's expense
defines love and hope. He deserts Belinda for his profession. He
marries Mary for convenience but humors himself that they
"managed a bit of love along the way" (*Perfect*, 473). He falsely
implicates Sir Boyd with their preparatory school's headmaster and
then leads the search for Boyd's accuser. He respects Brotherhood,
Britain, and the Firm but feeds Jack disinformation, steals national
secrets, and jeopardizes Anglo-American relations. He reveres Axel
for liberating his mind but betrays him and eventually deserts him.
He adores his son, Tom ("He's the dearest thing I have"), but provides him with no better model than Rick was and entrusts his future
to Brotherhood, the spymaster whom he believes to have con-
tributed to his duplicity.

Closing his narrative with his actual death brings Magnus full circle, as surely as writing *A Perfect Spy* closed David Cornwell's spiritual wounds. Magnus has destroyed because he loves, not hates.
Once exposed, this displaced man dies without a clear national or
individual identity. Yet Magnus dies with the knowledge that his
greatest treacheries, those inherent in principles higher than patriotism, have made him a good man.

The Russia House

The Russia House follows recurrent le Carré themes, dissecting
intelligence agencies and their motivations, lamenting the ambiguity
of human relationships, and charting its agents' spiritual decline, all
in the new Russia of *perestroika*. This novel entangles the dual
themes of inadequate or unconsummated love with the possibility of
redemption through love and therefore hints at an optimistic resolution. Echoes of Turner's rage, Westerby's naïveté, and Charlie's
hopeful resurrection sound against a political landscape filled with
"chauvinist drumbeats" (*Russia House*, 286). And the novel's hope-

ful protagonist, Barley Blair, achieves an ironically heroic status because he betrays.

This shorter, less labyrinthine novel than either *Drummer Girl* or *Perfect Spy* derives its hopefulness from the tentative democratic reforms commenced in the late 1980s by Soviet and Warsaw Pact citizens. The people rejected outdated cold war mentalities, but espionage bureaucracies continued to distrust one another. A long history of repression cannot be easily dismissed, and in this novel Western espionage bureaucracies, inured to spying on allies and their enemies (i.e., the KGB and Moscow Centre), find the changes disconcerting. What do spies do when "the old isms" die and the "contest between Communism and capitalism" ends "in a wet whimper" (*Russia House*, 286)? Rather than detailing again the despairing violations of human decency, the novel gives voice to Dwight D. Eisenhower's assessment that "people want peace so much that one of these days governments had better get out of their way and let them have it." Despite this unfamiliar optimism, the novel's method is vintage le Carré.

The dispirited narrator, Horatio Benedict "Harry" dePalfrey, is comfortable with his duplicitous inactivity. Known as Old Palfrey to his colleagues in the Russia House – the Firm's headquarters for this operation – Harry is a world-weary, Smileyesque legal consultant. Sitting in his nondescript office, he recounts Barley Blair's recruitment and betrayal. Words shield Harry from action. He immerses himself in the details of Barley's case to expunge his complicity. Harry laments his failed relationships with his son, Alan, and his married mistress, Hannah. Amused yet frightened, he sanitizes the Firm's report on Barley's treason. From Harry's viewpoint the tortuously planned, painstakingly verified operation – lyrically codenamed "Bluebird" – failed because Barley chose a slim hope for love over allegiance to his controllers.

The linchpin this time is the Dickenesque protagonist Bartholomew "Barley" Scott Blair. Barley is a vaguely left-wing, middle-aged publisher whose Eton and Cambridge education qualifies him, at least in Harry's eyes, as an honorable schoolboy and a potentially perfect spy.[10] Seedy, feckless, cantankerous, and usually drunk, Barley follows his father's lead in heading a decrepit publishing house known for its director's incompetent management. Barley's father and his legacy to his son are far cries from Rick Pym and his legacy to his son. The Firm's hierarchy dismisses the elder Blair as an eccentric who sympathized with the Soviets during World War II: he died financially and emotionally bankrupt at Stalin's repression. The CIA, however, is more suspicious. It sees Barley's father as "a Communist sympathizer, latterly disenchanted" (*Russia House*, 235), who must have instilled in his son an undiscerned political fervor. The truth is far more prosaic and hence incomprehensible to Barley's espionage handlers. Barley's father represents the mixed blessing of his own frustrated dreams and, to some extent, those of his country as well.

Barley also opts to play jazz, mimic authority, and carouse rather than act responsibly. He has casual affairs and avoids sincere attachments to anyone, most of all to his family. Yet Barley is pragmatically philosophical. He gives himself to those he loves, such as his "guru on mortality," dying jazz musician Andrew George Macready (alias "Andy"), and Katya Orlov, the mysterious, beautiful Russian editor/courier for whom Barley betrays his country. Just as easily, he lies by absenting himself from a man he admires, Ned, the Firm's top linguist and interrogator, and one agent he cannot respect, Richard Sheriton, the Agency's TECHINT expert.

Barley's background and irresponsibility make him a singularly inappropriate recruit. He is not a company man – the espiocrats' prime requirement for working the field – but an unpredictable individualist. He agrees to the Firm's mission not for patriotism but for friendship. In short time Barley develops a kinship with his physical and psychic double, Ned – his British controller – and with Ned's Russia House agents. Simultaneously he gains a sense of responsibility to Soviet physicist and betrayer "Goethe" that escapes even Barley's full understanding.

As a regular part of his publishing business, Barley travels overseas to solicit manuscripts. During one such trip he partakes of a noteworthy "bender" in a writer's dacha community near Russian writer Boris Pasternak's grave in Peredelkino. Here, to his hosts' delight, he delivers a drunken speech on global disarmament and peace. Barley, the accomplished actor, is "Mr. Wonderful . . . Star of the stage and screen. Western, courteous, and specious" (*Russia House*, 76). Barley privately acknowledges his innocuous deception, however. He admits to Ned that the "Sovs are the only people daft enough to listen to my bullshit" (*Russia House*, 76).

In Barley's audience is a thin, mysterious bearded man, about Barley's age. "Tall. Dark suit, black tie. Hollow face. . . . Black hair. Drunk" (*Russia House*, 75), this dissident commands respect from fellow writers. Goethe (so named because "he was born with two souls, just like Faust" [*Russia House*, 85]) is the renegade Russian physicist Yakov Savelyev. Goethe's idealism and humanitarian outlook suggest Andrei Sakharov, but his intensity approaches that of Dostoyevski's tortured souls.[11] His years of state service have made him distrust "the sanity of experts and the superior ignorance of its bureaucrats" (*Russia House*, 207). Yet Goethe without cogent reasons loves the English; they are "the moral leaders of Europe, the secret steadiers, and the unifiers of the great European ideal" (*Russia House*, 86). Goethe condemns his country's leaders for confusing the relationship between words and actions; le Carré tacitly lets the criticisms apply to the West. Bureaucrats fear action because it means forfeiting their positions and facing the malaise they created. If they don't know how to change, officials should simply and rightly get out of their people's way.

Goethe is entranced by Barley's impertinent argument – that freedom supersedes responsibility – because of Barley's nationality and his own drunkenness rather than the argument's logic. Goethe decides he must abandon abstractions and thought for courageous, selfless action. The incongruity between what Barley says and what Goethe hears should discredit Goethe's resolution to act. Instead, his commitment to redress real and imagined deceits provides the novel's tension and the philosophical model for Barley's change from nihilistic acceptance of his fate to sentimental participation in its direction.

Years after this meeting Goethe entrusts three cheap notebooks with his sometime lover Yekaterina ("Katya") Orlov, with instructions that she give them to Barley and that Barley publish them unchanged. Katya, a divorcée with two children, cannot obtain permission to leave Russia. She presses Goethe's manuscript on book salesman Nicki Landau, one of Barley's more colorful publishing-world doubters. Landau assumes the notebooks are another outburst of Soviet dissent angst, but he is suspicious enough to look. The notebooks are filled with wild sociopolitical ramblings, mathematical formulas of uncertain application, scientific doubletalk, and secret diagrams and information. They also contain Goethe's description of his country's "involvement in the preparation of anti-humanitarian weapons of mass destruction" (*Russia House*, 158). Goethe portrays incompetence, massive corruption, criminal mismanagement, and ethical shortcomings "in all fields of the defence-industrial complex" (*Russia House*, 158). He alleges that Soviet telemetry is a cruel hoax that would disgrace Russian citizens if they knew about the costly shambles. Western allies need not fear weaponry that lacks accuracy and reliability. "The American strategists can sleep in peace," Goethe writes assuredly. "Their nightmares cannot be realised. The Soviet knight is dying inside his armor" (*Russia House*, 18) – a realistic prediction of contemporary events.

Goethe's motives come under immediate scrutiny by British and American experts. Is he a KGB plant, promoting a clever disinformation plot to destabilize Western alliances, or is his information real? The latter possibility alarms these sober, eminently sane agents. If the West's massive defense complex is being perpetuated to fight a phantom empire, Western politicians can expect public censure. Politicians anxious to disavow their complicity will turn on the espionage bureaucracy for promoting years of overspending. Peddling the arms race becomes impossible, one espionage professional complains, "when the only asshole you have to race against is yourself" (*Russia House*, 246).

Moreover, Goethe's information, if true, changes the rules of espionage and leaves active agents ill-suited to the new game. The ethics of collecting intelligence threatens to supersede accuracy. The cynical agents – Ned, Walter, Clive, and their American counterpart Richard Sheriton – become obsessed with preserving their positions by discrediting Goethe. They do not want to be humiliated by an often-drunken, possibly mad Russian physicist. Even more alarming to them, they do not want to look into their mirrored world of deception and realize that they are the enemy they seek.

Players long accustomed to the game refuse, however, to retreat quietly. Ned, Harry, Clive, and a host of American experts attempt to lure Barley into their ranks. They conduct an interrogation/conversion scene that mocks the complexity of the conversion scenes in *Drummer Girl*. These neither evil nor singular espiocrats are naive bumblers, and Barley, increasingly distrustful, seems a decent humanitarian. Accustomed to engineering ignominious defections, the agents perceive Barley as a lower-class womanizer, perpetually insolvent and thus susceptible to bribery. But Barley lacks illusion and so rejects patriotic or financial appeals. They present Barley with a compromise familiarly offered to people of uncertain loyalties and presumed psychological failings. If he will give himself to their reality, take the "second vow" of *Looking-glass*, Barley will never need to come to terms with himself; they will provide reality for him. Barley, however, lacks theatricality and hence rejects these appeals. Ned correctly assesses Barley's weaknesses but ignores the very real possibility that Barley may fall in love. Ned's mistake encourages Barley's treason.

The KGB, the novel's silent protagonist, is sharply and unrealistically distinguished from Western intelligence agencies by its humanity. A nearly clinical detailing of the Firm's actions confirms the duplicity and wickedness of which Western intelligence agencies are capable. Yet the KGB, shrouded in the same mysteriousness Karla enjoyed, enters into deals Barley naively construes as honorable because "they don't break their promises" (*Russia House*, 352). The idealistic suggestion, promoted throughout the novel, is that Russian espiocrats are unlike their Western counterparts because they can accommodate radical political change within their bureaucracy. The KGB is described as possibly embracing humanitarian ideals espoused yet neglected by Western agents.

Barley ignores history, a damning myopia throughout le Carré's canon, to believe that a totalitarian and brutal agency would exchange his lover and her family for his treason. In fact, the novel's characterization of the KGB, meant to underscore the difficulty of trust, is so historically improbable that it compromises the question of trust.[12] Barley's trust grows from his goodheartedness and his business dealings. Barley does not succumb to Leamas's and Smiley's fate; nor does he sell himself for a vaguely defined ideology, as Else Fennan and Haydon did. He betrays when he opens himself up to trust and releases an exuberant romanticism, as Westerby did. He takes the risk that, by compromising some values, he may experience greater joy than he now experiences. Barley has no reason other than his love and trust in the Soviet's acceptance of revolutionary change to believe that, if he betrays Ned's manipulative organization, the KGB will honor its deal. The more cynical, cold war view is that Moscow manipulated Barley so that the KGB could quietly execute Goethe as an embarrassment to the authorities and that the authori-

ties agreed to spare Katya and her family to secure the list of questions the British prepare for Goethe that reveal the lacuna in British
intelligence. Either resolution fits the facts as Barley knows them.
Barley ends up alone in Lisbon, unable and unwilling to return to
England and unsure of when – or if – Katya will be allowed to join
him.

Working from *perestroika*, however, demands a trust alien to the
superpower services but acceptable to individuals. Goethe was ill,
too fragile to meet with Barley more than once in Leningrad. Barley
ends up a long-distance lover like Harry, but an optimistic one. As he
tells Ned, his hope arises from Katya's love and an individualism that
dictated his betrayal of his British masters. Love, not political ethic,
ennobles him. For Barley, it is a naive and sentimental trust posed as
a choice between obvious alternatives. Barley ends a traitor and a
free man who in his compromise "signed nothing, . . . accepted
nothing, . . . wanted nothing, . . . conceded nothing, . . . owed nothing, and . . . wished the living lot of us, without anger, to the Devil"
(*Russia House*, 352-53). His controllers stay impotent and scared, as
all are in Harry's trade, "of people of good instinct."

The Secret Pilgrim

Less a novel than loosely connected short stories, *The Secret Pilgrim*
brings George Smiley out of retirement long enough to impress new
Circus recruits, trained by *Russia House*'s Ned, with the rituals, allegiances, and potential for self-betrayal promised by clandestine
behavior. The Firm has demoted Ned to Sarratt because he botched
the Barley Blair exchange. Now close to retirement, Ned's conscience incessantly bothers him. Whereas he and Smiley could justify
their patriotism around ideological stalemates but, at least for Smiley,
condemn institutional callousness, these recruits have no anchor at
all. The cold war is gone, and Ned in particular fears what will
replace it.

Smiley's somewhat unexpected presence at the graduation dinner as well as his advice and ancedotes trigger Ned's recollections of
his career. The stories shift back and forth in time, recalling and contrasting moral ambiguity, wry triumphs, and humorous mishaps with
brutality and worldly compromises. Ned still delights in his profes-

sional and personal conquests. He makes little effort to repudiate his compromised morality. He has, he freely admits to himself, succeeded in operations, romanced intelligent women, dealt with honorable counterparts, and watched his country's ideological frameworks dominate other nations' absolutist doctrines. He reminisces about his liaison with Bella, Slavic sea captain Brandt's lascivious mistress. He recalls with pleasure his country's besting of the Americans in passing them the Circus's fatuous mercenary, Hungarian professor Teodor.

More often he remembers with genuine sorrow how his actions destroyed others. His best friend and fellow spy, Ben, unintentionally compromised an entire network. Ned, seeking to protect him, clumsily led Smiley to him and even more ineptly fell in love with Ben's lover, Stephanie, a passion he keeps secret throughout his life. He grieves for how his interrogation drove cypher clerk Cyril Arthur Frewin to suicide. Ironically, Ned recalls how he admired Frewin for his integrity, as it was Frewin who alerted Ned's superiors to his guilt.

As he remembers, Ned analyzes his world and predicts what his recruits' society will be like. Throughout he struggles with his emotions and his sense of duty to these newcomers. He wonders what moral foundations he, Smiley, and others have left. Their professional legacy is bankrupt: more than 40 years were wasted in cold war espionage. Ned perceives that Sarratt's neophytes inherit the mentality and convictions of those who, like him, protect themselves by their cynicism. He laments Smiley's modest insight that "spying is eternal." Both professionals know that "if governments *could* do without it, they never would. They adore it."[13] Still, after all the compromises Ned optimistically hopes for a better time that will justify his sacrifices for his service and give him absolution from his questions.

Ned's memories of his profession rehearse well-known le Carré characters and tropes. There are eccentrics, such as Polish spy and torturer Colonel Jerzy, British agent Henry (the Chinese son of a Kuomingtang warlord), and Arabist and distinguished bridge player Giles Latimer. There are accepted characters, such as Harry dePalfrey, Peter Guillam, and Toby Esterhase. And, of course, there are darker figures, such as Bill Haydon and Karla. In Ned's memory the past (Before the Fall) intrudes on the present (After the Fall) with lessons still unlearned. The agency haphazardly trains and abandons disreputable émigrés doing the service's bidding; embittered dons compromise themselves for a dishonorable occupation; and an Anglo-Dutch father's true passion for his Eurasian daughter degrades both his commitment and his life. The Circus represents "any other British institution" (*Pilgrim*, 103), and responsible characters (i.e., Ned, Ben, Hansen, Frewin) continue to question actions and condemn their own when warranted.

The Russia House mishaps haunt Ned's position and force him, as his last official act, to deal with the new enemy, Sir Anthony Joyston Bradshaw. Bradshaw is a particularly unsavory representative of what Ned suspects will be the Circus's new adversary. DePalfrey sends Ned (alias Mr. Carlisle) groveling to Sir Anthony to keep him from exposing secrets about the government's financial and espionage dealings. Sir Anthony is "one of England's natural shits," recruited and sponsored by Percy Alleline, who may have used his Circus cover for a "string of shady transactions of dubious value to anybody but Sir Anthony" (*Pilgrim*, 327). Secure in a powerful position, Sir Anthony's extreme arrogance leaves him shallow and uninteresting, even for a typical le Carré eccentric. Karla, as shadowly as he is, represents moral ambivalence more completely than Bradshaw ever can. Moreover, Bradshaw is clearly worse than his espionage progenitors Maston, Control, and Percy Alleline. He merges a proletariate vulgarity with his shady business ability and the insufferable attitudes of the "Foreign Office types." The combination disgusts Ned personally and humiliates any pretense of honor. Smiley, Ned, and their ilk defeated communism; now, with the likes of Bradshaw as the new enemy, Sarratt's graduates "were going to have to set about defeating capitalism" (*Pilgrim*, 334). The battle promises to be bloodier because the Bradshaws, unlike Ned's cold war enemies, respect no ideology.

For more than 30 years le Carré has written about people struggling with ideological conflicts and about the irreconcilable problems dispirited agents face in trying to maintain their humanity in light of impossible situations.[14] Freed from the contorted motives for betrayal found in *Drummer Girl* and the mazed, mirrored world of *Perfect Spy*, le Carré sees *The Russia House* as "the beginning of what for me would be an exciting rejuvenation – personally, in my writing."[15] He describes *The Secret Pilgrim* as a challenge to anyone writing contemporary espionage fiction.[16]

Yet this optimism does not necessarily prevail in these later novels. The murky complexity of *The Russia House* inadequately justifies its obvious plotting, clichéd mood, and slight analysis of motivations. The caricatures of *The Secret Pilgrim* do not exploit ambiguity as much as they lament that the wrong people – Smiley's embittered dons and, in the 1990s, England's lower-middle-class nouveaux riches – continually set the moral standards.[17] To his credit he makes love and individuality – not spy fiction's superficial patriotism or modern literature's manifested self-awareness – determine a protagonist's fate throughout all his novels. In fact, le Carré insists on this variation over the genre's often-slapdash formulas. He couples it with his concern for credible characters and settings, and creates a multitextured fiction that indicts absolutist loyalty, challenges liberalism, and exemplifies the degradation individuals face with the moral ambiguity of espionage. If a character can prevail, he does so because his trust opens up new realms of imaginative speculation.

Chapter Seven

Shaking the Tree:
The Achievement of John le Carré

I am trying to reconcile the novel of action with that wretched *Message* which is constantly shoving its nose under the wire. And was it not Conrad who once grumbled that sometimes his characters stood for so much that they didn't stand up at all? I know that feeling only too well.

– "The Clandestine Muse" (1986)

The most popular British espionage novelist of the twentieth century, John le Carré writes a hybrid fiction. He merges romance and thriller formulas with the experimental techniques prevalent in contemporary "literary" fiction. In the tradition of John Buchan and Eric Ambler, le Carré assesses the political and moral vitality of his society. Moreover, he redefines the borders of genre fiction by exploring the dark sides of contemporary life, while giving temporary solutions to the pervasive chaos of moral uncertainty. Throughout he reminds readers that agents committed to secrecy are capable only of societal and emotional subversion. Intelligence agencies and their employees anxiously delude themselves. Agents are fragmented antiheroes, fighting ambiguous battles against boredom and drudgery in decidedly unglamorous and unappreciative worlds. No one wins in a le Carré novel, because no victories are possible.

His novels turn on themes of betrayal. He contrasts private morality and public accountability, thought and action, duty and love, and ideological commitment and personal betrayal. He mixes characters' interjections, opinions, and insider's information into sometimes confusingly sequenced dialogues. Double agents are le Carré's primary vehicles for exploring spiritual and moral bankruptcy. They serve two masters but are true to neither controllers nor themselves. Their assignments reproduce the perpetual disloyalties endemic in most human relationships. Treason is nurtured into habit and inevitably kills the human spirit.

With great skill le Carré integrates this basic theme with several secondary themes. He insists that characters question fascism, the authority of political institutions, and the nature of ethics. His more developed characters know that love must underlie and unify an individual's sense of moral rules – a fairly romantic and sentimental viewpoint. Repeatedly, he argues that failing to question adequately means continuing a duplicity that invariably defeats both betrayer and betrayed. Yet despite their questioning, his characters cannot redirect democratic or moral ideology – symbolized in the collectives they serve. Honorable questioners like George Smiley, Barley Blair, and Ned stumble, resort to a means-ends position that meets their private moral codes, and survive only because they force themselves to walk away from sure manipulation.

A second variation on betrayal arises when individuals evaluate themselves by how well they conform to their collective's values. These agents attribute to their unworthy institutions motivations similar to their own dreams and, without adequate justification, adopt the institution's goals as their own. Institution men, realizing the power they hold, encourage individuals to take Leclerc's "second vow" and relinquish their humanity for the institution's suspect goals.

Le Carré presses the issue further by suggesting how various institutions mirror the ethical nature of all society. Because a collective cannot survive without subsuming individuals, it follows, then, that Western society is hypocritical for praising individualism while devaluing individuals. Throughout the novels honorable characters – the individuals who question and those who love – find that their triumphs are, in practical terms, meaningless. The balance of power stays with institutions; individualism ensures only existential anguish and empty theatricality.

Love, the opposite of apathy, finds expression in the virtues of friendship (i.e., Peter Guillan and Smiley), companionship (i.e., Hilary and Connie Sachs), and family (i.e., Drake and Nelson Ko, Katya and her family). Love, however, makes a character vulnerable to betrayal. Seemingly admirable intentions lead to tragic consequences as heroes pursue their quests for true love. Yet repeatedly "love is what you can betray," the last illusion of illusionless agents.

The redemption love promises comes to nothing, and those innocent
bystanders who become the objects of agents' affection suffer
unjustly.

For all the intricate variations le Carré invests in these themes,
his characters frequently come across as one-dimensional eccentrics
or Dickensian caricatures. Gestures rather than slowly developed
motivations clue trained professionals that a character's intentions
are furtive. How characters speak betrays them more than what they
say. Repetition numbs these subtleties and denies even major figures
like George Smiley true psychological depth. Character types recur
because le Carré restricts his attention to variations of divided loyalties. There are goodhearted patriots (i.e., Jim Prideaux, Jerry Westerby) who share both physical characteristics and a vulnerability
born of patriotism and comradeship. Variations on patriotism gone
wrong set up other characters. Maston, Leclerc, Bill Haydon, Saul
Enderby, and Sir Anthony Joyston Bradshaw, though enhanced with
individual eccentricities, are sycophants whose sophistication makes
their patriotism suspect. To trained eyes their loyalty is as studied as
their clothing or manners. Smiley's professionalism and constant
questioning are disingenuously restated in Kurtz, who easily bal-
ances reason and feeling and reconciles ends with means. Reality is
endlessly distorted to meet immediate purposes.

Contrasting characters and parallel plot lines are fundamental to
le Carré's narrative technique. Le Carré wants readers to accept his
fictional world as plausible and his judgments about that world's
immorality as sound. He releases ambiguous fragments of information piecemeal, until a protagonist finally assembles the jigsaw puzzle
in full view of readers. Random events and contrapuntal flashbacks
fragment reality, interrupt anecdotes, and invite realistic digressions.
Agents invest small matters, courtesies, or incidental encounters with
great significance. Offhanded comments, gaps in interrogations, and
subordinate clauses buried within a character's forced admission
provide key information. Characters' abbreviated explanations and
skewed memories pervert past events. These atypical genre techniques force close attention on characters' motives. Uncertain agents
replicate the chaos that so frequently is a part of contemporary existence. Their involvement promotes questioning, the sort alien to a
Leclerc or Kurtz but compulsory for conscientious thinkers.

Central to this narrative technique – and one of the limitations imposed on his fiction – is le Carré's love for constructing parallels. Characters, situations, agencies, and operations duplicate each other almost to distraction. Individual agents fight their countries' opposing causes with identical methods. The hunter invariably becomes the hunted. Most noticeably, each novel sets up dark/light dopplegängers who symbolize each other's limitations and moral degradation. Tatiana's schizophrenia feeds her dual identity as Alexandra Ostrakova and Karla's daughter. She clings to the illusion of her twin fathers, one who sacrifices everything for her and the other who is too powerful to exist for her. The Israelis and Palestinians fictionalize themselves as freedom fighters rather than terrorists. Charlie realizes this lie when she analogizes going between the Israeli and Palestinian camps to repeated trips through the looking glass. Smiley belatedly sees not only Karla as a twin mirage (an unfeeling spymaster and a loving father) but himself as Karla's professional and psychological twin. Karla must exist for Smiley to exist as surely as Barley needs Goethe or Cassidy is incomplete without Shamus. The effect of le Carré's doubling reinforces his preoccupation with betrayal. Each doubled character comes to understand how he must interpret all life as duplicitous. Conspiracy, the lifeblood of espionage, has a human face very like each agent.

Accustomed to a labyrinth of moral ambiguities, le Carré revels in wordplay. Words focus attention on the constant boredom and threat of betrayal and on the Gordian knots of specific institutions. Jargon becomes one way espionage novices validate their membership. They quickly learn how to substitute dishonest euphemism for legitimate argot, a practice le Carré mocks throughout his fiction. The insider's language enmeshes readers in these secret worlds and alerts them to question not only content but the speaker. Le Carré borrows terms (i.e., *fieldmen, surveillance, case officer, courier, cryptonym,* and *deskman*) from an established espionage vocabulary but refuses to accept only their clichés. He endows otherwise-neutral words with sinister implications (i.e., *alimony* = delayed payments to agents; *competition* = rival intelligence agencies; *customer* = government office buying intelligence; *funny* = intelligence service operative; *hardware* = electronic equipment; *recycle* = bring agents in from the cold; and *tradecraft* = espionage techniques) and parodies the meanings of other words (i.e., *honor, lover, naive, quality*). He replaces common terms with ironically metaphoric codenames (i.e., *Nursery* = the Circus's training base or "charm school for outward bound penetration agents"; *mothers* = senior secretaries; *housekeepers* and *burrowers* = researchers; and *the Sandman* = Moscow Centre's head assassin, Karla). The Circus's support sections – the *scalphunters* (blackmail and murder specialists), *lamplighters* (domestic intelligence agents), and *babysitters* (spymasters' bodyguards) – chaotically serve active agents and their *Joes* (recruited spies), *wranglers* (codebreakers), *shoemakers* (forgers), and *tradesmen* (mercenaries). The *stinks-and-bangs school* (responsible for electronic and chemical apparatus) erratically interacts with the Circus's central command. Agents include *pavement artists* (experts at tailing), *gorillas* (Soviet watchdogs of Soviet spies), and *occasionals* (part-time agents); *espiocrats* (intelligence bureaucrats) secure in their *safe houses* far away from the *Cousins* (the untrustworthy CIA) *unpack* (interrogate) double agents, or *moles*, who were compromised by *honey-traps* (sexually compromising blackmail schemes).[1]

Adept mimicry marks a character's class and persona. Sefton Boyd's clipped speech defines his upper-class status as immediately as Syd Lemon's cockney dialect identifies his inferior social rank. Magnus Pym designs his reserved, measured syntax to hide information from all those he loves. Betrayer Mikhel and his victim Vladimir Miller, like all le Carré's nonnative speakers, misplace words in their English sentences. Jerry Westerby's errors, however, are imitations of Craw's journalistic chatter, contrived to get himself accepted as a "good old boy." This linguistic play is neither haphazard nor unintentional: it serves to place readers imaginatively and ideologically within le Carré's intelligence worlds.

Le Carré consistently dismisses arguments on his place in mainstream or genre fiction as a concern more for literary critics than for an active novelist. Critical opinion stays divided about his place in contemporary British fiction. Many reviewers find that le Carré's linguistic dexterity, plausible characters, plot labyrinthine machinations, and emphasis on espionage's drudgery, boredom, and moral ambiguity, as well as its dark vision of contemporary society, move his fiction away from entertainment to an art form. Some critics put le Carré in the company of Anthony Burgess, Joseph Conrad, John Fowles, William Golding, Graham Greene, and Iris Murdoch for his "exciting, disturbing, therapeutic fantasies of action and intrigue" as well as his abilities to engage political, moral, and psychological complexities (Rutherford, 147).

Moderate critics view le Carré's novels as repetitive in the manner of John Galsworthy's or Arnold Bennett's fiction. His is a conscious narrative technique of increasingly sophisticated variations on basic themes, places, history, and characters. Quality, in these terms, arises not from startling ideas but from familiarity with a topic and genre; it is in the technical expertise of drawing out textured characters and atmospheres.

Readers who bear in mind that le Carré chooses to write espionage fiction can better assess his artistic contribution to British fiction. The strengths of le Carré's fiction are his considerable talents at manipulating this genre and his relentless moral vision. He has enriched espionage fiction with complex motivations, ingenious metaphors, and political dilemmas. Memorable characters, reminiscent of Dickens's best caricatures, reappear inhabiting not just espionage but ordinary life. Their actions remind readers that decency, love, and the line between betrayal and loyalty are precarious.

To present this world and its characters credibly, le Carré exchanged action, the mainstay of genre fiction, for psychological debate and ethical paralysis. Convoluted plots end with little or no change in the status quo; passages twist in on themselves, sometimes overly complicating what action there is.

His at-times-pretentious writing is le Carré's effort to turn the genre novel into a novel of political philosophy and manners. His novels assess the moral conditions of society and culture but avoid the excesses of some of contemporary fiction's more self-conscious experimenters. His efforts to push the limits of the genre and his attempts to abandon espionage fiction altogether explain why his successful novels restrict him to that genre. When he strays outside espionage fiction's narrative limits and expected deception, as he did in *The Naive and Sentimental Lover* and, to a limited degree, in some of his later novels, his preoccupation with themes and issues overwhelms his writing. Espionage fiction gives him a ready form, and he has marketed his version of this commercially popular form into artistic success. His considerable appeal is therefore simply explained. The best of his novels – *Tinker, Tailor, Soldier Spy*, *Smiley's People*, and *The Little Drummer Girl* – borrow some traditional conventions from popular thrillers and introduce some experimentation from literary fiction. John le Carré explores difficult subjects while keeping his books engaging, lucid, and within the boundaries of the genre that he now defines.

Notes and References

Chapter One

1. "In England Now," *New York Times Magazine*, 23 October 1977, 34; hereafter cited in text as "In England."

2. Joseph Lelyveld, "Le Carré's Toughest Case," *New York Times Book Review*, 16 March 1986, 44.

3. *A Perfect Spy* (New York: Knopf, 1986), 75; hereafter cited in text as *Perfect*.

4. Stefan Kanfer, "The Spy Who Came in for the Gold," *Time*, 3 October 1977, 67; hereafter cited in text.

5. Melvin Bragg, "A Talk with John le Carré," *New York Times Book Review*, 13 March 1983, 22; hereafter cited in text.

6. Tony Cornwell remembers how he and David joked about Ronnie's plans for them: "We were allowed to be anything we wanted, so long as it was a barrister or solicitor" (Kanfer, 67).

7. Interestingly, le Carré educated his sons at British public schools.

8. Bhaskara Rao, "John le Carré," in *Critical Survey of Long Fiction*, ed. Frank N. Magill (Englewood Cliffs, N.J.: Salem Press, 1984), 1609.

9. *Tinker, Tailor, Soldier, Spy* (New York: Knopf, 1974), 10; hereafter cited in text as *Tinker, Tailor*.

10. "England Made Me," *Observer*, 13 November 1977, 25. Graham Greene's 1935 novel *England Made Me* merges the hunter and hunted identities.

11. Michael Dean, "John le Carré – the Writer Who Came in from the Cold," *Listener*, 5 September 1974, 306; hereafter cited in text.

12. Mark Abley, "Le Carré's People: The Writer Who Came in from the Cold," *World Press Review*, 30 (May 1983): 34; hereafter cited in text as Abley 1983a.

13. "Don't Be Beastly to Your Secret Service," *Times*, 23 March 1986, 41.

14. Early on David Cornwell claimed that "le Carré" (French for "the square" or "straightforward") was the name of a London shop he once passed, but no one can find the shop in any city directory (see James Cameron, "The Case of the Hot Writer," *New York Times Magazine*, 8 September 1974, 63; hereafter cited in text). Later Cornwell admitted that

he invented the story to satisfy the American press (see Mark Abley, "John le Carré's Trail of Terror," *Maclean's Magazine*, 7 March 1983, 51; hereafter cited in text as Abley 1983b). Other possibilities abound. The late-nineteenth-century British spy Thomas Beach once used the covername Henri le Caron, and in the 1940s British intelligence captured a German mole named Mathilde Carré (see Peter Lewis, *John le Carré* [New York: Ungar, 1985]). "Le Carre" also designates a whimsically tied fabric that hides an unsightly chair.

15. "To Russia, with Greetings: An Open Letter to the Moscow *Literary Gazette*," *Encounter* 26 (May 1966): 6; hereafter cited in text as "To Russia."

16. Henry Zieger, *Ian Fleming: The Spy Who Came in with the Gold* (New York: Duell, Sloane, & Pearce, 1965), 123.

17. Michael Barber, "John le Carré: An Interrogation," *New York Times Book Review*, 25 September 1977, 44.

18. David McCormick, *Who's Who in Spy Fiction* (London: Elm Tree Books, 1977), 108.

19. Jordan Bonfante, "The Spy-master Unmasked," *Life*, 28 February 1964, 40.

20. Introduction to *The Philby Conspiracy*, by Bruce Page, David Leitch, and Phillip Knightley (New York: Ballantine, 1981), 14, 5; hereafter cited in text as "Introduction." For Philby's defense, see Kim Philby, *My Silent War* (London: MacGibbon & Kee, 1968), hereafter cited in text; or Phillip Knightley, *The Master Spy* (New York: Knopf, 1989).

21. "Spying on My Father," *Times*, 16 March 1986, 33.

22. Pierre Assouline, "John le Carré: Spying on the Spymaster" [excerpt from *Lire*], *World Press Review*, August 1986, 59.

23. Stephen Schiff, "The Secret Life of John le Carré," *Vanity Fair*, June 1989, 189; hereafter cited in text.

24. *The Russia House* (New York: Knopf, 1989); hereafter cited in text as *Russia House*.

25. Even with the end of the cold war, le Carré finds espionage a fruitful genre and places himself forthrightly within its traditions. Interviewed at the publication of *The Secret Pilgrim*, le Carré confidently declared the end of spy fiction premature: "To say the spy writer has had his toys taken away from him is ridiculous" (William Boyd, "Oh, What a Lovely Cold War," *New York Times Book Review*, 6 January 1991, 3).

Chapter Two

1. *The Spy Who Came in from the Cold* (London: Victor Gollancz, 1963; New York: Coward-McCann, 1964), 213; hereafter cited in text as *Spy*.

2. Useful discussions of espionage fiction's history include "I Spy with My Little Eye," *Economist*, 4 January 1975, 81-83; Christoher Andrew, *Her*

Majesty's Secret Service (New York: Penguin Books, 1985), 34-85; le Carré, "Don't Be Beastly," 41-42; John Gardner, "The Espionage Novel," in *Whodunit?*, ed. H. F. R. Keating (London: Windward Publishers, 1982), 70-78; Jerry Palmer, *Thrillers: Genesis and Structure of a Popular Genre* (London: Edward Arnold, 1978); Jerry Palmer, "Thrillers," in *Popular Fiction and Social Change*, ed. Christopher Pawling (London: Macmillan, 1984), 76-98; John Atkins, *The British Spy Novel: Styles in Treachery* (London: John Calder, 1984); David A. T. Stafford, "Spies and Gentlemen: The Birth of the British Spy Novel, 1883-1914," *Victorian Studies* 24, no. 4 (Summer 1981): 489-509; and Julian Symons, "A Short History of the Spy Story," in *Mortal Consequences* (New York: Schocken Books, 1972), 230-46.

3. David French, "Spy Fever in Britain, 1900-1915," *Historical Journal* 21, no. 2 (1978): 355-70.

4. MI-5, formerly section 5 of the British Military Intelligence, roughly compares with the Federal Bureau of Investigation or the Soviet Committee for State Security (the KGB). MI-6 is Britain's version of America's Central Intelligence Agency. Traditionally, the administrative directors of the agencies are known only by the initials of the sections' first heads, "K" in MI-5 for Sir Vernon Kell and "C" in MI-6 for Commander (later Captain Sir) Mansfield George Smith-Cumming (see Andrew, 174-202).

5. According to Phillip Knightley in *The Second Oldest Profession: Spies and Spying in the Twentieth Century* (New York: Norton, 1986), Le Queux's novel *The Invasion of 1910* "sold more than one million copies in twenty-seven languages – including Icelandic and Urdu" (19).

6. Both George Orwell and U.S. congressional representative Bernard Baruch are credited with the first use of "cold war." The phrase figuratively describes the political and ideological rivalries that divided the United States and its World War II allies from the Soviet Union and the Warsaw Pact allies until economic tensions forced Mikhail Gorbachev to abandon those rivalries and adopt more Western political and economic structures.

7. For a detailed comparison of detective and espionage fiction, see R. Austin Freeman, "The Art of the Detective Story," in *The Art of the Mystery Story*, ed. Howard Haycraft (New York: Carroll & Graff Publishers, 1924), 7-17, and Glenn W. Most, "The Hippocratic Smile: John le Carré and the Traditions of the Detective Novel," in *The Poetics of Murder: Detective Fiction and Literary Theory*, ed. Glenn W. Most and William W. Stowe (New York: Harcourt Brace Jovanovich, 1983), 342-65.

8. Robert Gillespie, "The Recent Future: Secret Agents and the Cold World War," *Salmagundi* 13 (Summer 1970): 45-60; David Monaghan, "John le Carré and England: A Spy's-eye View," *Modern Fiction Studies* 29, no. 3 (Autumn 1983): 569-82.

9. Maugham claimed that British intelligence authorities forced him to destroy at least 14 Ashenden stories because the stories gave his own code-

name ("Ashenden"), home address, descriptions of other agents, and details of several assignments (see Andrew, 149-53).

10. Eric Homberger, *John le Carré* (London: Methuen, 1986).

11. Julian Symons (243), among others, equates the split between spy and espionage fiction to that between classical and hard-boiled detective fiction.

12. Melvin Bragg, "The Things a Spy Can Do: John le Carré Talking," *Listener*, 22 January 1976, 90.

13. *Call for the Dead* (London: Victor Gollancz, 1961; New York: Walker, 1962), hereafter cited in text as *Call*; *A Murder of Quality* (London: Victor Gollancz, 1962; New York: Walker, 1963), hereafter cited in text as *Murder*.

14. Speculations on Smiley's model vary. The *Guardian* (11 March 1981) nominated Sir Maurice Oldfield, the former head of MI-6; le Carré roundly denounced this suggestion ("Unlicensed to Quote," *Times*, 17 March 1981, 13). Nicolas Parsons in *The Book of Literary Lists* (New York: Facts on File, 1989) offers retired intelligence officer John Bingham (b. 1908), Lord Clanmorris, as Smiley's model. Le Carré claims Smiley is a composite of James Skardon, the man who interrogated Klaus Fuchs, the nuclear scientist who sold American atom bomb secrets to the Soviets, and Vivian Green, the history don who taught Cornwell at Oxford and married him to Ann Sharp (see Abley 1983b, 51).

15. During the 1940s Lady Ann rebelliously drops the final "e" from Sercombe.

16. The Circus, founded by a small group of Oxbridge intellectuals, moves from Knightsbridge to Cambridge Circus in central London in the early 1940s. Its geographic location suggests an irony beyond the obvious paradox found with its name because Kim Philby was recruited from Cambridge.

17. The Matthew Arnold quotation, which supplies the title for le Carré's closing chapter in *Call for the Dead* and John Halperin's analysis of le Carré's fiction in "Between Two Worlds: The Novels of John le Carré" (*South Atlantic Quarterly* 79, no. 2 [Spring 1980]: 17-37), is taken from "Stanzas from the Grande Chartreuse": "Wandering between two worlds, one dead, / The other powerless to be born, / With nowhere yet to rest my head."

18. The revelations are factual and establish an air of credible realism in the novel. The cypher clerk le Carré refers to is Soviet Igor Gouzenko, whose defection in September 1945 revealed that Soviet agents had successfully infiltrated American, British, and Canadian intelligence. Le Carré mixes in other factual references, including one to Klaus Fuchs and British traitor Donald Maclean.

19. Abraham Rothberg dissents in "The Decline and Fall of George Smiley: John le Carré and English Decency," *Southwest Review* 66, no. 4 (Autumn 1981): 377-93.

20. Dedicated "To Ann," *Murder* begins with le Carré's disclaimer that "there are probably a dozen great schools of whom it will be confidently asserted that Carne is their deliberate image. But he who looks among their common rooms for [the characters] will search in vain."

21. See Lewis's discussion (45-46) of le Carré's use of the word *quality*.

Chapter Three

1. John F. Kennedy's ability to bluff Nikita Khrushchev during the Cuban Missile Crisis (16-27 October 1962) is one telling example of the few successes intelligence has provided political leaders (see Knightley, 317-22).

2. David Monaghan argues in *The Novels of John le Carré* (New York: Basil Blackwell, 1985) that le Carré's novels evaluate how individuals can remain fully human "in a society whose institutions have lost . . . connection with individual feeling" (11). Eric Homberger in *John le Carré* refines Monaghan's position, adding that, at least for *Spy*, le Carré's constant theme is "a conflict between ways of living, and ultimately of social systems, which are rooted in respect for individualism, and those which are not" (50).

3. Alan Watson, "Violent Image," *Sunday Times*, 30 March 1969, 55.

4. As critics like Peter Lewis (*John le Carré*, 67) note, le Carré's original title for the novel, *The Carcass of the Lion*, obscures the novel's ambiguous irony.

5. Andrew Rutherford in *The Literature of War: Five Studies in Heroic Virtue* (London: Macmillan, 1978) argues that *Spy* is written "in the manner of a moral fable" (146; hereafter cited in text).

6. Le Carré's suggestion in *Looking-glass* seems chillingly real in light of the Soviet Union's 1983 destruction of Korean Air Lines flight 007 and the United States' 1984 downing of an Iranian Air Lines passenger jet. The Soviets argued that KAL 007 was on a reconnaissance mission; the United States believed that IAL was preparing to attack navy vessels in the Persian Gulf.

7. *The Looking-glass War* (London: Heinemann, New York: Coward-McCann, 1965), 29; hereafter cited in text as *Looking-glass*.

8. Le Carré says an agent taking the second vow "experiences self-knowledge but does not withdraw" (Granville Hicks, "Spies without a Sense of Mission," *Saturday Review* 24 [July 1965]: 40).

9. Tony Barley in *Taking Sides* (Philadelphia: Open University Press, 1986) records that the frontispiece to the British edition of *Looking-glass* is a line from Lewis Carroll's *Through the Looking Glass*: "I wouldn't mind being a Pawn, if only I might join [the game]" (49). As Barley comments,

the full quotation serves as a central theme for much of le Carré's fiction:
" 'I declare [the Red Queen's garden] is marked out just like a large chess-
board!' Alice said at last. 'There ought to be some men moving about
somewhere – and so there are!' she added in a tone of delight, and her
heart began to beat quick with excitement as she went on. 'It's a great huge
game of chess that's being played – all over the world – if this is the world
at all, you know. Oh, what fun it is! How I wish I was one of them! I
wouldn't mind being a Pawn, if only I might join [the game] – though of
course I should like to be a Queen, best' " (Lewis Carroll, *The Annotated
Alice: Alice's Adventures in Wonderland and Through the Looking Glass*
[New York: Bramhall House, 1960], 207-8).

10. *A Small Town in Germany* (London: Heinemann, New York:
Coward-McCann, 1968), 37; hereafter cited in text as *Town*.

11. This time it is Harting's uncle who serves as le Carré's paternal
scoundrel. The elder Harting survived the war years making "pills in a
machine. Dried fruit. Squashed them all up and rolled them in sugar, then
put them in the tins, see. Used to spit on them, Leo did, just to spite his
uncle. . . . He hasn't had the love, see, not what you've had" (*Town*, 89).

Chapter Four

1. Arthur Cooper, review of *The Naive and Sentimental Lover, Saturday Review*, 8 January 1972, 34.

2. *The Naive and Sentimental Lover* (New York: Knopf, 1972);
hereafter cited in text as *Lover*.

3. "You Can't Sack a College Boy," *Spectator*, 27 November 1964, 699,
700.

4. "Dare I Weep, Dare I Mourn?" *Saturday Evening Post*, 28 January
1967, 54, 56, 60.

5. "What Ritual Is Being Observed Tonight?," *Saturday Evening Post*,
60-62, 64, 65.

6. Koorp's description anticipates *The Looking-glass War*'s Fred Leiser:
Koorp "was a fat, flossy, tidy man, quite nimble. . . . They had always
laughed at Koorp; laughed at his cowardice and his precision, . . . laughed
at his early dignity and his attachment to the law, laughed at his monetary
caution" ("Dare I Weep," 54).

7. "Wishful Thinking," *Times Literary Supplement*, 24 September
1971, 1138. H. F. R. Keating in "Life without Roots" (*Times*, 4 July 1974),
however, found the novel a "splendid romantic fantasy . . . that shoulders
its way into the front ranks of art" (10), and the *Times Literary Supplement*
("Hunt the Sleeper," 19 July 1974) attempted to rescue the novel as "a
brilliant and ambitious *roman à clef* . . . which was not so much ignored by
the critics as vilified in a striking display of smallmindedness" (761).

8. James Kennaway and Susan Kennaway, *The Kennaway Papers* (New York: Holt, Rinehart & Winston, 1981), 7; hereafter cited in text. Susan Kennaway attempts by annotating her husband's personal papers to secure his literary reputation. Alternately brilliant and petulant, James created insulting scenes, initiated fights to spark his creativity, and was incorrigibly unfaithful yet compulsively confessional. In *Some Gorgeous Accident* (New York: Atheneum, 1967) he translates his own self-destructive impulses into James Link, a scheming Irish-American war photographer who "arrested attention and invited passion with dangerous facility; dangerous because, as he welcomed life, seized it by both hands and pulled it in the door, he let destruction in as well" (245). Link's passions alienate him from the lovers he wants to control, fashion editor Susan Steinberg and Dr. Richard David Fiddes (Kennaway's visions of his wife and Cornwell). Link recognizes, as *Lover's* antagonist Shamus cannot, that no one "had body enough, substance enough to invade Link's isolated absorption with Link . . . that mirror land of Link and Link and again Link from that Linkified Paradise, that hell . . . of Link's own doing" (245).

9. Trevor Roper's biography of Kennaway, *James and Jim* (Edinburgh: Mainstream Publishing, 1983), supports the image of Kennaway's divided character as *The Kennaway Papers* and *Some Gorgeous Accident* do.

10. David Monaghan in *The Novels of John le Carré* argues that Schiller's dichotomy explains the metaphoric substance of all of le Carré's fiction (2-41).

11. Chapter 23 of *Lover* begins, "An unusual silence fills the house and no birds sing," the last four words apparently taken from Keats's "La Belle Dame sans Merci." Peter Lewis in *John le Carré* puzzles over this quotation, finding it "a piece of gratuitous jokiness, and . . . meretriciously showy" (115). The Keats reference does, however, illustrate Schiller's dichotomy here as clearly as le Carré's references to Goethe throughout his espionage fiction ("In the beginning was the deed") contrasts past and present.

12. Le Carré interprets the theme of *Lover* as "not as far from its predecessors as you might suppose," because it removes "that vast superstructure of plot and politics" to reveal "beneath it the man I have always known: bewildered, aspiring, comic, loving, weak and oddly loyal" (Lewis, 114).

13. Peter Wolfe in *Corridors of Deceit* (Bowling Green, Ohio: Popular Press, 1987) argues that *Lover's* repeated white imagery underscores Cassidy's search for his maternal "first course of objective reality and nourishment" (170). The futile search for this denied nurturing defines Cassidy's tragic flaw.

14. Various reviewers criticize the novel but skirt the issue of le Carré's vision of Cassidy as powerful yet ceaselessly insecure. Geoffrey Wolfe in "All Naked into the World of Art" (*New York Times Book Review*, 9 January 1972) finds Cassidy a "gray little man" in a "world of gray little men" who

fails to "shake the world" (7). Peter Wolfe questions the character's plausibility, commenting that "either le Carré doesn't know how hard it is to acquire money and power in competitive industry or he has misrepresented Aldo" (173). Cassidy's character inconsistencies are a direct result of le Carré's retreat from his routine of recording action arising from characters in conflict. In *Lover* le Carré privileges personal experience over plot *and* character.

15. Peter Wolfe construes *bavers* as British slang for "rubbish" (169).

16. After embarrassing Cassidy at a corporate exhibition, Shamus leaves Aldo a note identifying himself as "your obedient humble servant Shamus P. Scardanelli (Vendor)" (*Lover*, 182). The surname serves Shamus's immediate purpose only.

17. As Peter Wolfe comments, "the Few" and "the Many-too-Many" are adapted from John Fowles's *Aristos* (178).

15. Eric Homberger in *John le Carré* chides le Carré for ducking "the problem of portraying a real artist, and of confronting the situation which artists actually face in post-war England" (71).

Chapter Five

1. These comments from, respectively, H. R. F. Keating ("Life without Roots," 10), Peter S. Prescott ("Shamus and Aldo," *Newsweek*, 10 January 1972, 64), Julian Symons ("Criminal Activities," *New Review*, July 1974, 61), and Auberon Waugh ("Piers Paul Read and Other Novelists," *Spectator*, 25 September 1971, 449) represent the range of criticism *Lover* received.

2. Abley (52) reports that le Carré trained two whippets, Mach II and Whisper, to growl at the word *critic*.

3. Paul Vaughan, "Le Carré's Circus: Lamplighters, Moles, and Others of that Ilk," *Listener*, 13 September 1979, 339. Ever vigilant, le Carré acknowledged that "For good trade reasons one doesn't like to announce one's going to write a trilogy. If the book's a flop you're landed with the other two, or you have to crawl out of the tunnel."

4. Northrop Frye in *Anatomy of Criticism* (Princeton, N.J.: Princeton University Press, 1957) delineates the structural principles of romance and quest literature. Christopher Booker in "Spymasters and Spy-Monsters" (*Spectator*, 9 February 1980, 16-17) argues that le Carré intentionally patterns *Smiley's People* as a classic quest. And Lars Sauerberg in *Secret Agents in Fiction* (London: Macmillan, 1984) applies Frye's principles to novels by le Carré, Ian Fleming, and Len Deighton, praising le Carré's novels as the most literary, as they translate quest motifs into contemporary images.

5. Le Carré in "Closing the File" (*Radio Times*, 18-24 September 1982) had in mind ending Smiley before *Smiley's People*. Smiley and Karla would destroy each other, "Smiley by an act of professional absolutism, Karla by a

lapse into humanity. It was to be the moral Reichenbach Falls with no happy moment when Smiley returns to his bee keeping" (cited in Lewis, 165).

6. *The Honourable Schoolboy* (London: Hodder & Stoughton, New York: Knopf, 1977), 533; hereafter cited in text as *Schoolboy*.

7. Le Carré's inventiveness pleases many critics but not all espionage insiders. Critics enjoy the irony implicit in le Carré's retooling one of Guy Burgess's aliases, Jim Andreyevitch Eliot, into Jim Prideaux's covername, "Jim Ellis." Espionage insiders scoff.

8. In *My Silent War* Philby vigorously defends his ideological motivations, while carefully concealing the specifics of his recruitment.

9. Philby's literary legacy is also considerable. His betrayal has been the subject of numerous fictional and nonfictional works, including Alan Bennett's *The Old Country*, Reginald Hill's *The Spy's Wife*, Joseph Hone's *The Private Sector*, and Alan William's *Gentleman Traitor*. Graham Greene's effort, *The Human Factor* (1978), invites comparison with *Tinker, Tailor*. Greene translates Philby's story into a psychological investigation of private morality. Unheroic and emotionally torn, Maurice Castle gives voice to Greene's condemnation of espionage as psychological warfare. Unlike Philby or Bill Haydon, Castle is saved from pathos or horror by love. He betrays his country but not his wife; their sad separation further confirms Castle's honor, an image with which le Carré tries to cloak Smiley.

10. Homberger in *John le Carré* (84-86) argues that the seeds of Smiley's conversion to Control's perspective are sown in *Spy*. Hence Smiley's continued presence as a force for morality results more from his persistent compassion for his service than from his unsullied character.

11. *Smiley's People* (London: Hodder & Stoughton, New York: Knopf, 1980), 288; hereafter cited in text as *Smiley's*.

12. Le Carré's use of the "Sandman" tale marries the trilogy's romance-quest motif to its doubling imagery (see Barley, 126-30).

13. Holly Beth King in "Child's Play in John le Carré's *Tinker, Tailor, Soldier, Spy*" (*Clues* 2 [Fall-Winter 1982]: 87-92) argues that le Carré's literary maturity allows him to use children's vision to expose the emotions and motivations professionals hide.

14. David Monaghan in *The Novels of John le Carré* notes that le Carré's description of Hong Kong's brightness is rare, suggesting "a direct relationship between the presence of light in [le Carré's] Hong Kong and the society's ability to retain contact with . . . basic human urges" of family, trust, and loyalty (66). H. D. S. Greenway in "Travels with le Carré" (*Newsweek*, 10 October 1977, 102) argues that le Carré's descriptive accuracy enriches Westerby's characterization and sets him up as Lord Jim's ironic counterpart. James Fenton, however, in "Le Carré Goes East" (*New*

Review, October 1977, 31-34) soundly denounces le Carré's superficial geographic and political descriptions as impoverishing the characterization.

15. Homberger in *John le Carré* suggests that *Schoolboy* follows the Aristotelian pattern for tragedy of "exposition," "initiating action," "rising action leading to crisis," "falling action," and "denouement" (80).

16. Westerby's first artistic interest, like le Carré's, is illustration, an interest that contributes to his vivid imagination. Also like his creator, he abandoned a career in visual art early on.

17. Louis Finger in "Manly One" (*New Statesman*, 23 September 1977) condemns le Carré's preference for eccentrics "with [little] more than two or three identifying traits" (415).

18. Peter Wolfe in *Corridors of Deceit* (200) finds each major character in *Schoolboy* wounded by family losses, a theme le Carré introduces in *Call for the Dead* and replays in all his novels.

19. Richard West in "Local Colour" (*Spectator*, 10 September 1977) argues that *Schoolboy* fails to integrate its overworked themes: "It's easy to agree or disagree with *The Quiet American*; it's difficult to find the heart in *The Honourable Schoolboy*" (20).

20. Lewis in *John le Carré* (144-45) argues that the techniques (i.e., baffling plots for verisimilitude, protagonist without omniscient knowledge, and characterization superseding adventure) affirm that le Carré is more than a clever genre novelist.

21. In *Tinker, Tailor* Smiley tells Peter Guillam that Karla married a Leningrad woman who committed suicide when she learned Karla was imprisoned; in *Smiley's People* Karla orders his mistress's death for her antisocialist views of history. Thus it is unclear whether Tatiana's mother is Karla's wife or his mistress.

22. Lewis in *John le Carré* (131) finds Smiley's meeting with Ann both a romance convention and an image of moribund Britain.

Chapter Six

1. Arthur Koestler, *The Age of Longing* (New York: Danube Edition, 1970), 30-31. Additionally, le Carré maintains that Charlie is loosely based on his half-sister, Charlotte Cornwell, a successful British actress.

2. *The Little Drummer Girl* (New York: Knopf, 1983), 114; hereafter cited in text as *Drummer*.

3. *The Little Drummer Girl* stirred up considerable disagreement among critics. David Pryce-Jones in "Drumming up Hatred" (*Spectator*, 16 April 1983, 9-10) discredited it as a patently pro-Palestinian adventure story centered on a bizarre love story; John Wyver in "Fiction" (*City Lights*, 1 April 1983) found the book pro-Israeli because only Israelis voice reason and "sophisticated good sense" (22), whereas Palestinians advocate strident, instinctive brutality. While professing that he condemns both

sides, le Carré commends the Palestinians for showing him "the Palestinian heart" and the Israelis for their excellent professional techniques.

4. Lewis in *John le Carré* (192-93) argues that the Mossad's reputation and le Carré's choice to center the action on the Israelis give the novel an air of verisimilitude. It is equally logical to question the Mossad's assumed operational skill because its successes came largely in the 1967 and 1973 wars.

5. T. J. Binyon in "Theatre of Terror" (*Times Literary Supplement*, 25 March 1983, 298) condemns the novel's closing scene as impossible sentimentality degrading into kitsch.

6. Homberger in *John le Carré* (99-101) finds Pym and Charlie central nothingnesses who allow their families to possess and define them. The same holds true for le Carré protagonists who define themselves by their professions.

7. Harold Bloom in his "Editor's Note" to *John le Carré* (New York: Chelsea House, 1987) finds Pym a less impressive version of Conrad's Decoud (*Nostromo*) and Greene's Pinkie (*Brighton Rock*).

8. Susan Laity, " 'The Second Burden of a Former Child': Doubling and Repetition in *A Perfect Spy*," in *John le Carré*, ed. Bloom, 138.

9. Smiley leaves a copy of this book at Roddy Martindale's club in *Tinker, Tailor*.

10. "Barley," a nickname for the English way to call time-out in competitive sports, ideally suits Blair's character.

11. Le Carré met Sakharov in Leningrad. To le Carré Sakharov symbolized guilt, "because he's the man who gave [the Soviets] the hydrogen bomb, and his opinion of the recipients of his talent was not high." Unlike the Cambridge spies, who "took the secret road in an open society where protest could be voiced," Sakharov chose "the much braver road of public protest in a closed society" (Craig R. Whitney, "Now the Other Side Warms to le Carré," *New York Times*, 22 May 1989, C13, C18).

12. Sergi L. Petrov, "The Little Drummer Boy: What John le Carré Does Not Know about Russia," *New Republic*, 21 August 1989, 30-33.

13. *The Secret Pilgrim* (New York: Knopf, 1991), 174; hereafter cited in text as *Pilgrim*. This loosely connected set of tales is dedicated to Sir Alec Guinness, who played Smiley in the BBC production of *Tinker, Tailor, Soldier, Spy*.

14. Katherine Stephen, "A Mast of Cold War Greets the Era of Glasnost," *Los Angeles Times*, 31 May 1989, 1.

15. Charles Trueheart, "John le Carré: The Spy Spinner after the Thaw," *Washington Post*, 25 May 1989, D2.

16. "I Was Heartily Sick of It," *New York Times Book Review*, 6 January 1991, 3.

17. Richard Grenier in "Better the $6 Bread than the le Carré" (*Washington Times*, 20 June 1989) found *The Russia House* a "thin, mushy 'peace' drivel worked up by a pretentious thriller writer out of surly antipathy toward his own society and a strange obsequiousness toward its adversaries" (F3). Ian Buruma in "After the Fall" (*New York Review of Books*, 28 March 1991, 8-9) deplores the novel's anti-American sentiments, overly broad caricatures, heavy irony, and predictability.

Chapter Seven

1. David Monaghan's dictionary *Smiley's Circus* (New York: St. Martin's, 1986) defines the operations and jargon used in seven of the espionage novels that feature George Smiley.

Selected Bibliography

PRIMARY WORKS

Fiction

Call for the Dead. London: Victor Gollancz, 1961; New York: Walker, 1962.

"Dare I Weep, Dare I Mourn?" *Saturday Evening Post*, 28 January 1967, 54, 56, 60. Short story aired as television play on "ABC Stage 67" later that year.

The End of the Line. Play produced at the Armchair Theatre on 29 June 1970.

The Honourable Schoolboy. London: Hodder & Stoughton, New York: Alfred A. Knopf, 1977.

The Incongruous Spy: Two Novels of Suspense. New York: Walker, 1964. Reissue of *Call for the Dead* and *A Murder of Quality*.

Introduction to *The Philby Conspiracy*, by Bruce Page, David Leitch, and Phillip Knightley. New York: Ballantine Books, 1981.

The Little Drummer Girl. London: Hodder & Stoughton, New York: Alfred A. Knopf, 1983.

The Looking-glass War. London: Heinemann, New York: Coward-McCann, 1965.

A Murder of Quality. London: Victor Gollancz, 1962; New York: Walker, 1963. Rewritten as screenplay, 1990.

The Naive and Sentimental Lover. London: Hodder & Stoughton, 1971; New York: Alfred A. Knopf, 1972.

A Perfect Spy. New York: Alfred A. Knopf, 1986.

The Quest for Karla. New York: Alfred A. Knopf, 1982. Reissue of the Smiley trilogy *Tinker, Tailor, Soldier, Spy, The Honourable Schoolboy,* and *Smiley's People*.

The Russia House. New York: Alfred A. Knopf, 1989.

The Secret Pilgrim. New York: Alfred A. Knopf, 1991.

A Small Town in Germany. London: Heinemann, New York: Coward-McCann, 1968.

Smiley's People. London: Hodder & Stoughton, New York: Alfred A. Knopf, 1980.

The Spy Who Came in from the Cold. London: Victor Gollancz, 1963; New
    York: Coward & McCann, 1964.

Tinker, Tailor, Soldier, Spy. London: Hodder & Stoughton, New York:
    Alfred A. Knopf, 1974.

"What Ritual Is Being Observed Tonight?" *Saturday Evening Post,* Novem-
    ber 1968, 60-62, 64-65.

"You Can't Sack a College Boy." *Spectator,* 27 November 1964, 699-700.

Biographical Articles

"England Made Me." *Observer,* 13 November 1977, 25.

"In England Now." *New York Times Magazine,* 23 October 1977, 34-35, 86-
    87.

"Spying on My Father." *Sunday Times,* 16 March 1986, 33-35.

Nonfiction

"An American Spy Story." Review of *The Man Who Kept the Secrets: Richard
    Helms and the CIA,* by Thomas Powers. *New York Times Book Review,*
    14 October 1979, 1, 46-48.

"At last, It's Smiley." *Sunday Telegraph Magazine,* 21 October 1979:105,
    106, 111, 112.

"Betrayal." *Observer,* 3 July 1983, 23-24. Part of a series of articles commis-
    sioned by the newspaper and published in conjunction with *The Little
    Drummer Girl.*

"The Clandestine Muse." *Johns Hopkins Magazine* 38 (August 1986): 11-16.
    Abbreviated version appears as "Readings: Le Carré: The Dishonorable
    Spy." *Harper's,* December 1986, 17-19.

"Don't Be Beastly to Your Secret Service." *Sunday Times,* 23 March 1986,
    41-42.

"Exiles in the White House." *Observer,* 26 June 1983, 25-26. Part of a series
    of articles commissioned by the newspaper and published in conjunc-
    tion with *The Little Drummer Girl.*

"Hughes of Hong Kong." *Sunday Times,* 8 January 1984, 9a-9b.

"In a Small Place in Cornwall." *Sunday Telegraph Magazine,* 6 September
    1974, 39, 40, 45, 46.

"Inside Books: John le Carré on Perfect Spies and Other Characters."
    Writer's Digest, February 1987, 20-21.

"McCullin's World." *Sunday Times Magazine,* 26 October 1980, 50, 51, 53,
    55, 57, 58, 61. Reprinted as the Introduction to *Hearts of Darkness,* by
    Don McCullin (New York: Alfred A. Knopf, 1981).

"Memories of a Vanished Land." *Observer,* 13 June 1982, 9-10. Part of a
    series of articles commissioned by the newspaper and published in
    conjunction with *The Little Drummer Girl.*

"Optical Illusion." *Times*, 22 March 1982, 11.

"Siege." *Observer*, 1 June 1980, 25.

"The Spy to End Spies: On Richard Sorge." *Encounter*, November 1966, 88-89.

"Tinker, Tailor, and the Mole That Never Was." *Manchester Guardian*, 7 November 1979, 14.

"To Russia, with Greetings: An Open Letter to the Moscow *Literary Gazette*." *Encounter* 26, no. 5 (May 1966): 3-6.

"Unlicensed to Quote." *Times*, 17 March 1981, 13.

Vanishing England (with Gareth W. Davies). New York: Salem House Publishers, 1987.

"Vocation in a World of Pain." *Sunday Times*, 25 October 1970, 25.

"Well Played, Wodehouse." *Sunday Times*, 10 October 1971, 35.

"What Every Writer Wants to Know." *Harper's*, November 1965, 142-45.

"World Service." *Times*, 1 July 1981, 15.

"A Writer and a Gentleman." *Saturday Review*, 30 November 1968, 4, 6.

"The Writer and the Spy." *Daily Telegraph*, 29 March 1964, 18.

"Wrong Man on Crete." *Holiday*, December 1965, 74-75.

SECONDARY WORKS

Interviews

Assouline, Pierre. "John le Carré: Spying on the Spymaster." *World Press Review*, August 1986, 59-60. Excerpt from *Lire*.

Barber, Michael. "John le Carré: An Interrogation." *New York Times Book Review*, 25 September 1977, 9, 44, 45.

Blades, John. "Spy Novel Superpower." *Chicago Tribune*, 19 June 1989, 1, 5.

Bragg, Melvin. "The Little Drummer Girl: An Interview with John le Carré." In *The Quest for le Carré*, edited by Alan Bold, 129-43. New York: St. Martin's, 1988. Interview that was first transmitted on the ITV network on 27 March 1983.

———. "A Talk with John le Carré." *New York Times Book Review*, 13 March 1983, 1, 22.

———. "The Things a Spy Can Do." *Listener*, 22 January 1976, 90.

Chiu, Tony. "Behind the Best Sellers: John le Carré." *New York Review of Books*, 6 January 1980, 30.

Crutchley, Leigh. "The Fictional World of Espionage." *Listener*, 14 April 1966, 548-49.

Dean, Michael. "John le Carré: The Writer Who Came in from the Cold." *Listener*, 5 September 1974, 306-7. Originally taped from the BBC2 network.

Gross, Miriam. "A Labyrinth of Espionage: On the Trail of a Master Spy Novelist." *World Press Review*, May 1980, 62.

____. "The Secret World of John le Carré." *Observer*, 3 February 1980, 33, 35.

Hodgson, Godfrey. "The Secret Life of John le Carré: A *Book World* Interview." *Washington Post Book World*, 9 October 1977, E1, E6.

Kucherawy, Dennis. "Romance in Russia: A Spy Novelist Comes in from the Cold." *Maclean's Magazine*, 19 June 1989, 55.

Leitch, David. "The Ultimate Spy." *Sunday Times Magazine*, 13 September 1987, 50-51.

Orlik, Viktor. "Spies Who Come in from the Cold War: A Session between John le Carré and the Soviets." *World Press Review*, October 1989, 28-30.

Sanoff, Alvin P. "The Thawing of the Old Spymaster." *U.S. News & World Report*, 19 June 1989, 59-61.

"The Secret Life of John le Carré: The Enigmatic Author of Some of This Century's Best Spy Stories Has Lived What He Writes About." *Reader's Digest-Canadian*, November 1989, 63-68.

Vaughn, Paul. "Le Carré's Circus: Lamplighters, Moles, and Others of That Ilk." *Listener*, 13 September 1979, 339-40.

Wapshott, Nicholas. "Tinker, Tailor, Soldier, Novelist." *Times*, 6 September 1982, 7.

Watson, Alan. "Violent Image." *Sunday Times*, 30 March 1969, 55, 57. Originally aired as "The Spymaker Comes in from the Cold" on the BBC in 1969.

Yardley, Jonathan. "Le Carré's Drumbeat: Defending His 'Equation' on the Palestinians." *Washington Post*, 6 April 1983, B1.

Books and Parts of Books

Adams, Michael. "John le Carré/David John Moore Cornwell." In *Critical Survey of Mystery and Detective Fiction Authors*, edited by Frank N. Magill, 1041-47. Englewood Cliffs, N.J.: Salem Press, 1989.

Barley, Tony. *Taking Sides: The Fiction of John le Carré*. Philadelphia: Open University Press, 1986.

Bloom, Harold, ed. *John le Carré: Modern Critical Views*. New York: Chelsea House, 1987. Collection of previously published essays by Andrew Rutherford, LeRoy L. Panek, Abraham Rothberg, Holly Beth King, Helen S. Garson, Glenn W. Most, Lars Ole Sauerberg, and David Monaghan; reviews by Stefan Kanfer and William F. Buckley; an introduction by Bloom; and a commissioned article by Susan Laity.

Bold, Alan Norman. Introduction to *The Quest for le Carré*, edited by Alan Bold, 9-24. New York: St. Martin's, 1988.

Cawelti, John G., and Bruce A. Rosenberg. "The Complex Vision of John le Carré." In *The Spy Story*, 156-86. Chicago: University of Chicago Press, 1987.

Crehan, Stewart. "Information, Power, and the Reader: Textual Strategies in le Carré." In *The Quest for le Carré*, edited by Alan Bold, 103-28. New York: St. Martin's, 1988.

East, Andy. "CWF 41: Le Carré, John." Chapter in *The Cold War File*. Metuchen, N.J.: Scarecrow Press, 1983.

Edwards, Owen Dudley. "The Clues of the Great Tradition." In *The Quest for le Carré*, edited by Alan Bold, 41-68. New York: St. Martin's, 1988.

Giddings, Robert. "The Writing on the Igloo Walls: Narrative Technique in *The Spy Who Came in from the Cold*." In *The Quest for le Carré*, edited by Alan Bold, 188-210. New York: St. Martin's, 1988.

Green, Vivian. "*A Perfect Spy*: A Personal Reminiscence." In *The Quest for le Carré*, edited by Alan Bold, 25-40. New York: St. Martin's Press, 1988.

Homberger, Eric. *John le Carré*. New York: Methuen, 1986.

Jeffares, A. Norman. "John le Carré." In *Contemporary Novelists*, 21st ed., edited by James Vinson, 793-95. New York: St. Martin's, 1976.

"John le Carré." In *Current Biography Yearbook 1974*, edited by Charles Moritz, 232-35. New York: H. W. Wilson, 1974.

"John le Carré." In *World Authors: 1950-1970*, edited by John Wakeman, 841-42. New York: H. W. Wilson, 1975.

Lewis, Peter. *John le Carré*. New York: Frederick Ungar, 1985.

McCormick, Donald. "John le Carré." In *Who's Who in Spy Fiction*, 108-12. London: Elm Tree Books, 1972.

Massie, Allan. *The Novel Today: A Critical Guide to The British Novel, 1970-1989*. New York: Longman, 1990.

Masters, Anthony. "John le Carré: The Natural Spy." In *Literary Agents: The Novelist as Spy*. New York: Basil Blackwell, 1987.

Monaghan, David. *The Novels of John le Carré: The Art of Survival*. New York: Basil Blackwell, 1985. Chapter 2, " 'A World Grown Old and Weary': Description as Metaphor in le Carré's Novels," is reprinted in *John le Carré*, edited by Harold Bloom, 117-36. New York: Chelsea House, 1987.

———. Monaghan, David. *Smiley's Circus: A Guide to the Secret World of John le Carré*. New York: St. Martin's, 1986.

Most, Glenn W. "The Hippocratic Smile: John le Carré and the Traditions of the Detective Novel." In *The Poetics of Murder: Detective Fiction and Literary Theory*, edited by Glenn W. Most and William W. Stowe, 341-65. New York: Harcourt Brace Jovanovich, 1983. Reprinted in *John le Carré*, edited by Harold Bloom, 81-102. New York: Chelsea House,

1987. Reprinted in *The Quest for le Carré*, edited by Alan Bold, 144-68. New York: St. Martin's, 1988.

O'Neil, Philip. "Le Carré: Faith and Dreams." In *The Quest for le Carré*, edited by Alan Bold, 169-87. New York: St. Martin's, 1988.

Panek, LeRoy L. "John le Carré." Chapter in *The Special Branch: The British Spy Novel 1890-1980*, 236-57. Bowling Green, Ohio: Bowling Green State University Press, 1981. Reprinted as "Espionage Fiction and the Human Condition," in *John le Carré*, edited by Harold Bloom, 27-48. New York: Chelsea House, 1987. Connects le Carré's fiction to the mainstream British novel.

Rao, K. Bhaskara. "John le Carré." In *Critical Survey of Long Fiction: English Language Series*, edited by Frank N. Magill, 1606-19. Englewood Cliffs, N.J.: Salem Press, 1984.

Rowe, Margaret Moan. "Women's Place in John le Carré's Man's World." In *The Quest for le Carré*, edited by Alan Bold, 69-86. New York: St. Martin's, 1988.

Rutherford, Andrew. "The Spy as Hero: Le Carré and the Cold War." Chapter in *The Literature of War: Five Studies in Heroic Virtue*. New York: Barnes & Noble, 1978. Reprinted in *John le Carré*, edited by Harold Bloom, 13-26. New York: Chelsea House, 1987.

Sauerberg, Lars Ole. *Secret Agents in Fiction: Ian Fleming, John le Carré, and Len Deighton*. London: Macmillan, 1984. The chapter "Fear of Extremes: England's Relationship with Germany and America" is reprinted in *John le Carré*, edited by Harold Bloom, 103-12. New York: Chelsea House, 1987.

Scanlan, Margaret. "Philby and His Fictions." In *Traces of Another Time: History and Politics in Postwar British Fiction*, 87-115. Princeton, N.J.: Princeton University Press, 1990. First published in *Dalhousie Review* 62 (Winter 1983): 533-53.

Royle, Trevor. "Le Carré and the Idea of Espionage." In *The Quest for le Carré*, edited by Alan Bold, 87-102. New York: St. Martin's, 1988.

Smith, Myron J., Jr. "Le Carré, John." Chapter in *Cloak and Dagger Bibliography: An Annotated Guide to Spy Fiction, 1937-1975*. Metuchen, N.J.: Scarecrow Press, 1976.

Snyder, John. "John le Carré." In *Twentieth Century Crime and Mystery Writers*, edited by John M. Reilly, 933-35. New York: St. Martin's, 1980.

Steinbrunner, Chris, and Otto Penzler. "John le Carré." In *Encyclopedia of Mystery and Detection*, 242-43. New York: McGraw Hill, 1976.

Wolfe, Peter. *Corridors of Deceit: The World of John le Carré*. Bowling Green, Ohio: Bowling Green Popular Press, 1987.

Articles in Periodicals

Abley, Mark. "John le Carré's Trail of Terror." *Maclean's Magazine*, 7 March 1983, 47-52.

———. "Le Carré's People: The Writer Who Came in from the Cold." *World Press Review* 30 (May 1983): 33-35.

"Atticus." "Words with the Much-Wooed Spyman." *Sunday Times*, 21 June 1964, 31.

Banks, R. Jeff, and Harry Dawson. "Le Carré's Spy Novels." *Mystery Fancier* 2 (September-October 1978): 22-25.

Barzun, Jacques. "Spies and le Carré: A Response to Walter Laqueur." *Commentary*, October 1983, 16-17.

Bell, Pearl K. "Coming in from the Cold War." *New Leader*, 24 June 1974, 15-16.

Best Crime Books Awards. *Times*, 17 April 1964, 25b.

Bonfante, Jordan. "The Spy-master Unmasked." *Life*, 28 February 1964, 39, 40, 42.

Brady, Charles, A. "John le Carré's Smiley Saga." *Thought*, 60 (September 1985): 275-96.

Calendrillo, Linda T. "Role Playing and 'Atmosphere' in Four Modern British Spy Novels." *Clues: A Journal of Detection* 3 (Fall-Winter 1982): 111-19.

Cameron, James. "The Case of the Hot Writer." *New York Times Magazine*, 8 September 1974, 55, 57, 59, 64-66.

Dawson, Harry D. "The Fathers and Sons of John le Carré." *Mystery Fancier* 5 (May-June 1981): 15-17.

———. "John le Carré's Circus." *Armchair Detective* 13 (Spring 1980): 150.

Diamond, Julie. "Spies in the Promised Land: A Review Article." *Race & Class* 25 (1984): 35-40.

Dobel, J. Patrick. "The Honorable Spymaster: John le Carré and the Character of Espionage." *Administration and Society* 15 (August 1988): 191-215.

Garson, Helen S. "Enter George Smiley: Le Carré's *Call for the Dead.*" *Clues: A Journal of Detection* 3 (Fall-Winter 1982): 93-99. Reprinted in *John le Carré*, edited Harold Bloom, 73-80. New York: Chelsea House, 1987.

Gelber, Alexis, with Behr, Edward. "The Spymaster Returns." *Newsweek*, 7 March 1983, 70-74. Incorporates Peter S. Prescott's review of *Drummer Girl*.

Geoghegan, Jack. "The Spy Who Served Me: A Thriller Starring John le Carré." *New York Times Book Review*, 4 December 1988, 1, 16.

Halperin, John. "Between Two Worlds: The Novels of John le Carré." *South Atlantic Quarterly* 79 (Spring 1980): 17-37.

Henissart, Paul. "Of Spies and Stories." *Writer*, May 1978, 15-18.

Hughes, Celia. "Serious Reflection on Light Reading: The World of John le Carré." *Theology* 84 (July 1981): 274-79.

Hunter, Evan. "Spies and Moles and Other Entertainers." *New York Times Book Review*, 24 January 1982, 12, 17.

Johnson, Douglas. "Three Cards of Identity." *New Society* 42 (3 November 1977): 247-48.

Kakutani, Michiko. "Mysteries Join the Mainstream." *New York Times Book Review*, 15 January 1984, 1, 36-37.

Kanfer, Stefan, with Fischer, Dean. "The Spy Who Came in for the Gold." *Time*, 3 October 1977, 58-60, 67-68, 72. Reprinted as "'Our Impudent Crimes': *The Honourable Schoolboy*." In *John le Carré*, edited by Harold Bloom, 7-12. New York: Chelsea House, 1987.

King, Holly Beth. "Child's Play in John le Carré's *Tinker, Tailor, Soldier, Spy*." *Clues: A Journal of Detection* 3 (Fall-Winter 1982): 87-92. Reprinted in *John le Carré*, edited by Harold Bloom, 65-72. New York: Chelsea House, 1987.

_____. "George Smiley – the Reluctant Hero." *Clues: A Journal of Detection* 2 (Spring-Summer 1981): 70-76.

Kirk, John. Introduction to *The Incongruous Spy: Call for the Dead and Murder of Quality*. New York: Walker & Co., 1963.

Knight, Stephen. "Re-formations of the Thriller: Raymond Chandler and John Le Carré." *Sydney Studies in English* 12 (1986-87): 78-91.

Laqueur, Walter. "Spies and le Carré: A Response to His Critics [Barzum, Rose, and Windholz]." *Commentary*, October 1983, 18.

Lasseter, Victor. "John le Carré's Spy Jargon: An Introduction and Lexicon." *Verbatim* 8 (Spring 1982): 1-2.

Lord, Graham. "What a Charming Crook of a Father Did to le Carré." *Express*, 16 March 1986, 6.

McIlvanney, Hugh. "The Secret Life of John le Carré." *Observer Magazine*, 8 March 1983, 18-22.

Maddocks, Melvin. "Le Carré at His Best with an Ethical Spy." *Life*, 25 October 1968, 6.

Maddox, Tom. "Spy Stories: The Life and Fiction of John le Carré." *Western Quarterly* (Autumn 1986): 158-70.

Monaghan, David. "John le Carré and England: A Spy's-eye View." *Modern Fiction Studies* 29 (Autumn 1983): 569-82.

Moss, Norman. "Charlie: Fact and Fiction." *Telegraph Sunday Magazine*, 15 July 1984, 16-17.

Neuse, Steven M. "Bureaucratic Malaise in the Modern Spy Novel: Deighton, Greene, and LeCarré." *Public Administration* 60 (Autumn 1982): 293-306.

Noland, Richard W. "The Spy Fiction of John le Carré." *Clues: A Journal of Detection* 1 (1980): 54-70.

Oakes, Philip. "Goings On: Hard Cash and le Carré." *Sunday Times*, 11 September 1977, 35.

Rose, Gideon. "Spies and Le Carré: A Response to W. Laqueur." *Commentary*, October 1983, 17.

Rothberg, Abraham. "The Decline and Fall of George Smiley: John le Carré and English Decency." *Southwest Review* 66 (Autumn 1981): 377-93. Reprinted in *John le Carré*, edited by Harold Bloom, 49-64. New York: Chelsea House, 1987.

Sauerberg, Lars Ole. "Literature in Figures: An Essay on the Popularity of Thrillers." *Orbis Litterarum: International Review of Literary Studies* 38 (1983): 93-107.

Silver, Brenda R. "Woman as Agent: The Case of le Carré's *Little Drummer Girl*." *Contemporary Literature* 28, no. 1 (1987): 14-40.

"Spymaster Holds the Mirror up to His Own Secrets." *Sunday Times*, 1 November 1987, 16.

Stout, Rex. "The Man Who Came in from the Cold." *Mademoiselle*, July 1964, 60, 61.

Symons, Julian. "Criminal Activities." *New Review* 1 (4 July 1974): 60-61.

Van Tilburg, Barry. "Dossier #17: George Smiley." *Mystery Fancier* 4 (May 1980): 27.

Walker, Christopher. "Le Carré Dodges the Glasnost Grilling." *Times*, 20 May 1987, 7a.

Wallace, Douglas. "John le Carré: The Dark Side of Organizations." *Harvard Business Review* 63 (January-February 1985): 6, 7, 10, 12, 14.

Windholz, Thomas B. "Spies and le Carré: A Response to W. Laqueur." *Commentary*, October 1983, 17.

Selected Book Reviews

Call for the Dead

Fleischer, L. "Deadly Affair." *Publishers Weekly*, November 1966, 63.

"More le Carré Capers." *Time*, 29 May 1964, E2, E4.

"Rewards and Buffets of the Paperback Round." *Times*, 15 December 1966, 16e.

The Honourable Schoolboy

Binyon, T. J. "A Gentleman among Players." *Times Literary Supplement*, 9 September 1977, 1069.

Burgess, Anthony. "Peking Drugs, Moscow Gold." *New York Times Book Review*, 25 September 1977, 9.

Crispin, Edmund. "The Sinister Circus." *Sunday Times*, 11 September 1977, 39.

Fenton, James. "Le Carré Goes East." *New Review* 4 (October 1977): 31-34.

Finger, Louis. "The Manly One." *New Statesman*, 23 September 1977, 414, 415.

Fremont-Smith, Eliot. "Thriller of Dignity, Diller of Distaste." *Village Voice*, 24 October 1977, 103, 105.

Greenway, H. D. S. "Travels with le Carré." *Newsweek*, 10 October 1977, 102.

James, Clive. "Go Back to the Cold!" *New York Review of Books*, 27 October 1977, 29-30.

Leavis, L. R., and Bloom, J. M. "Current Literature in 1977." *English Studies* 59 (October 1978): 447.

Painter-Downes, Mollie. *New Yorker*, 3 October 1977, 163.

Prescott, Peter S. "Smiley vs. the Mole." *Newsweek*, 17 June 1977, 103-4.

"Random Notes." *National Review*, 19 August 1977, 948.

Sigal, Clancy. "Smiley's Villains." *Manchester Guardian*, 8 September 1977, 12.

Stern, Laurence. "The Secret World of George Smiley." *Washington Post Book World*, 9 October 1977, E1, E6.

Vaizey, Lord. "Futile Jerry." *Listener*, 29 September 1977, 409.

West, Richard. "Local Colour." *Spectator*, 10 September 1977, 19-20.

The Little Drummer Girl

Binyon, T. J. "Theatre of Terror." *Times Literary Supplement*, 25 March 1983, 289.

Broyard, Anatole. *New York Times*, 25 February 1983, 21.

Buckley, William F., Jr. "Terror and a Woman." *New York Times Book Review*, 13 March 1983, 1, 23.

Champlin, Charles. *Los Angeles Times Book World*, 13 March 1983, B1.

Cremeans, John E. "Would You Prefer a Fat, Bald Spy?" *Washington Post*, 10 May 1983, A18.

Fuller, Edmund. *Wall Street Journal*, 21 March 1983, 16.

Harper, Michael. *Los Angeles Times*, 13 November 1983, 7.

Kaufman, Gerald. "John le Carré's Israeli Thriller." *Jewish Chronicle*, 1 April 1983, 17.

Laqueur, Walter. "Le Carré's Fantasies." *Commentary*, June 1983, 62-67.

Prescott, Peter S. "In the Theater of the Real." *Newsweek*, 7 March 1983, 72-73.

Pryce-Jones, David. "Drumming Up Hatred." *Spectator*, 16 April 1983, 9-10. Reprinted as "A Demonological Fiction" in *New Republic*, 18 April 1983, 27-30.

Shipp, Randy. *Christian Science Monitor*, 30 March 1983, 9.

Waugh, Auberon. "Mixed Up by a Master." *Daily Mail*, 31 March 1983, 7.

Will, George F. "Le Carré's Unreal Mideast." *Washington Post*, 28 April 1983, A19.

Wolcott, James. "The Secret Sharers." *New York Review of Books*, 14 April 1983, 19-21.

Yardley, Jonathan. *Washington Post*, 14 March 1983, B1.

The Looking-glass War

Ambler, Eric. "John le Carré Escapes the Follow-up Jinx." *Life*, 30 July 1965, 8.

Barrett, William. "Tradition of the Spy." *Atlantic*, August 1965, 124-25.

Boston, Richard. "What Became of Harting?" *New York Times Book Review*, 27 October 1968, 5, 70.

Campbell, Alex. "Thrillers for Eggheads." *New Republic*, 3 July 1965, 25.

Elliott, George P. "It's the Spy Who Counts." *New York Times Book Review*, 25 July 1965, 8.

Enzenberger, Howard. "Up the Circus." *Spectator*, 25 June 1965, 827.

Freeling, Nicolas. "Crime Novels." *Times Literary Supplement*, 24 June 1965, 539.

Grella, George. "Murder and Loyalty." *New Republic*, 31 July 1976, 23-25.

Hicks, Granville. "Spies without a Sense of Mission." *Saturday Review*, 24 July 1965, 39-40.

Marcus, Stephen. "Grand Illusions." *New York Review of Books*, 5 August 1965, 20-21.

Tomalin, Claire. "Looking Glass." *Observer*, 26 September 1971, 9.

A Murder of Quality

Boucher, Anthony. "Criminals at Large." *New York Times Book Review*, 8 September 1963, 45.

Fleischer, L. "Deadly Affair." *Publishers Weekly*, November 1966, 63.

"More le Carré Capers." *Time*, 29 May 1964, E2, E4.

"Rewards and Buffets of the Paperback Round." *Times*, 15 December 1966, 16e.

The Naive and Sentimental Lover

Bannon, Barbara A. *Publishers Weekly*, 18 October 1971, 42-43.

Cooper, Arthur. *Saturday Review*, 8 January 1972, 34-35.

Curley, Arthur. *Library Journal*, November 15, 1971, 3777.

Prescott, Peter S. "Shamus and Aldo." *Newsweek*, 10 January 1972, 64.

Raphael, Frederic. "Looking-glass Hero." *Sunday Times*, 26 September 1971, 38.

Waugh, Auberon. "Piers Paul Read and Other Novelists." *Spectator*, 25 September 1971, 448-49.

Weeks, Edward. *Atlantic*, February 1972, 107-8.

"Wishful Thinking." *Times Literary Supplement*, 24 September 1971, 1138.

Wolff, Geoffrey. "All Naked into the World of Art." *New York Times Book Review*, 9 January 1972, 7.

A Perfect Spy

Annan, Noel, "Underground Men: *A Perfect Spy.*" *New York Review of Books*, 29 May 1986, 3, 4, 6, 7.

Bannon, Barbara A. "Generations of Intrigue." *Commonweal* 113 (23 May 1987): 308-9.

Barnes, Anne. "A Perfect Mess of Spies." *Times*, 2 May 1987, 17a.

Burgess, Anthony. "Defector as Hero." *Observer*, 16 March 1986, 25.

Conroy, Frank. "Sins of the Father." *New York Times Book Review*, 13 April 1986, 1, 24.

Edwards, Thomas R. *New Republic*, 19 May 1986, 32.

Heald, Tim. "Cracking the Code of Hidden Shoals." *New York Times*, 20 March 1986, 11.

Kamins, Morton. *Los Angeles Times Book Review*, 20 April 1986, 2.

Klett, Rex E. *Library Journal*, 1 April 1986, 162.

Lelyveld, Joseph. "Le Carré's Toughest Case." *New York Times Magazine*, 16 March 1986, 40, 43-44, 46,79, 90-91.

Morrison, Blake. "Love and Betrayal in the Mist." *Times Literary Supplement*, 14 March 1986, 380-81.

Prescott, Peter S. *Newsweek*, 21 April 1986, 78.

Rose, Lloyd. *Atlantic*, May 1986, 94.

Sheppard, R. Z. "A Tale of the Acorn and the Tree." *Time*, 28 April 1986, 71-72.

Sutherland, John. "Le Carré on Spying." *London Review of Books*, 3 April 1986, 5-6.

Symons, Julian. "Matters of Deceit and Betrayal." *Manchester Guardian*, 20 March 1986, 20.

The Quest for Karla

Broyard, Anatole. "Reading and Writing: Le Carré's People." *New York Times Book Review*, 29 August 1982, 23.

The Russia House

Gray, Paul. "A Master Hits His Old Pace." *Time*, 29 May 1989, 86.

Grenier, Richard. "Better the $6 Bread than the Le Carré."*Washington Times*, 20 June 1989, F3.

Higgins, George V. "Le Carré's Glasnost." *Chicago Tribune*, 21 May 1989, sec. 14, pp. 1, 9.

Hitchens, Christopher. "Le Carré's Glasnost Thriller." *Elle*, August 1989, 132, 134.

Koenig, Rhoda. *New York Magazine*, 5 June 1989, 56.

Lehmann-Haupt, Christopher. "Into the Age of Perestroika." *New York Times*, 18 May 1989, C28.

Locke, Richard. *Wall Street Journal*, 30 May 1989, A14, A20.

Mathews, Tom, "In from the Cold." *Newsweek*, 5 June 1989, 52-57.

O'Brien, Conor Cruise. "Bad News for Spies." *New York Times Book Review*, 21 May 1989, 3.

Petrov, Sergi L. "The Little Drummer Boy: What John le Carré Does Not Know about Russia." *New Republic*, 21 August 1989, 30-33.

Rawlinson, Nora. *Library Journal*, 15 March 1989, 61.

Schiff, Stephen. "The Secret Life of John le Carré." *Vanity Fair*, June 1989, 146-50, 152, 154, 188-89.

Steinberg, Sybil. *Publishers Weekly*, 21 April 1989, 79.

Trueheart, Charles. "John le Carré: The Spy Spinner after the Thaw." *Washington Post*, 25 May 1989, D1-D3.

Waugh, Harriet. "The Spy Who Went Out to the Warm." *Spectator*, 1 July 1989, 26-27.

Whitney, Craig R. "Now the Other Side Warms to le Carré." *New York Times*, 22 May 1989, C13, C18.

Yardley, Jonathan. "From Russia with Love." *Washington Post Book Review*, 4 June 1989, 3.

The Secret Pilgrim

Boyd, William. "Oh, What a Lovely Cold War," *New York Times Book Review*, 6 January 1991, 3.

Buruma, Ian. "After the Fall." *New York Review of Books*, 28 March 1991, 8-9.

Prescott, Peter S. " 'To End the Time I Lived In': A Fading Spy Offers a Valediction to His Profession." *Newsweek*, 31 December 1990, 63.

Raphael, Frederic. *Sunday Times*, 13 January 1991, 1.

A Small Town in Germany

Keating, H. F. R. "From Bonn: A Literary Bundle." *Times*, 2 November 1966, 22.

"Labyrinthine Ways." *Times Literary Supplement*, 31 October 1968, 1218.

Rosenthal, T. G. "Thriller into Novel." *New Statesman*, 8 November 1968, 641.

Turner, E. S. "Chancery Creeps." *Listener*, 31 October 1968, 588.

Smiley's People

Alvarez, A. "Half-angels versus Half-devils." *Observer*, 3 February 1980, 39.

Booker, Christopher. "Spymasters and Spy-monsters." *Spectator*, 9 February 1980, 16-17.

Broyard, Anatole. *New York Times*, 12 December 1979, C29.

Brunner, Richard Kepler. *Christian Science Monitor*, 14 January 1980, B3.

Caute, David. "It Was a Man." *New Statesman*, 8 February 1980, 209.

Clark, Lindley H., Jr. *Wall Street Journal*, 11 December 1980, 22, 26.

Condon, Richard. "Buried Treasure." *New York Magazine*, 24 December 1979, 66.

Foot, M. R. D. "Open Secrets." *Economist*, 15 March 1980, 51-54, 56-58.

Fuller, Edmund. *Wall Street Journal*, 14 January 1980, 14.

Jacobs, Arthur L. "On the Intelligence Bookshelf." *Periscope* 5 (Spring 1980): 6.

Lekachman, Robert. "Good Boys, Bad Boys, Old Boys." *Nation*, 26 April 1980, 504-6.

McLellan, Joseph. "George Smiley's Revenge." *Washington Post Book World*, 23 December 1979, 1, 4.

Moynaham, Julian. *New Republic*, 19 January 1980, 31-32.

Prawer, S. S. "The Circus and Its Conscience." *Times Literary Supplement*, 8 February 1980, 131.

Pritchett, V. S. "A Spy Romance." *New York Review of Books*, 7 February 1980, 22-24.

Ratcliffe, Michael. "George's Black Grail." *Times*, 7 February 1980, 12.

Stokes, Geoffrey. "The Reluctant Cowboy." *Village Voice*, 14 January 1980, 33.

Wood, Michael. "Spy Fiction, Spy Fact." *New York Times Book Review*, 6 January 1980, 1, 16, 17.

The Spy Who Came in from the Cold

Adams, Robert M. "Couldn't Put It Down." *New York Review of Books*, 5 March 1964, 13-14.

Allsop, Kenneth. "Is This the Private Nightmare of a Master Spy?" *Daily Mail*, 12 September 1963, 10.

Boucher, Anthony. "Temptations of a Man Isolated in Deceit." *New York Times Book Review*, 12 January 1964, 5.

Iles, Francis. "Criminal Records." *Manchester Guardian*, October 1963, 9.

"Inside Job?" *Newsweek*, 3 February 1964, 80.

"New Fiction." *Times*, 12 September 1963, 13b.

"Ruthless Is as Ruthless Does." *Time*, 17 January 1964, 88, 90.

Voinov, V. "John le Carré: Spy Tamer." *Literaturnaya Gazeta*, 16 October 1965.

Tinker, Tailor, Soldier, Spy

Connolley, David. "Tinker, Tailor, Soldier, Swot." *New Scientist*, 14 April 83, 91.

Coyne, John. R. Jr. "Twentieth Century Heroes." *National Review*, 2 August 1974, 880.

"Crime Compendium." *Spectator*, 6 July 1974, 21.

Foote, Timothy. "Playing Tigers." *Time*, 24 June 1974, 88, 91, 93.

Gadney, Reg. "Triple Agents?" *London Magazine* 14 (October-November 1974): 73-77.

"Hunt the Sleeper." *Times Literary Supplement*, 19 July 1974, 761.

Keating, H. F. R. "Life without Roots." *Times*, 4 July 1974, 10.

Locke, Richard. "The Spy Who Spies on Spies." *New York Times Book Review*, 30 June 1974, 1-2.

Mahon, Derek. "Dolls within Dolls." *Listener*, 4 July 1974, 30.

Miller, Karl. "Gothic Guesswork." *New York Review of Books*, 18 July 1974, 24-27.

Sale, Roger. "Fooling Around, and Serious Business." *Hudson Review* 27 (Winter 1974-75): 621-35.

Index

Western politicians, 48, 132;
and Western principles, 21-
23, 26, 29, 36, 47-49, 53, 55,
60, 69, 91, 93, 109, 110, 126,
139
"deskman" (agent reassigned to
paperwork), 141
detective fiction, 19, 24, 26, 36,
47
détente, 7, 68, 92
Dickens, Charles, ix, 13, 34, 111,
129, 140, 143; his character
Mr. Micawber, 2, 111
didacticism, 111: political, ix, 13,
23, 70, 138; social, ix, 125
dishonesty, 2
disillusionment, 3, 11, 23, 26, 32,
92, 97-98, 118, 122, 139
disinformation, 128, 132
"dogsbody" (working drudge),
50
doppelgänger, 5, 12, 29, 32, 55,
77, 92, 108, 141
Dostoyevski, Fyodor, 131
doubling imagery, 10, 13, 28, 29,
32, 33, 35, 44, 51, 66, 84, 86,
106-7, 124-26, 130-32, 138,
139, 141-43
Doyle, Arthur Conan, 8; his
character Sherlock Holmes,
27, 28
dream (deceit) versus reality, 25,
30-33, 44, 52, 58, 62-64, 66-
67, 85, 100, 118, 121, 124,
130
dream-turned-nightmare, 36, 38,
48, 66, 121
Drug Enforcement Agency
(DEA), 100
duality, 33, 107
duplicity, 3, 5, 12, 28, 34, 36, 42,
43, 53, 69, 105, 114, 128,
129, 133, 136, 139, 141
duty, 28, 34, 54, 88, 99, 109, 113,
138

Eastern totalitarianism, 36
East-West conflict, 5
Eisenhower, Dwight D., 129
Eliot, T. S., 108
ends-means argument, 11-12, 16,
47, 49, 51, 52-54, 57, 59, 70,
77, 83, 93, 105, 109-11, 115-
17, 139, 140
enemies-turned-friends/friends-
turned-enemies, 20, 34-35,
47, 56, 65, 111
Eton College, 7, 9, 129
"espiocrats" (espionage
bureaucrats), 112, 130, 132-
34, 142
espionage fiction, x, 1, 7-8, 14-
15, 16, 22-23, 47-49, 70, 71,
88, 136, 138
ethics: codes of, 5, 18, 23, 25, 38,
46-47, 49, 52, 53, 55-56, 61,
69, 86, 92-93, 103, 113, 119-
20, 132, 139; le Carré's sense
of, 2-3, 5, 10-11, 13, 50, 51,
60, 86, 103, 106, 111, 112,
116; paralyzed, 106, 143;
political, 31, 55-56, 92, 134,
138, 139
European Economic Community
(EEC), 65, 68, 69
Eustace, Valerie Jane, 10

facism, 139
family, x, 2-4, 9, 13, 24-26, 28, 33-
34, 37-38, 51, 62, 65, 71, 74,
78-80, 82, 84, 86, 91, 99,
100, 102, 103, 111-12;
dysfunctional, 113-15, 116,
119, 122, 124
fathers, 2, 3, 5; le Carré as a
father, 8-9, 12; Smiley as
father figure, 30, 53, 56, 58,
63, 72-73, 75, 78, 81, 91,
102, 107, 111, 113; Kurtz as

The Author

LynnDianne Beene is an associate professor of English at the University of New Mexico, Albuquerque, where she has taught writing, literature, and popular culture since 1981. She is the author of *Argument and Analysis* (with Krystan V. Douglas), *Solving Problems in Technical Writing* (with Peter L. White), and *The Riverside Handbook of Rhetoric and Grammar* (with William Vande Kopple). She is completing a bibliography of explications of nineteenth- and twentieth-century prose fiction writers and monographs on Wilkie Collins and Margaret Oliphant.